Foreign Aid
Its Defense and Reform

Perhaps in these spheres the right thing
has always to be done for the wrong reasons.
Arthur Koestler, *Arrival and Departure.*

Foreign Aid
Its Defense and Reform

Paul Mosley

THE UNIVERSITY PRESS OF KENTUCKY

Published in the United States by
The University Press of Kentucky

Scholarly publisher for the Commonwealth, serving Bellarmine
College, Berea College, Centre College of Kentucky, Eastern
Kentucky University, The Filson Club, Georgetown College, Kentucky
Historical Society, Kentucky State University, Morehead State
University, Murray State University, Northern Kentucky University,
Transylvania University, University of Kentucky, University of
Louisville, and Western Kentucky University.

Editorial and Sales Offices: Lexington, Kentucky 40506–0024

Library of Congress Cataloging-in-Publication Data

Mosley, Paul.
  Foreign aid, its defense and reform.

  Bibliography: p.
  Includes index.
  1. Economic assistance—Developing countries.
I. Title.
HC60.M67   1987   338.91′09172′4   86-23400
ISBN 0-8131-1608-2

For Helena
and for my friends in the
Independent Group on
British Aid

Contents

Tables

Figures

Preface

In this book I present a personal view of how overseas aid is allocated and what effect it has had. I argue that it is a two-edged sword which can cut through knots which cannot be undone by any other agency, but which at the same time is capable of inflicting serious damage on the poor people and countries that it aims to help. On balance, as the title implies, I feel that its achievements are sufficient to argue for its retention and reform, rather than for it to be wound down. But there is no doubt that it has disappointed many of the more extravagant claims that have been made for it, particularly as an instrument of national self-interest.

These are scarcely startling or novel insights, but it is a fact that aid, even more than religion or capital punishment, corrodes the objectivity of those who write about it, so that the people who describe the wounds inflicted by aid are seldom the same as the people who describe its positive achievements. Since many of the stories on both sides of the argument derive from third-hand accounts of what may have happened on one project in one developing country, the possibilities for confusion are multiplied; and on so vital a subject as world poverty, the public, who finance the aid in the first place, do not deserve to be confused.

This book is primarily for that public, so I have taken care to avoid abstruseness, and in particular mathematical modelling, in the main text. But since one of my main criticisms of the existing literature is that it fails to express the linkage between aid and the targets that it is meant to influence in a testable form, I have set out in the appendices to Chapters 3, 5 and 6 my own attempts to model this linkage. These are first attempts only, and I shall be very grateful to hear from readers who have been able to modify the models or to replicate the tests there reported.

I have been continuously involved with overseas aid ever since, in 1979–80, I spent a year as an economic adviser at the UK Overseas Development Administration working on issues of aid policy and management, and I would like to thank John Healey and James Winpenny, two of my colleagues at that time, for their sane and practical encouragement then and ever since. Four years later I worked as consultant to a study of aid effectiveness commissioned by the Development Committee of the World Bank and IMF; much of the analysis of this book stems from ideas generated then, and I am particularly grateful for the intellectual stimulus provided by Adrian Hewitt, Michael Lipton and John Toye, three of my fellow-consultants on that study. Bron Gyngell typed an immaculate final draft of the book. The University of Manchester, which now employs me, gave me the necessary time to write the book by appointing me to a Hallsworth Fellowship for the academic year 1985/6. Finally, my two greatest debts are acknowledged in the dedication. My six colleagues in the Independent Group on British Aid have been, for four years now, an inspiration in showing that it is possible for people from widely varying professional backgrounds to work together in pursuit of greater public participation in, and a better quality of, overseas aid. And Helena Dwornik lived, and helped the book, through nearly all of the book's uncomfortable gestation period in the winter of 1985/6. Although the support and criticism of these people enriched the final version of the book beyond measure, it goes without saying that none of them bear any responsibility for what follows, and that any errors therein are mine alone.

Paul Mosley
Hayfield, Derbyshire   April 1986

Part I
Introduction

1 The Theoretical Case: Overseas Aid as a 'Public Good'

Overseas aid, for the purposes of this book, is money transferred on concessional terms by the governments of rich countries to the governments of poor countries.[1] It is big business: about $35 billion in 1985, about three-quarters of it transferred direct, and the remaining quarter through multilateral institutions such as the World Bank and the UN family of agencies. This $35 billion, as illustrated by Table 1.1, amounts to about one-third of all capital inflows into the Third World as a whole, and for the poorer countries it is a great deal more. In this book we shall seek to argue that, on balance, these flows do good, and should continue. But before we get there we must first ask, why do they exist in the first place?

The most obvious answer is compassion. It is clearly wrong in most people's judgement that most people in rich countries should be able to lead lives of considerable luxury whilst a thousand million people—a quarter of the world's population—do not even get enough to eat.[2] But individual taxpayers in these countries, because of selfishness or ignorance, may not recognise this moral imperative; if they recognise it, they may not know what they can do about it as individuals; if they do know what they can do, namely give to voluntary agencies, they may be reluctant to give unless assured that others will also contribute their share.[3] Lacking such an assurance, they look to governments to provide on an international basis, through aid, the same functions of income redistribution which they supply on a national basis through the progressive income tax and the various institutions of social security.[4]

Table 1.1: Capital flows into developing countries from all sources in selected years 1970–85 ($ billion)

		1970	1975	1980	1982	1983	1984	1985
(1)	*Official development assistance* of which:	8.1	20.1	37.5	34.7	33.6	34.6	35.2
	bilateral	7.0	16.2	29.7	27.2	26.1	26.8	27.7
	multilateral	1.1	3.9	7.8	7.5	7.5	7.8	7.5
(2)	*Grants by private voluntary agencies*	0.9	1.3	2.3	2.3	2.2	2.6	3.1
(3)	*Non-concessional capital flows* of which:	10.9	34.3	59.4	60.4	63.9	47.8	44.8
	Official — total	3.9	10.5	24.5	22.0	19.6	17.6	15.8
	Export credits	2.7	5.6	13.6	9.8	7.6	5.4	3.0
	'Hard' loans from multilateral agencies	0.7	2.5	4.9	6.6	7.0	8.2	8.8
	'Hard' loans from bilateral agencies	0.5	2.4	6.0	5.6	5.0	4.0	4.0
	Private — total	7.0	23.8	34.9	38.4	44.3	30.2	29.0
	Direct investment	3.7	11.4	10.5	11.9	7.9	10.4	8.0
	Bank lending	3.0	12.0	23.0	26.0	36.0	17.4	13.0
	Bond lending & other private	0.3	0.4	1.4	0.5	0.5	2.4	8.0
(4) = (1)+ (2)+(3)	*Total capital flow to developing countries*	19.9	55.7	99.2	97.4	99.7	85.0	83.1
$\frac{(1)}{(4)}$	Official development assistance as percentage of total capital flow	40.7	36.0	37.8	35.6	33.7	40.7	42.3
$\frac{(2)}{(4)}$	Grants by voluntary agencies as percentage of total capital flow	4.5	2.3	2.3	2.3	2.2	3.0	3.7

Source: World Bank. *World Development Report 1985*. Table 2.3. Updated for 1984 and 1985 from OECD, *Financial Resources for developing countries: 1985 and recent trends*, press release PRESS/A (86)27, 18 June 1986.

Governments' own motives for fulfilling these functions, of course, go well beyond the desire to put leverage behind the compassionate motives felt by individuals. Foreign and defence ministries have seen aid as a means of winning, and holding, the political and military support of Third World countries; trade and employment ministries have seen it as a means of winning a foothold in the markets of Third World countries and hence creating jobs at home; ministries of overseas development and, in some cases, finance have seen it as a means of promoting growth in Third World countries for the benefit of both those countries and the world economy. These three objectives, as will already be obvious, overlap only tenuously with one another and with the compassionate motive for aid expressed by members of the public. The fundamental point at issue in this book is whether overseas aid flows can do anything useful towards realising any of these objectives and whether, if they can, it is best done by government.

Whether they do any good, in any of the senses considered above, is an empirical question, to be settled by investigation of the facts; the whole of Part III is devoted to such an investigation. Let us for a moment hold that question in suspense, and ask whether, if aid does confer benefits, government provision is the best way of conveying them. In economic theory there exist several justifications for intervention by the government in the economy.[5] Some things which give happiness, pleasure or comfort might never exist if their provision were left to the free market (such as public parks and police protection); this is called *total market failure*. Some things which probably would exist in a free market may be supplied in inadequate measure if it is difficult to get beneficiaries to pay for them (road maintenance), if consumers are ignorant about the nature of the service being provided for them (health care) or if the agency which provides the service does not benefit financially from doing so (pollution control); all of these are cases of *partial market failure*. If the distribution of income or wealth is thought to be unjust, the government is the only institution with the resources of compulsory taxation which make it possible to redistribute income on a large scale. Finally, many schools of macroeconomics argue that it is possible for a number of markets in modern economies, in particular the market for labour, to remain in disequilibrium for a substantial time and that it is a major function of governments to stabilise the economy by stimulating aggregate demand when it is deficient and reducing demand when it is excessive.

It will be very obvious that governments, by our earlier argument, are the only institutions capable of fulfilling the *redistributive* function of aid. Voluntary transfers, as we saw in Table 1.1, only account for some 3 per cent of the total flow of resources into developing countries and are about one-twelfth the size of official flows; there is little prospect, therefore, that if that official flow were to be redistributed through voluntary agencies on a large scale, the administrations of voluntary agencies would be capable of handling the extra money and making sure it was effectively used. If even the amount of redistribution between rich and poor countries that aid currently achieves is desired, therefore, it can only be done by governments and by multilateral agencies acting on their behalf.

The extent to which government-to-government aid can improve the allocation of resources or stabilise the world economy is harder to assess. The allocative case for aid rests on the presumption that the international capital market is imperfect, and in particular does not work in such a way as to provide significant private finance for development in the poorest and least developed countries.[6] It is imperfect because of the presence of enormous uncertainties concerning the yield on capital, which in turn derive from the structure of the economy. In very poor countries, characteristically, four-fifths of national income or more derives from agriculture, animal husbandry and fishing; such activities, being dependent on biological processes, are subject to vagaries of climate and disease which do not affect most industrial processes. Furthermore, any attempts made to raise productivity in these fields are, of their very nature, experimental: the approach which turns out to be right for a given area will only be right for the soil conditions, climate and social conditions of that particular area, and may take a long time to find, in particular because the information available for lenders on the profitability of different technical specifications for a project is so poor. The uncertainties involved in finding it may well deter, and on the evidence of Table 1.2 do deter, foreign private capital from investing in the least developed countries, even though potentially profitable projects do exist as much there as in richer countries.[7] Investments in primary education may have an average expected economic rate of return of 30 per cent, and in agricultural research an average expected rate of return of 10 to 15 per cent, but such estimates of the mean rate of return will be no attraction to lenders if the variance around the mean is suspected to be excessive, the economic benefits hard to capture in financial terms and the payback period long.[8] Outside the dominant natural resources sectors, prospects for private investment are little better in the least developed countries, for reasons of small domestic markets and lack of skilled manpower. The situation is particularly bad in sub-Saharan Africa, where in 1983 only 16 per cent of incoming capital flows were from non-official sources.[9] Domestic capital, meanwhile, must contend, as soon as it ventures outside the urban business districts, not only with these uncertainties, but also with high interest rates which reflect the uncertainties themselves. In a poor and remote rural area, borrowers with good projects who intend to repay their loans cannot be distinguished from potential delinquents; nor is the legal system usually able to recover owings from those borrowers who do default on their debts. All borrowers, as a consequence, must be charged the same (high) interest rate, with the consequence that, as Anderson and Khambata have written: 'those with good projects either are driven out of the market or must reduce their investments substantially. In both cases there is a loss of economic efficiency.'[10]

The imperfections of capital markets outside the 'formal sector' of developing countries do not end here. For the expected rate of return on development projects in these areas is not a constant, but can be expected to rise over time as a consequence of complementary investment and 'learning by doing' effects.[11] Consider, as a hypothetical case of such a project, a scheme to develop the export of

Table 1.2: Twenty poorest countries: inward capital flows on concessional and non-concessional terms, 1960–80

Country	(1) Official development assistance as percentage of GNP (average 1960–80)	(2) Non-concessional flows (official and private) as percentage of GNP (average 1960–80)	(3) (2) as percentage of (1)
Chad	13.3[a]	0.8[a]	6[a]
Ethiopia	3.2	0.7	21
Mali	11.9	0.6	5
Zaire	5.9	1.2	20
Uganda	2.1	0.9	43
Somalia	19.4	2.7	14
Madagascar	4.6	1.1	24
Nepal	3.4	0.1	3
Niger	9.7	2.0	21
Mozambique	1.3	0.4	31
Bangladesh	9.0[a]	0.1[a]	1[a]
Burma	2.7	0.6	22
Pakistan	4.8	0.4	8
India	2.0	0.1	5
Sri Lanka	4.9	0.5	10
Malawi	9.8	1.8	18
Upper Volta	10.7	0.3	3
Rwanda	11.3	0.1	1
Tanzania	7.0	1.6	23
Sudan	3.6	1.9	53
Weighted average, twenty poorest countries	4.6	0.5	11

Source: OECD, *Geographical Distribution of Financial Flows to Less Developed Countries*. successive issues from 1965 to 1983.
Notes: For countries denoted[a], data relate to the period 1970–80 only.

handicrafts from an area of the Nepalese Himalayas which is three days' walk from the nearest road. If money is put into this scheme over a period of several years, then it can be expected that, first, the cost per garment produced will fall over time as trainees become more skilled on the job, and, second, the existence of an export trade in garments will stimulate the building of local roads by private or commercial enterprise. But such effects, operating through time, appear not to be correctly anticipated by local capitalists in any rate the poorest developing countries.[12] In such circumstances there is a case for external agencies to act as a 'market substitute' and to provide concessional finance on a transitory basis for what is in effect an infant-industry subsidy.

The argument so far may be summarised by Figure 1.1.

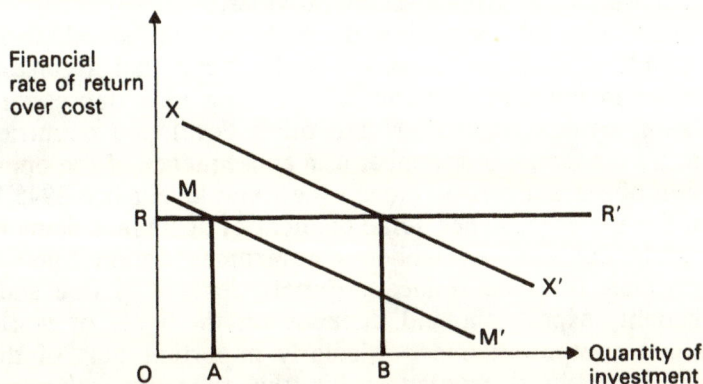

Figure 1.1: Allocation arguments for overseas aid

RR' is the minimum tolerable rate of return (say 10 per cent), *XX'* is the actual (*ex post*) rate of return on investment, and *MM'* is the *minimum ex ante* rate of return on investment, as anticipated by local and foreign businessmen in a typical very poor country. The quantity of investment is *OA* if businessmen make the most pessimistic assumptions possible about future rates of return, but *OB* if they could make correct forecasts of rates of return.

We have argued that:

(1) potential investors will make highly pessimistic forecasts of future rates of return on account of the presence of many risks against which they cannot insure;

(2) imperfections in the credit market will pull down MM' and XX' below the positions which they would occupy if information were perfect;

(3) both MM' and XX' will tend to rise over time as a consequence of 'learning by doing effects' and complementary investments, which may not be correctly anticipated by the private sector.

For all these reasons there is a case on allocative grounds for public overseas aid in the form of 'pump-priming investment' to supplement the inadequate capital investment which the private sector provides.

The case for providing overseas aid on stabilisation grounds is a simple extension of the Keynesian argument for an increase in government spending in a depression. Unemployment in Britain and other developed countries has no tendency to disappear as a consequence of the operation of market forces, indeed the trend level since 1945 is on the increase, hence some element of aggregate demand must be expanded by deliberate government action if unemployment is to be reduced. Export demand is one such element; export demand depends on the level of world output; output in one particularly important part of the world can be expanded, using the allocative argument already developed, by increases in the level of overseas aid. These may not only *increase* export demand in the Third World, but also *reduce its instability*, with probably beneficial effects for the growth of investment catering to such demand. A particularly important route by which they can do this is by compensating for the instability of private international capital flows. More even than other forms of investment, international lending by banks is subject to waves of euphoria and panic, the latter often caused by and tending to aggravate world recession: for example, in the most recent slump, between 1980 and 1983, long-term export credits to sub-Saharan Africa fell from $1.25 billion to $250 million. International aid flows can act in a counter-cyclical manner to cushion the effect on the poorest countries of such abrupt fluctuations in the availability of capital.[13]

This argument for aid is not new: it was first deployed, to the author's knowledge, by Lord Milner, the British Colonial Secretary from 1919 to 1921. Writing in the *Observer*, he argued that:

What these countries (i.e. the colonies) need ... is economic equipment— roads, railways, engines, tractors, and in some cases, notably the Sudan, irrigation works. It would increase employment and purchasing power at home as well as in the countries where the work of development is proceeding ... Their development is a question of money—and money from outside.[14]

However, the case for money aid flows to 'prime the pump' for economic recovery in Western countries has become more powerful since colonial times. The openness of all advanced economies to international trade and capital flows has markedly increased in the postwar period—for example, Britain's average propensity to import rose from 19 to 44 per cent between 1946–51 and 1976–81[15]—and in Stewart's view this increased openness has augmented the deflationary bias which financial markets impose on the world economy. 'Whereas deflationary policies adopted by a particular country tend to be validated and reinforced by the responses of the world financial community', he argues that expansionary policies are likely to be weakened or reversed,[16] citing as examples the case of Britain in 1976 and France in 1982, both of whom were compelled to abandon mildly reflationary macroeconomic policies by a flight of international capital from the low interest rates and relatively high inflation which those policies were provoking. No such discipline operates to provoke a reversal of policy by a government whose macroeconomic stance is too restrictive. Deflation in one country is perfectly possible (and, of course, repeatedly enjoined by the International Monetary Fund (IMF)) whereas reflation in one country is wellnigh impossible in a capitalist economy.

There is, therefore, a particularly strong case at the present time for reflation in all Organisation for Economic Co-operation and Development (OECD) countries through the 'surrogate' medium of international capital flows; such was, of course, the message of the Brandt Commission (1980,

1983) which eloquently argued the case for international aid as a self-interested rather than a moral or redistributive act.[17] Whether these capital flows take the form of concessional aid or of non-concessional flows such as bank lending is, of course, a quite separate question. There is no reason to suppose that a dollar of concessional aid will generate more or less imports from the West than a dollar of non-concessional credit, but current American initiatives (Autumn 1985) towards a 'Brandt-type strategy' favour non-concessional credit and hence the more prosperous developing countries.[18]

We have therefore established:

first, a *redistributive* case for aid, based on the value judgement that the conditions of life available to the poorer people of the Third World today are not acceptable, and should be relieved by transfers of income from those who have more;

second, an *allocative* case for aid, based on multiple imperfections in the market for capital investment and loan finance in developing countries;

third, a *stabilisation* case for aid, based on the proposition that aid flows can augment world aggregate demand and relieve unemployment, particularly in developed countries.

These three justifications for aid can be considered *universal*, that is, they are valid for the world taken as a whole. There are two further arguments for aid which are *particular*, that is, they are valid only for individual countries and not for the world as a whole. These are that bilateral aid by one country can (a) buy political support for that country, and (b) increase exports from that country. As we saw earlier, these particularistic arguments for aid underlie much of the domestic political pressures for aid in donor countries. It is tempting to sneer at these arguments, on the ground that what good they do for individual donor countries can only be at the expense of other donor countries, and possibly the recipient as well. But, as the quotation at the front of this book reminds us, aid, like anything else, can do good even if transferred for the 'wrong' motive. A major purpose of this book will be to find out whether aid, for whatever motive it is given, actually achieves any of the functions of redistribution and reallocation of resources that it ought to be achieving. We shall consider aid's ability to win political support in the next chapter, its ability to promote growth in Chapter 5;[19] its ability to redistribute income in Chapter 6, and its ability to promote exports in Chapter 7.

The reader will be aware that a theoretical case has been made against aid as well as for it, and before we turn to the business of empirical verification it will be useful to consider how this case relates to the abstract case for the defence presented thus far. Overseas aid is one of those topics which unites the radical right and the radical left against the middle. But the two groups of radicals arrive at the same conclusion—distaste for aid flows—by a different process of reasoning. The case of the radical right, repeatedly articulated by Professor Bauer but stridently popularised in recent years by newspapers such as the London *Times* and *Sun*, is allocative: aid will, first of all, reduce the cost of 'leisure' in relation to 'effort' for the recipient government, and thus reduce the amount of effort the recipient is prepared to make towards development.[20] In terms of the popular metaphor which likens international to domestic redistribution of goods and services, the recipient government is turned into a 'pauper' by being offered a 'crutch'.[21] In the second place, aid flows impede the international division of labour by encouraging misguided attempts towards 'self-sufficiency' or 'inward-looking' economic policies by recipient governments. Bauer frequently alleges, in particular, that inflows of overseas aid are the cause of acts of nationalisation and expropriation of multinational companies by host governments.[22] By contrast the argument of the radical left is essentially redistributive; by redistributing money now, it contends, you make it harder in the long run to redistribute to the poor the really crucial thing, which is power, and indeed you entrench in power regimes which are anxious to continue expropriating the poor.[23] Sometimes, however, the argument is supplemented by the allocative proposition that aid increases capital intensity or reduces the propensity to save in recipient countries.[24] To summarise, the right argue that the *allocative* case for aid is undone by side-effects on the supply of effort and on private investment in recipient countries, whereas the left argue that the *redistributive* case is undone by an improper focus by analysts on the distribution of income rather than on the distribution of power. The second of these propositions is a matter of differing priorities or value judgements, and as such not susceptible to empirical analysis. The first, however, is eminently a testable proposition, and will be examined in Chapter 5.

In what follows it will be important to lay repeated stress on one critical point. This is that to demonstrate, as we have done, that there exist gaps which aid ideally *ought* to fill is not to demonstrate that the system of international aid that we have *actually does* fill those gaps. The very word 'system', although we shall be using it from time to time, is of course a misnomer. It has rightly been said of the British tax system (by Kay and King) that 'nobody would design such a system, and nobody did'.[25] The comment applies with even greater force to the cluster of redistributive measures which constitute international aid. Not only has the system grown piecemeal, like national fiscal systems, but in addition, unlike those systems, it is not under the control of any one authority. It is under the control of many authorities, national and supranational, frequently in bitter rivalry and often trying by means of this one instrument of policy to realise a large number of incompatible objectives. But it is the only system that we have, and the relevant question is, of course, not whether some idealised system of aid would do more good but whether the one which we have, plus any reforms which may be thought feasible, is worth having and if so what those reforms are.

The task of this book, then, is to draw up a balance sheet: to catalogue the ways in which aid improves on the operation of the market, and the ways in which, as at present constituted, it appears to make matters worse. The poor quality of many of the data we shall be handling means that our conclusions must often be tentative. Those conclusions are, as the title of the book implies, that aid is an activity which should be reformed and defended, not dismantled; but there is much that can and must be reformed at once, and much more that ought to be reformed if it were not for the presence of what seem to be immovable political and administrative constraints within the developing countries. The first step, therefore, is to get a feel for the way in which the politics of aid operate. This is done in the next three chapters. Having thus defined the constraints, we can then turn to questions of aid effectiveness: of whether aid actually does what idealists would like it to do.

NOTES

1. There are minor exceptions to this generalisation: some aid for development is given by voluntary agencies (*see* next paragraph); some aid is given not to governments in less developed countries, but to private-sector agencies such as development banks (*see* Chapter 7 below); some aid such as food aid is given in kind rather than in cash.
2. World Bank, *World Development Report 1984*, pp. 5–6.
3. The 'Bowles Report' on *Attitudes to official development assistance* (Bowles, 1978) sheds interesting light on these matters.
4. The international redistribution of income achieved by aid may be seen, therefore, as an 'international public good': a service desired by many which, however, cannot be satisfactorily brought into existence by the efforts of individuals acting in isolation.
5. *See*, for example, Brown and Jackson (1982), Chapter 2.
6. One strand in the birth of overseas aid in the 1940s, indeed, was a desire to stimulate the economies of poor countries at a time when the government-to-government bond market had been moribund since the inter-war great depression; see Chapter 2.
7. The World Bank (1982a) p. 11 reports that economic rates of return for poverty-focused projects (most of which were in agriculture) were, on average, no lower than rates of return for other projects. In their 1985 *World Development Report*, at p. 1, they go further and claim: 'Capital has long flowed from richer to poorer countries. It has done so because it is relatively scarcer in economies that are at earlier changes of development and the expected rate of return tends to be correspondingly higher.'
   As between rich and poor countries this theoretical expectation may be confirmed by the facts. But it is not true as between poor countries: rates of return achieved by the World Bank in sub-Saharan Africa, the poorest region, over the period 1960–80 are only 14.7

per cent by comparison with 21.2 per cent in South and South-East Asia, the most prosperous. World Bank, *Ninth Annual Review of Project Performance Audit Results* (Washington, 1983); *see also* Chapter 5, Note 27.

8. These figures are from World Bank, *World Development Report 1985*, p. 99.

9. World Bank, *World Development Report 1985*, p. 88.

10. Anderson and Khambata (1985), p. 350. The problem is one of 'quality uncertainty' as identified by Akerlof (1970), similar to that faced by the buyer of a used car: lacking the information with which to distinguish a good car from a 'lemon' the buyer may withdraw altogether from the market rather than contend with the small probability of buying a 'lemon', leading in extreme cases to a collapse of the demand side of the market and partial or total market failure. Quality uncertainty can lead to failure in the capital markets of developed as well as developing countries: individual investors working from home often have enormous difficulty in getting venture capital houses to back what are often brilliant and cost-effective inventions (*see Sunday Times*, London, 14 October 1984). And in other markets too, notoriously the market for artistic talent. The argument for government intervention in each of these markets, as argued here for the specific case of capital markets in developing countries, is essentially the same.

11. Arrow (1962) demonstrates that: 'the presence of learning means that an act of investment benefits future investors, but this benefit is not paid for by the market. Hence it is to be expected that the aggregate amount of investment under the competitive model ... will fall short of the socially optimal level.'

12. This problem is particularly severe with projects which do not yield tradable output directly or yield it only over a long period of 20 or 30 years (in particular infrastructure such as water supply, transport, power, telecommunications, health) since most private investors expect to recoup their capital over a short period of 7–8 years maximum and are reluctant to attach any weight at all to benefits which are expected to materialise any further into the future.

13. World Bank, *World Development Report 1985*, box 7.2 p. 96. On private capital flows during the 1980–3 recession *see also* United Kingdom, House of Commons, Fourth Report from the Treasury and Civil Service Committee, (session 1982–3) *International Monetary Arrangements*, 3 vols.

14. Lord Milner, writing in the *Observer*, 1923; quoted in Ian M. Drummond, *British Economic Policy and the Empire 1919–39* (London, Allen and Unwin, 1974), p. 40.

15. Data from successive issues of *Economic Trends*.

16. Stewart (1983), p. 60.

17. *See* in particular Brandt Commission (1980), Chapter 3, and for a critical symposium covering many of the issues raised by the Com-

mission, the entire issue of the *Third World Quarterly* for October 1980.

18. The 'Baker plan', launched by the US Secretary of the Treasury James Baker at the Seoul Conference of the World Bank and IMF in October 1985, urges Western commercial banks to lend an extra $20 billion, and the World Bank and other development banks an equivalent amount, over the period 1986–8 to the fifteen most financially indebted countries. Most of these (e.g. Argentina, Brazil, Mexico, South Korea, Philippines) are middle-income countries.

19. On this question depends empirical support for both the allocation and the stabilisation arguments, since if aid cannot promote growth in the recipient country, it cannot stabilise demand in the world economy.

20. Whether it is appropriate to personify a government in this way is an open question.

21. At the present time this image of aid recipients as 'spongers' on an international 'welfare state' is being relentlessly pursued by the London *Times*; *see* for example editorial entitled 'Privatising aid' in the issue for 9 July 1985.

22. A typical statement of Bauer's position is as follows:

Almost all recipients of foreign aid restrict the inflow and deployment of private foreign capital. During the last decade or so these restrictions have increasingly developed into expropriation of foreign capital, often accompanied by the expulsion of the owners and their employees. As a result, the inflow of foreign aid is matched by an outflow of both domestic and foreign private capital. Bauer (1965), pp. 45–6.

23. Hayter and Watson (1985), Chapter 10; Lappe (1980), *passim.*

24. *See*, for example, Griffin (1970).

25. Kay and King (1982), preface p. vii.

Part II
Historical and Theoretical Background

2 The International Politics of Aid

2.1 DONORS: OUTLINE HISTORY

Overseas aid, so named, is a by-product of decolonisation: the expression 'overseas aid' is not found in newspapers or official documents until after the Second World War. But since the nineteenth century it has been a common practice for governments to transfer money on concessional terms to the governments of their colonies under the label of 'grant in aid', 'budgetary subsidy' or some such term. The governments of Britain, France, Germany and the United States all gave 'infant colony subsidies' of this sort before 1914,[1] but invariably on a temporary basis and without the slightest connotation of moral obligation or aid for 'development', a word which itself was not part of the vocabulary of the time.[2] Very frequently, indeed, 'aid' of this sort had to be kept going longer than planned because the colonies' budgets had been thrown into deficit by unexpected expenditures arising from the suppression of revolts by the indigenous people.[3] In those days, as now, grants-in-aid by colonial authorities to their colonies fulfilled the function of propping up the bottom end of the international capital market. Private capital, then as now, was scarcely interested in the poorer developing countries; it has been estimated that in 1914, at the climax of the golden age of international capital movements, 75 per cent of all overseas assets were held in North and South America, Europe and Oceania.[4].

During the inter-war period, the United States took over from Britain as the major source of new capital flows;

however, the period witnessed a major contraction of overseas investment under the stress of the great depression,
the adoption of protectionist policies by very many
countries, and ultimately a default on loan repayments by
most Latin American countries in 1931 and 1932. It is
against the background of a depressed world economy and
stagnation in private capital markets that, for the first time,
the idea of overseas aid for *development* enters political
discussion. As we have seen, it was proposed principally as
a pump-priming device to relieve unemployment in the
aiding country. Lord Milner's impassioned plea, quoted in
the previous chapter,[5] was but the first of many attempts
to argue, sixty years before the Brandt Commission, for aid
as a means of promoting 'mutual interests' in development.[6]
The actual amounts of development aid disbursed during the
inter-war period, by provisions such as the British Colonial
Development Act of 1929, were minute. Abbott estimates
that total expenditure under the Act was some £6 million
over the entire decade of the 1930s, or less than 0.1 per
cent of British national income;[7] most of it was allocated to
the development, through technical assistance and through
infrastructure, of imperial resources of raw materials such
as Ugandan cotton for the Lancashire cotton mills.

During the Second World War imperial sources of raw
materials became more important for both Britain and
France, and the scope of their colonial development programmes was enlarged to include in particular provision for
projects to enlarge the 'human capital stock' through health
and education projects.[8] In the post-war period the continuing dollar shortage caused these programmes to be
expanded to embrace grandiose schemes for imperial self-
sufficiency in food, notoriously the 'Groundnut Scheme' in
Southern Tanzania into which £20 million was poured
between 1946 and 1952 for a return of zero:[9] the world's
first 'white elephant' aid project, and one which still yields
valuable lessons for present policy. These are discussed in
Chapter 6.

It is in the early 1950s that one sees the beginning of aid
in its present-day sense, as a transaction between sovereign
states, with the beginning of the US development pro-

gramme in South-East Asia. At the conclusion of the Korean War, in 1951, the United States Government felt very uncertain of being able to contain the spread of communism in Asia unless it could provide some demonstration that the capitalist economy worked better there than the centrally planned economy.[10] Such a demonstration, it was felt, could be provided by transfers of concessional money, which might vitalise the poor countries of Asia on the communist periphery—South Korea, South Vietnam, Taiwan—in much the same way as Marshall Aid, which was also free, had revitalised the rich but war-damaged countries of Europe between 1948 and 1952. These, of course, were the years in which physical capital was seen as the key limiting factor in economic development, and the 'incremental capital–output ratio' as a fairly dependable link between capital investment and growth.[11] The difference between 'reconstruction' and 'development' operations was not, at that stage, apparent to most people. The figures of Table 2.1 show the degree of concentration of American aid in 'key' Asian countries in the 1950s.

The early 1950s were also the years in which the World Bank[12] switched its attention from Reconstruction to Devel-

Table 2.1: US aid commitments to selected countries, fiscal year 1954–5

Destination	Amount ($m)	% of total aid budget
South Vietnam	324	18
South Korea	301	17
Taiwan	132	7
Turkey	90	5
India	86	5
Pakistan	63	3
Other Asian (including Near East)	362	20
Total Asia	1,358	75
Total world-wide	1,821	100

Source: White (1974), p. 202, supplemented by *Economic Report of the President and Annual Report of the Council of Economic Advisers for 1955.*

opment. The Bank, set up at the Bretton Woods conference in 1944 as one of the pillars of the international post-war economic order, was the first and is still the most important vehicle for multilateral transfers of money from rich to poor countries, although a large proportion of its loans are made on quasi-market terms and hence do not formally count as 'aid'.[13] By the middle 1950s its task of lending for the repair of war damage in Europe and Japan was over, and the Bank had become exclusively a development institution, lending at this stage largely to Asia and South America.

During the second half of the 1950s the Soviet Union became, for the first time, a substantial donor of aid. Until Stalin's death in 1953 the sole financial link between the USSR and the developing countries had been its support for local communist parties. But after the first conference of 'non-aligned' countries at Bandung in 1955 it became clear that the world could not be rigidly divided into pro-communist and anti-communist governments, and that there existed a group of countries, most of them underdeveloped, who were for the superpowers what floating voters are for competing political parties: objects of persuasion. The Soviet Union formally announced its acknowledgement of this point in 1956.[14] The obvious instrument of persuasion was development aid. The five countries which thus became the principal objects of superpower competition in development aid from the middle 1950s on were Egypt, Iran, Afghanistan, Indonesia and, most important of all, India. India's Second Five-Year Plan, introduced in 1956, was much influenced by Soviet ideas of comprehensive planning with priority to heavy industry, and was centred on the expansion of the steel industry through the construction of three new plants at Bhilai, Durgapur and Rourkela. The contracts for the Durgapur and Rourkela plants went to firms in Britain and West Germany, respectively, on commercial terms; the Russians financed the Bhilai steel mill with a highly concessional loan.

During the later 1950s and early 1960s the African colonies of both Britain and France became independent in quick succession. This led to a very rapid expansion of the aid programmes of those two countries, which in many cases took over responsibility not only for the development budget but also for large lumps of the recurrent budget such as the salaries of expatriate civil servants. Some of these countries, notably Ghana, Nigeria, Kenya and Zambia, also became the object of competitive offers of aid from the United States and the Soviet Union. It was also in the early 1960s that Japan, West Germany, Holland and the Scandinavian countries, none of whom had ever been colonial powers on any scale, became substantial donors of aid for the first time, as illustrated by Table 2.2. The market for aid transfers had moved rather rapidly from virtual United States monopoly in the early 1950s, to US–Soviet duopoly in selected countries in the late 1950s, to a situation of fairly free actual or potential competition between donors by the early 1960s. And as it did so, the scope for political or other leverage by any one donor was reduced, except in the unlikely event that it was able to conscript its 'competitors' into supporting the form of conditionality which it was trying to impose. We return to this point in section 2.4.

As the scope for crude political leverage was reduced, so donors began to lay more stress on the presumed developmental impact of aid. Cynically, this can be interpreted as competition between the donors based on the quality of their product. But there was more to the expansion of aid in the 1960s than intensification of competition between donors. This decade was the high-water mark of idealism concerning what overseas aid could achieve. It was the first United Nations Development Decade, in which for the first time a target was announced for the annual growth rate of GNP in the Third World (5 per cent) and for the ratio of aid to GNP for donors (0.7 per cent).[15] It was the decade in which most countries first began to formulate a policy towards the Third World, and in which an institution, the Development Assistance Committee of the OECD, was set up to co-ordinate the efforts and policies of the Western donor nations. It was a period of substantial multilateralisation of aid, as Tables 2.2 and 2.3 illustrate, with the EEC, the regional development banks and the World Bank's International Development Agency emerging as donors of aid which, it was hoped, might be free of the

Table 2.2: Total disbursement of concessional resources to developing countries 1951–84 (millions of current US dollars)

Bilateral donors (percentage of GNP in brackets)	1950–5 average	1961	1971	1981	1984	1985
United States	1,118(0.32)	3,026(0.57)	3,112(0.33)	5,760(0.19)	8,711(0.24)	9,555(0.24)
Japan	10(0.04)	108(0.20)	510(0.22)	3,170(0.28)	4,319(0.35)	3,797(0.29)
Great Britain	190(0.42)	457(0.59)	622(0.44)	2,194(0.43)	1,418(0.33)	1,531(0.34)
France	500(1.24)	903(1.36)	1,075(0.68)	4,177(0.73)	3,788(0.77)	4,022(0.79)
W. Germany	38(0.11)	366(0.44)	734(0.34)	3,182(0.47)	2,782(0.45)	2,935(0.47)
Netherlands	17(0.27)	56(0.45)	216(0.58)	1,509(1.07)	1,268(1.02)	1,135(0.91)
Sweden, Norway, Denmark	4(0.04)	23(0.10)	224(0.40)	1,789(0.80)	1,733(0.89)	1,836(0.89)
Other OECD	76	304	1,008	3,759	4,667	4,769
OECD Total	1,953(0.34)	5,243(0.54)	7,501(0.33)	25,540(0.35)	28,686(0.36)	29,580(0.35)
OPEC States	—	—	442(0.76)	8,364(1.51)	4,545(0.86)	3,000(0.56)
Centrally planned economies	—	1,605a	2,023b	2,991(0.21)	3,033(0.21)	3,1200.21)
Bilateral total	(1,953)	6,848	10,016	36,895	36,264	35,700
Multilateral donorsc						
World Bank Group	—	–122a	567b	1,952	2,533	..
United Nations agencies	—	463a	1,330b	2,771	2,739	..
European Economic Community	—	37a	895b	1,401	1,287	..
Other multilateral	—	–318a	196b	1,587	1,188	..
Multilateral total	—	60a	2,988b	7,711	7,747	..

Note: The disbursements quoted for bilateral donors include subscriptions to multilateral agencies. —=Data not available.
a1960–1. b1970–1. cConcessional flows only.
Source: OECD, Twenty-five Years of Development Cooperation: a Review, Paris 1985, Table III–I, p. 93. Updated from OECD, Financial resources for developing countries: 1985 and recent trends, press release PRESS/A (86)27, 18 June 1986.

Table 2.3: OECD donors: forms of aid 1960–83

| | Percentages of total aid flow committed in year stated | | | | | |
	1960	1965	1970	1975	1980	1984
Multilateral contributions	1.4	7.9	16.5	22.8	34.5	26.6
Bilateral —						
Project and sector aid			76.5	46.5	34.3	57.6
of which:						
agriculture				3.9	7.5	7.4
infrastructure	} 86.6	} 92.1		5.7	9.6	16.1
other				36.9	17.2	30.1
Programme aid				21.8	29.6	14.0
Food aid			7.0	8.9	2.0	1.8
Total	100	100	100	100	100	100

Sources: OECD, *Development Co-operations: Effects and Policies of the Members of the Development Assistance Committee*, Paris, 1984. Table II–E1 and corresponding tables in earlier issues.

economic and political costs imposed by much bilateral aid. Most strikingly, it was the period in which the largest bilateral donor, the United States, announced an intention to give aid to Third World countries 'not in order to contain the spread of communism, not because other nations are doing it, but because it is right'.[16] In intention, at least, overseas aid had transcended the concept of transnational bribery.

It was the end of the 1960s before one saw any signs of feedback from the process of development on the ground into aid policy. The feedback was of two kinds. At the level of efficiency, it was apparent that much aid, once committed, could not be spent on account of limits on the 'absorptive capacity' of recipient countries.[17] At the level of equity, research began to be published at the end of the decade which suggested that rapid growth of national income in developing countries was consistent with stagnation, or even decline, in the living standards of the lowest income groups in those countries;[18] and, by implication, that those most in need of aid were, at the least, getting no benefit from it.[19] The response to the first difficulty was for the bilateral donors, but not yet at this stage the multi-laterals, to release an increasing proportion of their aid budget as 'programme aid', that is, aid which is not tied to any specific project or training activity, but simply expands the recipient economy's capacity to import. Aid of this kind accounted, as Table 2.3 illustrates, for nearly 30 per cent of all bilateral aid by 1980.

The donors hoped at this stage that infusions of pro-gramme aid might remove foreign-exchange bottlenecks which domestic resources, for structural reasons such as flight of capital and the weakness of domestic tax systems, could not remove.[20] Some of them, especially the North American-based bilaterals and multilaterals, also hoped to use programme aid as a lever for bringing about changes in the policies of recipient countries towards the price of agricultural products, public utilities and foreign exchange, pressure for which has grown right through to the present day.[21]

Response by donors to the predicament of lower income groups was slower in coming. Not until 1973 did the World Bank announce,[22] under the stress of widespread famine in Africa, an intention to increase the proportion of its spend-ing which was intended to achieve a direct improvement in the welfare of poor people in rural areas and in shanty towns. This initiative was quickly copied by a number of bilateral donors, which by 1975 included all the Scan-dinavian countries, the Netherlands, Switzerland, the United States and the United Kingdom.[23] As illustrated in Table 2.3, disbursements of aid for agricultural projects rose rapidly in the second half of the 1970s. The 1970s were the decade of the 'integrated rural development project', in which aid donors—often acting in concert—poured comp-lementary inputs (e.g. roads, credit, extension advice, new seeds, fertilisers, irrigation) into the backward areas of developing countries in the hope of arresting the 'vicious circle of poverty'. This concentration on poverty reduction and equity in parts of the OECD aid community sat a little uncomfortably with the efforts being made in other parts of that community to make the economies of developing countries more efficient by 'getting prices right'.[24] The World Bank, however, insisted throughout the 1970s that the presumed conflict between equity and efficiency in aid policy did not exist and that 'redistribution from growth' in developing countries was possible.[25] But underneath the Bank's disclaimers, tension persisted, and within the OECD community a process of functional differentiation in aid policy was taking place. Britain, Canada, the United States and most stridently the World Bank moved to the 'efficiency' end of the spectrum and began, from 1980 on, to stress the quality of management and of price policy in developing countries as critical determinants of development; the programme loans which the World Bank gave to developing countries from 1980 on, called Structural Adjustment Loans, were in all cases made conditional on the implementation of 'supply-side' or incentive-boosting measures of policy, frequently involving privatisation of trade and industry by the recipient government.[26] So were many programme loans by the other donors mentioned. At the equity end of the spectrum, the governments of the Scandinavian countries and, more hesitantly, Holland and West Germany persisted with policies aimed at the poorest and continued to abjure conditionality as a means of raising the effectiveness of aid.

2.2 RECIPIENTS: WHO GETS WHAT AND WHY

It will be clear from Table 2.2 that development aid, once viewed as an instrument of the cold war, is now scarcely able to act in that role. Aid disbursements from centrally planned economies, which were around 31 per cent of the bilateral total in 1961, had by 1984 sunk to just over 8 per cent.[27] What is more, there is scarcely any overlap between the main recipients of aid from capitalist and communist countries. Table 2.4 shows the identity of the top ten aid recipients from OECD and from centrally planned economies respectively. If we look first at the data for 1983, we

Table 2.4: Major recipients of bilateral ODA from Western and Eastern bloc countries. Annual averages

(a) Percentages of total aid flow from OECD countries

	1960–1		1970–1		1982–3
India	11.4	India	11.5	Egypt	4.4
Algeria	7.4	Indonesia	7.2	Israel	4.0
Pakistan	4.8	S. Vietnam	4.8	India	3.0
South Korea	4.5	Pakistan	4.6	Indonesia	3.0
Brazil	3.4	South Korea	3.4	Bangladesh	2.4
S. Vietnam	3.3	Turkey	2.5	Turkey	1.7
Turkey	2.9	Brazil	2.0	*China*	1.6
Egypt	2.3	Papua N.G.	1.8	Tanzania	1.6
Yugoslavia	2.3	Colombia	1.4	Pakistan	1.5
Israel	2.2	Algeria	1.4	Sudan	1.4
Total	44.5		40.6		24.6

(b) Percentages of total aid flow from CMEA countries

		1976		1983
	Vietnam	30.1	Vietnam	35.2
	Cuba	20.6	Cuba	20.1
	Mongolia	15.9	Mongolia	18.4
	Iran	4.2	Afghanistan	9.7
	Iraq	3.7	*India*	1.4
	Egypt	3.4	Nicaragua	1.3
	Syria	3.1	*Syria*	1.3
	Laos	2.8	Ethiopia	1.2
	India	2.3	*Iraq*	0.9
	Pakistan	2.2	PDR Yemen	0.6
Total		88.3		90.1

Sources: For OECD countries, OECD, *Twenty-Five Years of Development Co-operation*, Paris 1985, Table III-11 for CMEA countries, United Kingdom Foreign Office, *Soviet, East European and Western Development Aid 1976–83*, Foreign Policy Document No. 108, London, December 1984.

Notes: CMEA = Council for Mutual Economic Assistance (COMECON) countries. Capitalist countries receiving aid from a communist source, and communist countries receiving aid from a capitalist source, are in italics.

find that the only country which appears both in the 'capitalist aid' and in the 'communist aid' list is India. The communist bloc has apparently been more willing to use economic aid to tempt neutral or ideologically opposed countries than the West, but as its aid has shrunk in purchasing power, so has it become concentrated on a few countries, with over 83 per cent in 1983 going to Vietnam, Cuba, Mongolia and Afghanistan. But if aid is not much used as an instrument of persuasion, it is certainly used to reward those countries which do cross the floor into the opposite camp. In the 1970s Egypt and Vietnam, after bitter wars, aligned themselves firmly on the capitalist and communist side respectively; they are now at the top of each bloc's list of aid recipients.

Attempts have been made to state formal hypotheses in explanation of the distribution of aid money. McKinley and Little, for example, have argued that the only statistically significant determinant of American, British, French and German aid disbursements in the 1960s was the 'foreign policy interests' of the donor, as measured by the existence or not of donor military bases and by the size of the Communist Party in the recipient country.[28] They have concluded that OECD aid flows are simply an instrument of power politics whose intentions are masked by 'developmental' rhetoric. This conclusion can be faulted on methodological grounds even for the 1960s.[29] But what is perhaps more important, it is confined to the 1960s, and cannot be in any case taken as a valid description of current aid allocation patterns.

What has happened since the 1960s, as we have seen, is that the number of donors to Third World countries has grown dramatically.[30] Most of the new donors, both bilateral (e.g. Japan, Scandinavia and West Germany) and multilateral (e.g. the International Fund for Agricultural Development, IFAD, and EEC) have no particular geopolitical interests to advance by means of their aid. As their numbers have grown, so the share of the US and the Soviet Union in the total aid flow has diminished, and the political leverage which they were able to exert by means of their own individual aid flows has diminished *pari passu*. The resulting pattern is one in which 'recipient need', as measured by income per capita, is by no means irrelevant as a determinant of aid flows. A crude demonstration of this is provided by Figure 2.1, which shows a broadly positive relationship between the poverty of Third World nations and the amount of aid, as a proportion of their GNP, which they receive. The relationship is statistically significant[31] but we may already note a number of deviations from it: small recipient countries (Mauritania, Lesotho) get a great deal more aid than the 'norm' and large countries (India, China) a great deal less; also those countries whose political support is thought to be essential to the donor will attract development aid over and above the 'norm' even if (Israel, Turkey) they are not really poor countries.

To sum up so far, we have found evidence both for the proposition that development aid is allocated according to the need of the recipient and for the proposition that it is allocated according to the political interest of the donor, but we have also found that 'political interest' is to be interpreted much more as the making of payments to allies to keep them faithful, than as the making of payments to neutrals or opponents in the hope of winning them over. The question which we now confront is whether even this strategy is an effective one. Frey has suggested that:

An industrialised country giving aid to a less developed country rarely does so unconditionally, but rather on the premise that the recipient country will take a political position favourable to the donor country, measured for instance by the proportion of votes it casts in line with the donor country's wishes in the United Nations.[32]

Is this expectation satisfied? In Table 2.5 we set out the proportion of votes cast in the UN General Assembly in support of the US by six major recipients of US aid, and in support of the Soviet Union by six major recipients of Soviet aid. India, as the only major recipient of aid from both Eastern and Western blocs, is in both categories. Each half of the table is subdivided into two groups, those who received an increasing share of the donor's aid and those who received a decreasing share. If Frey's prediction is correct, the former group should increase their level of

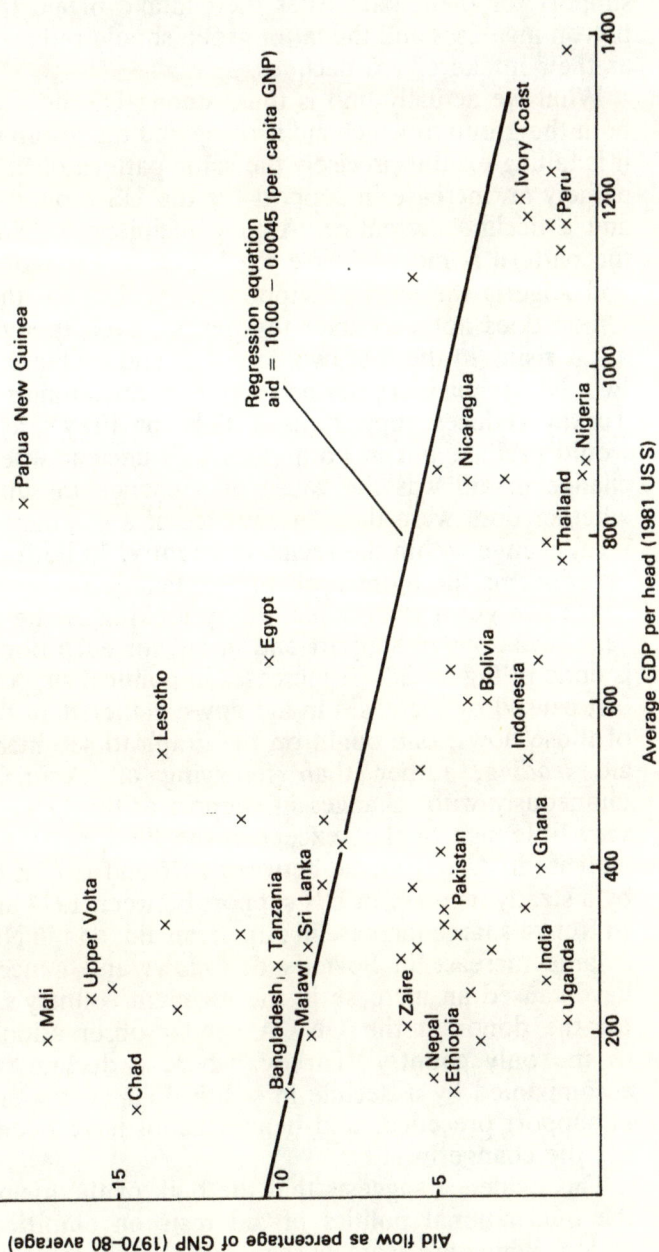

Figure 2.1 Poorer recipient countries: aid flows in relation to per capita GNP

support for their 'patron' as their intake of aid from that patron increases and the latter group should reduce support as their intake of aid declines.

What we actually find is that, among US aid recipients, both the group to which aid is rising and the group to which it is falling exhibit precisely the same pattern of behaviour, namely an increase in support for the US around 1978–80 and a decline thereafter. Among recipients of Soviet aid the pattern is more diverse. In Vietnam, Mongolia, India and Algeria the level of support in the UN for the Soviet Union does not vary over the period, even though Soviet aid is rising in the first two countries and falling in the last two. Nicaragua increases its support as Soviet aid rises, and Turkey reduces support as it falls, as Frey's hypothesis would predict, but in both cases it is unclear whether the change in aid was the cause of a change in support, or whether both were the consequence of a spontaneous political change within the recipient country. In both cases the latter seems the more probable explanation.

We can get a clearer picture by looking at the year-on-year variations in support and in aid for each donor. This is done in Figure 2.2. If increases in political support are in fact caused by increases in aid flows, rather than the cause of those flows, one ought on the graph to see increases in aid *leading*, rather than following or occurring simultaneously with, changes in support at the UN. There is very little sign of this, except in the Philippines where an increase in American aid between 1976 and 1977 is followed by a steady increase in UN support between 1977 and 1980. In Kenya a large increase in American aid, and in Nicaragua a large increase in Soviet aid, *follows* and hence cannot have caused an increase in the recipient country's support for the donor at the UN. A similar observation applies to the only country, Turkey, where a decline in aid is accompanied by a decline in political support: the decline in support preceded, and hence cannot have been caused by, the change in aid.

This evidence suggests that the bulk of theorising about the international politics of aid rests on empirical foundations which are scarcely secure. These theories take it as

Table 2.3: Voting pattern at UN General Assembly of six major recipients of aid from USA and the Soviet Union

Country	Level of aid ($m) from donor:		Proportion of votes[a] in UN General Assembly cast in support of donor. Session					
	in 1976	in 1983	31 (1976)	32 (1977)	33 (1978-9)	35 (1980)	36 (1981)	37 (1982-3)
(i) Major recipients of US aid								
(a) Aid inflow rising								
Kenya	13	74	5	0	19	19	15	10
Philippines	60	133	6	8	25	29	13	10
Somalia	2	46	10	0	16	25	15	17
(b) Aid inflow falling								
Pakistan	203	59	6	4	13	29	14	14
India	135	33	11	8	25	25	11	10
Tanzania	33	20	0	0	14	22	8	6
(ii) Major recipients of Soviet aid								
(a) Aid inflow rising								
Vietnam	500	1,025	NA	100	92	89	100	99
Mongolia	330	620	100	100	97	100	100	100
Nicaragua	—	45	50	46	47	89	94	97
(b) Aid inflow constant or falling								
India	41	50	88	91	75	74	88	90
Turkey	31	8	88	87	66	60	66	61
Algeria	23	5	95	100	86	84	93	96
Number of observations:			21	12	18	44	54	65

[a] The only votes considered in the analysis are those in which the US and the Soviet Union cast their vote on opposite sides.
Sources: Aid flows: OECD, Geographical Distribution of Financial Flows to Less Developed Countries, Paris, successive issues from 1976 to 1984. Aid is defined as net ODA in $ millions. Votes in UN: United Nations: General Assembly: Sessions 31 (1976) to 37 (1982-3): Index to Proceedings: annex.

(i) Countries for which aid on an increasing trend

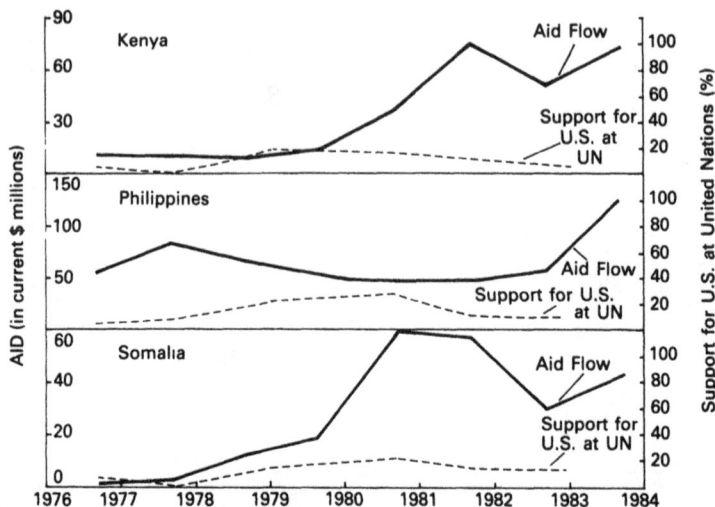

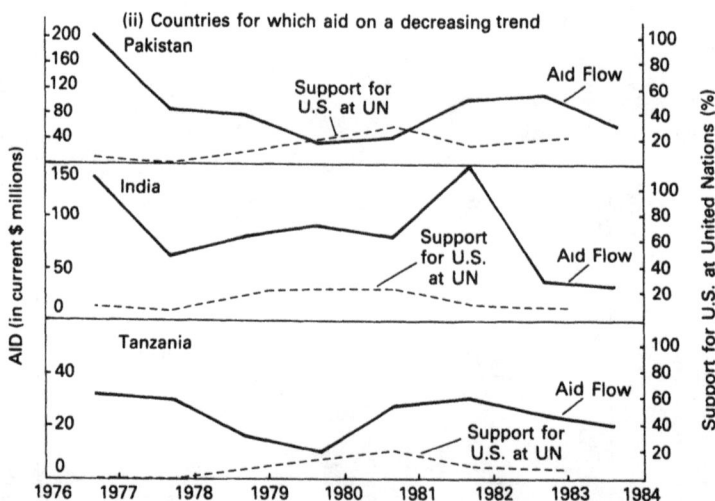

(ii) Countries for which aid on a decreasing trend

Figure 2.2 (a): Six major recipients of US aid: aid flows from US and support for US in United Nations General Assembly, 1976–83
Aid flows measured on left scale, support at UN on right scale. 'Support' is percentage of occasions in year stated when recipient supported US on an issue on which US and Soviet Union were in dispute.

Sources: *Aid flows: OECD, Geographical Distribution of Financial Flows to Less Developed Countries*, Paris, successive issues from 1976 to 1984. Aid is defined as net ODA in $ millions.
Votes in UN: United Nations: General Assembly: Sessions 31 (1976) to 37 (1982–83): *Index to Proceedings*: annex.

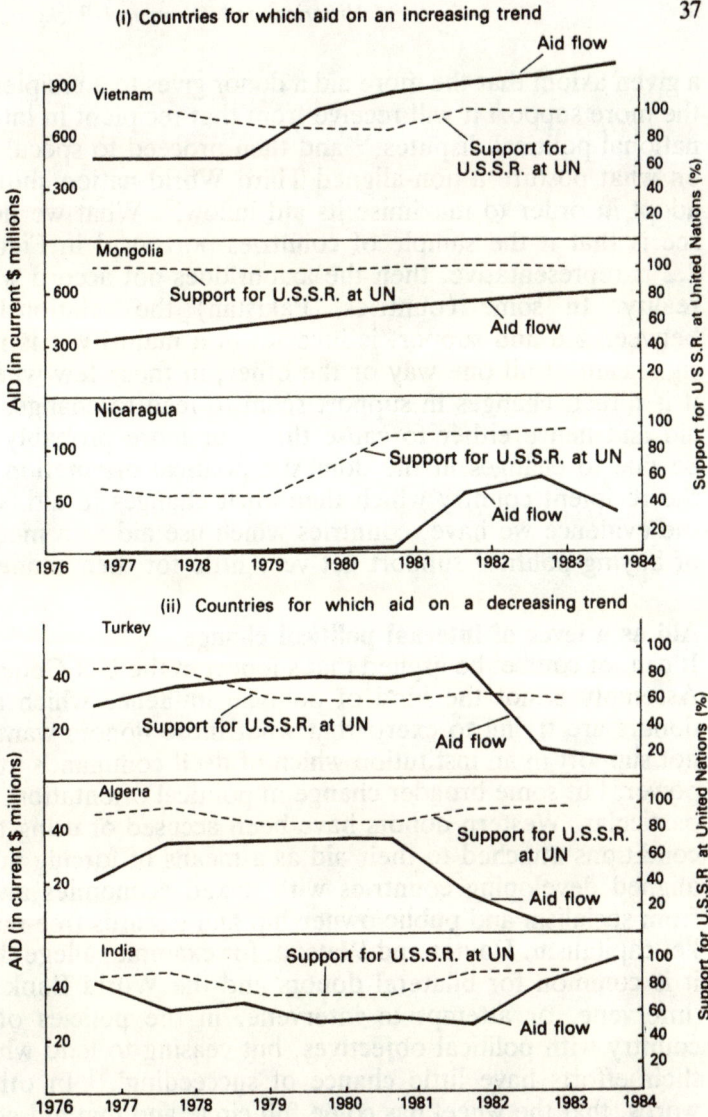

Figure 2.2 (b): Six major recipients of Soviet aid: aid flows from USSR and support for USSR in United Nations General Assembly, 1976–83 Aid flows measured on left scale, support at UN on right scale. 'Support' is percentage of occasions in year stated when recipient supported USSR on an issue on which US and Soviet Union were in dispute.

Sources: Aid flows: OECD, *Geographical Distribution of Financial Flows to Less Developed Countries*, Paris, successive issues from 1976 to 1984.
Votes in UN: United Nations: General Assembly: Sessions 31 (1976) to 37 (1982–83), *Index to Proceedings*: annex.

a given axiom that the more aid a donor gives to a recipient, the more support it will receive from that recipient in international political disputes,[33] and then proceed to speculate on what posture a non-aligned Third World nation should adopt in order to maximise its aid inflow.[34] What we now see is that if the sample of countries portrayed in Figure 2.2 is representative, then the axiom does not accord with reality. In some countries (Pakistan) the relationship between aid and support is inverse; in a majority it is not significant at all one way or the other; in those few where it is direct, changes in support seem to lead to changes in aid and hence either to cause them, or more probably to be due to changes in the domestic political orientation of the recipient country which then elicit changes in aid. On the evidence we have, countries which use aid as a means of buying political support get very little for their money.

Aid as a lever of internal political change

It can, of course, be argued that support in the UN General Assembly is not the kind of political influence which aid donors are trying to exert: that what those donors want is not support in an institution which of itself commands little power, but some broader change in political orientation. In particular, Western donors have been accused of using the conditions attached to their aid as a means of forcing non-aligned developing countries with mixed economies away from socialism and public ownership and towards free-market capitalism. Hayter and Watson, for example, allege that it is common for bilateral donors and the World Bank to 'intervene, or attempt to intervene, in the policies of a country with political objectives, but ceasing to lend when their efforts have little chance of succeeding'.[35] In other words, that the wheel has come full circle and that aid now perpetuates colonial relationships in a post-colonial world.

There is absolutely no doubt that a number of donors see it as vital to alter the 'policy environment' in less developed countries in a more growth-orientated direction, and to use their aid as a lever to effect this policy change. The World Bank's most recent report on sub-Saharan Africa argues that:

Distorted incentives and inefficient institutions are central to Africa's poor return on investment and therefore to its economic performance. Evidence from other countries shows that reforms of the kind required in Africa need large and sustained external support. In turn, donors can make their continuing support dependent on the reforms being maintained.[36]

The point at issue is how far pressure of this kind, which is quite overt, constitutes 'political interference', and how successfully it can be imposed on a reluctant government. We focus on the World Bank not only as a pioneer in the use of conditional aid, but also as the would-be ringleader for bilateral aid donors. In general, if bilateral donors do impose conditionality at the macroeconomic level where there are political overtones, it is only on programme loans or grants, and as a rule the conditionality consists of a requirement that the recipient adhere to policy conditions which the Bank, and sometimes also the IMF, have already laid down for the country.[37]

The kinds of conditions that the World Bank has insisted on in relation to its most ambitious programme of conditional programme aid,[38] the series of Structural Adjustment Loans (SALs) begun in 1980, is set out in Table 2.6. Ostensibly, the conditions there listed appear to have everything to do with raising the rate of economic growth and little to do with change in political system. But 'dissolve or reduce powers of state marketing boards', 'reduce or eliminate agricultural subsidies' and even the innocuous 'budget policy' imply, taken together, a severe limitation on the reach of central government. The intention behind the imposition of such conditions may be purely economic and efficiency based, but their consequence cannot but be political. Also, though the Bank itself has stressed that 'the key factor determining the efficiency of an enterprise is not whether it is privately owned, but how it is managed',[39] it has equated greater efficiency with privatisation too often to allow impartial observers to believe that it is politically neutral even in intent.

However, for political pressure to be effective, it must not only be applied; it must also be yielded to. On this matter, the bottom row of Table 2.6 is instructive. It shows

Table 2.6: *Essential components of World Bank structural adjustment operations 1980–5*

	Bolivia	Guyana	Ivory Coast I	Ivory Coast II	Jamaica I	Jamaica II	Jamaica III	Kenya I	Kenya II	South Korea I	South Korea II	Malawi I	Malawi II	Pakistan I	Pakistan II	Philippines I	Philippines II	Thailand I	Thailand II	Turkey I	Turkey II	Turkey III	Turkey IV	Mauritius I	Mauritius II	Yugoslavia	% of SAL's (to January 1986) subject to conditions in this area
1. Trade policy																											
Tariff reform and import liberalisation:																											
removal of quotas		X	X	X	X	X		X		X	X					X	X	X		X	X	X	X	X		X	66
tariff cuts						X			X								X		X								17
Export incentives and improved institutional support		X	X	X	X	X		X		X		X		X		X		X		X	X	X	X	X		X	83
2. Resource mobilisation																											
Budget policy		X			X	X		X	X	X	X	X	X	X				X		X	X	X	X	X		X	76
Interest rate policy		X			X	X		X	X			X	X								X	X				X	43
Strengthening of institutional capacity to manage external borrowing	X	X	X				X	X			X							X			X	X	X	X			54
Public enterprise financial performance		X	X		X	X		X		X	X	X				X		X		X	X	X	X	X	X		75
3. Efficient use of resources																											
Public investment programme: revision and review of structural priorities	X	X	X	X	X	X		X		X	X	X		X		X				X	X	X				X	71

Revise agricultural prices	X	X	X	X	X	X	X	X	X	X	X X X	75
Dissolve or reduce powers of state marketing boards		X									X	13
Agricultural input subsidies:												
reduce some		X	X								X X	20
eliminate some												
Revise energy prices	X		X	X	X	X	X	X	X	X	X X X	71
Conservation measures	X			X					X	X	X X X	50
Development of indigenous energy sources	X	X						X			X	42
Industry-revise incentive systems		X	X	X	X	X	X	X	X	X	X X	75
4. Institutional reforms												
Strengthening of institutional capacity to formulate and implement public investment programme		X	X	X	X	X	X	X	X	X	X X X	80
Institutional efficiency of public sector enterprises	X	X	X	X	X		X	X	X	X	X X	58
Improved institutional support to agriculture (marketing, etc.)	X	X	X	X			X	X	X	X	X	58
Institutional improvements in industry and sub-sector programmes		X	X		X		X	X			X	42
Proportion of conditions implemented to January 1986	20	82	95	95	63	39	95	90	81	82	96	
	58											

Source: Stern (1983) supplemented by World Bank, *President's Reports*, various and for bottom row of table, Mosley (1985c), Table 4.

that no country granted a SAL has complied with all the conditions imposed on it, and that some recipients, such as Bolivia, Guyana, Kenya and Malawi, have been quite startlingly remiss. Slippage on conditions imposed by donors, already noted by Killick in relation to the IMF,[40] is a relatively straightforward matter for a recipient which wishes to play the system and evade leverage, partly because some of the money must be handed over before the recipient can start complying with the conditions, partly because some conditions (e.g. 'rationalise the structure of protection') take years to monitor and are in any case ambiguous, and finally because not all donors practise conditionality, leaving the recipient with the option of turning to a donor whose yoke is relatively easy when other donors' conditions become too burdensome.[41] It is, in any case, not clear that all of the policy changes actually implemented by recipients of SALs were implemented only because they formed the subject of conditions imposed by the World Bank. In Turkey and Jamaica, two of the countries most energetic in implementing liberalisation programmes under the tutelage of the Bank, many of the reform measures listed in Table 2.6 formed part of the manifesto of the new governments installed in those countries in 1980. The Bank, indeed, is schizophrenic about the nature of its conditionality, sometimes referring to its conditional programme loans simply as *support* for local reform efforts (which by implication would have taken place anyhow) and sometimes as measures to *induce* changes in policy, which by implication would not have taken place in any case.

2.3   CONCLUSIONS

For these reasons we conclude that aid flows are scarcely more powerful as an instrument for inducing political change in LDCs than they are as a tool for purchasing support in international forums such as the United Nations. It is not that the donors are always unaware of the political implications of the changes they seek. Rather, it is that, as Table 2.4 demonstrates, the world has become partitioned into two sets of aid relationships, capitalist and communist, which scarcely overlap; and that in those cases where capitalist donors do attempt to impose policy changes on an unwilling 'capitalist' government, for example because it has become more socialist and the donors want to rein it back, those impositions can often be evaded, *if* the recipient government wishes. If it does not, and wishes to make the donor a scapegoat for its own internal economic troubles, then it can strike a posture towards the donor so unbending and truculent that aid relationships are broken off. In relation to the Bank, this seems to have happened in Chile under Allende, in Nicaragua in 1982, and to a lesser degree—involving a cooling rather than a severing of relationships—in Jamaica in the late seventies and in Tanzania between 1978 and 1982. But that the mere existence of a socialist government is no barrier to concessional aid from the US and World Bank is demonstrated by Burma, Mozambique, South Yemen, Yugoslavia, Hungary and most of all China,[42] and that substantial slippage on conditions need not force a breakage of the aid relationship is demonstrated by Malawi and the Philippines. If the desire to impose policy conditions is a powerful motive with donors, so also is the desire to forgive and redeem a Prodigal Son. As long as the recipient asserts willingness *in principle* to comply with the conditions set, the money will usually flow, from donors who are anxious to retain their own hold, regardless of how much compliance is occurring in practice. This gives recipients considerable power. It is only, as a rule, where those recipients choose to declare a reluctance in principle to comply with conditions that aid relationships are broken off.[43] And that is not leverage, but an acknowledgement of its failure.

We therefore reject the claim that aid, after its liberal hour in the 1960s and early 1970s, has returned to the function of sustaining colonial structures and relationships. Whether that is the intention of some of its spokesmen is not relevant: the point is that it is no longer capable of doing the job. There are a few cases, such as Mongolia, Réunion, the Falkland Islands and Montserrat, where the recipient is dependent for its economic survival on aid flows from one donor, but to list this bizarre miscellany is to demonstrate how rare this condition of dependence is. In all other countries recipients have taken care to diversify their sources of aid,[44] and in some cases they have industrialised to the point where they are far less dependent on aid as such. All of this increases their countervailing power in relation to donors—a power that has been understated both by those who see aid as an instrument of oppression and domination and by their opponents who see it as a powerful diplomatic tool. This power makes it hard for donors to induce, by means of aid, political changes which they are unable to induce by other means.[45] Aid does not, on the evidence available to us, capture support in international politics, nor does it compel many domestic policy changes which the recipient would otherwise have been reluctant to implement. If it is to be justified, then in our view it must be justified on grounds other than its potency as a tool of international persuasion.

NOTES

1. For records of such transactions by Britain in East Africa, *see* essays by Ehrlich in Harlow and Chilver (1965); by Germany in Tanganyika, *see* J. Iliffe, *Tanganyika under German Rule*, Oxford UP, 1963: by France, *see* the essay by Hugon in Stokke (1984).
2. For the history of this word *see* Kitching (1982) especially Chapters 1 and 2.
3. *See* Wolff (1974), Tables 3.1 and 3.2, pp. 49 and 50.
4. World Bank, *World Development Report 1985*, p. 12.
5. Chapter 1, p. 11.
6. Lord Milner, Colonial Secretary 1919, writing in the *Observer*, 1923; quoted in Mosley (1974), p. 157.
7. Abbott (1971), pp. 68–81. For comparison with the share of GNP disbursed in later years, *see* Table 2.1; and for further details of the Act, *see* Morgan (1980) Vol. I, Chapter 6.
8. The arguments for enlarging the human capital stock in those days were openly racialist. The following is typical: 'The real "development" needed in Africa today is not the investment of large sums of capital, but the improvement of the human material. The limiting factor is the low standard of health and intelligence of the average native.' (UK Public Record Office: CO852/118: File 15279/5 Economic of 1937: report by Earl de la Warr, Parliamentary Under-Secretary of State for the Colonies, on visit to Africa January–March 1937).

9. The Groundnut Scheme is described in detail in Morgan (1980), Vol. 2, Chapter 5. Over the entire 10 years to March 1956, £120 million was provided to all developing countries under the 1945 Colonial Development and Welfare Act.

10. *Economic Report of the President and Annual Report of the Council of Economic Advisors* (1952), p. 50.

11. For an authoritative statement of this approach, *see* United Nations (1951), especially Chapter VI, p. 35; 'In most countries where rapid economic progress is occurring, net capital formation at home is at least 10 per cent of the national income, and in some it is substantially higher. By contrast in most underdeveloped countries net capital formation is not as high as 5 per cent of the national income even when foreign investment is included. How to increase the rate of capital formation is therefore of great urgency.'

12. Set up in 1944 as the International Bank for Reconstruction and Development.

13. The World Bank group now comprises three agencies: the International Bank for Reconstruction and Development (IBRD), the International Development Association (IDA) and the International Finance Corporation (IFC). The IBRD borrows in the market, and normally lends at 0.5 per cent above this rate, but has a triple-A rating on the American stock market and so can lend to the governments of developing countries at an interest rate below the cost of any alternative source of credit. The IDA, established in 1959, obtains its money free in the form of donations from the aid budgets of developed countries, and makes only a service charge (currently ¾ per cent) by way of interest, and is thus indisputably an aid agency. The IFC, established in 1956, makes equity investments in private companies in less developed countries.

14. These countries, although they do not belong to the Socialist World system, can draw on its achievements in building an independent national economy and in raising their people's living standards. Today they need not go begging to their former oppressors for modern equipment. They can get it in the socialist countries, free from any political or military obligation.

Nikita Khrushchev to Twentieth Party Congress of the Communist Party of the Soviet Union, 1956, cited in Walters (1970), p. 30.

15. White (1974), p. 222. It has never come near to being achieved by OECD donors as a whole, although since the 1970s, as Table 2.2 shows, Holland, the Scandinavian countries and the OPEC states have as individual entities comfortably exceeded it.

16. President Kennedy's speech to Congress, April 1961: *see* White (1974), p. 199.

17. These limits seemed to be most serious in the 'least developed' countries. Bangladesh throughout the 1970s was unable to spend more than 15 per cent of the aid funds committed to it in any year: Faaland (1981), p. 32.

18. Three of the countries where this was most convincingly shown to

have happened were Brazil (*see* Fishlow, 1972), Mexico (Weisskopf, 1970) and Kenya (Hodd, 1976).

19. This implication does not, in fact, necessarily follow from the previous statement: aid projects can have a progressive effect in countries where the poor are getting poorer. But the data on the distributional effects of aid projects are very poor. For extended discussion *see* Chapter 6.

20. This is known as 'two-gap theory' (*see* Chenery and Strout (1966), McKinnon (1964)). Its implication, that domestic resources cannot be freely converted into foreign exchange and that there are therefore separate 'savings gaps' and 'foreign exchange gaps', has been much criticised. This justification for aid is further discussed in Chapter 5.

21. *See* pp. 38–43 below.

22. Robert MacNamara, *Annual address to the Board of Governors of the World Bank Group*, 1973, reported in World Bank, *Annual Report 1973*.

23. OECD, *Development Assistance* (1975), p. 65; (1976), pp. 153–72.

24. These tensions can manifest themselves right down to project level: for example, in the late 1970s the World Bank was trying to persuade the Kenyan government to charge beneficiaries of water projects at a fixed rate per gallon, and the Swedish International Development Authority was trying to persuade them to charge a variable rate according to the consumer's ability to pay. *See* Duncan and Mosley (1984), p. 123.

25. The original statement of this doctrine is contained in the book of that name which was published in the joint name of the World Bank and the Institute of Development Studies at Sussex University (Chenery *et al.*, 1974); it is repeated, notably, in World Bank (1982), which claims in particular that poverty-focused projects have as high a rate of return, and hence are as 'growth-inducing', as other aid-financed projects.

26. For discussion of these measures, *see* Mosley (1985c), (1986); also section 2 of this chapter and Chapter 8.

27. The exact figures are 30.6 and 8.3 per cent; data are from rows 11 and 12 of Table 2.2.

28. *See* McKinley and Little (1978a), (1979).

29. McKinley and Little reject the 'recipient need model' of aid allocation on account of finding no correlation between indicators of such need (e.g. the recipient's per capita income) and aid flows in an ordinary least squares regression equation. But ordinary least-squares estimation is inappropriate when, as in this case, there is a two-way relationship (recipient income affects the aid flow, and the aid flow affects the recipient's income). The use of an appropriate estimation technique confirms what intuition would suggest, namely that several factors other than donor political interest, including in particular the poverty of recipients, did affect aid flows. Estimated regressions by two-stage least squares over a cross-section of eighty-one recipient countries in 1977 are:

aid flow from $= 8.39** - 0.00042**$ (per capita GNP)
DAC countries   (3.46)   (2.82)
(percentage of
recipient GNP) $- 0.084$ (life expectancy) $- 0.015$ (literacy rate)
                  (0.51)   (0.98)

$- 0.0069*$ (population size); $r^2 = 0.3086$
(2.02)

Figures in brackets under coefficients are Student's t-statistics; *denotes significance at 5% level, ** at 1% level. DAC countries are members of the Development Assistance Committee of OECD (see p. 26 above), i.e. capitalist aid donors.

Often the mechanism triggering a response of aid to 'recipient need' would be a disaster in the recipient country, such as the famines in Bangladesh and Ethiopia in 1974; this aid, once begun, proved difficult to terminate. For a full critique of the McKinley and Little approach to the allocation of aid *see* Mosley (1981b).

30. The number of bilateral and multilateral donors giving aid to some of the largest aid recipients, according to successive issues of the OECD's *Geographical Distribution of Financial Flows*, is as follows:

	1961	1981
India	13	29
Indonesia	9	27
Kenya	6	28
Tanzania	8	32

31. The regression equation is:

aid (as percentage of GNP) $=$ 10.08**
                                  (7.07)
$- 0.0045**$ per capita GNP, $r^2 = 0.14,$
(3.17)

Ordinary least squares estimation, number of observations = 66.
32. Frey (1984), pp. 89–90.
33. *See* for example the diagrams in Frey (1984), Figure 5.1, p. 90, and the argument based thereon on pp. 90–6.
34. *See* for example Hirschman (1964).
35. Hayter and Watson (1985), p. 214.
36. World Bank (1984), p. 44.
37. For a detailed demonstration of this in the case of Kenya *see* Duncan and Mosley (1984), Chapter 4.
38. Formally, only a small part of the loans set out in Table 2.6 consists of 'aid' since, except in the case of Kenya, Pakistan and Malawi, they are given on 'hard' IBRD terms only slightly below the free-market interest rate.

39. World Bank, *World Development Report 1983*, p. 50.
40. Killick (1984), Vol. 1, Table 6.3 p. 194 and pp. 250–4, shows that devaluations were implemented as promised in only 1 per cent of cases between 1973 and 1981, and credit ceilings observed in only 55 per cent of cases between 1969 and 1978.
41. The determinants of slippage are explored in detail in Mosley (1985c).
42. The World Bank has current loan programmes (1985) in all of these countries. The United States has programmes of assistance to the first three. *See* OECD, *Geographical Distribution of Financial Flows to Developing Countries 1981–1984*, Paris 1985, individual country tables.
43. Aid relationships are also sometimes broken off when civil order breaks down and the safety of aid personnel cannot be guaranteed. (e.g. Uganda in 1972 and Ethiopia in 1976–7).
44. *See* statistical evidence for this in Note 30.
45. We are not, of course, asserting that they cannot bring effective pressure to bear on Third World countries, which they often do, either by invasion (e.g. the US in Grenada or the Soviet Union in Afghanistan) or by blockade (e.g. South Africa in Lesotho, early 1986). What we are asserting is that aid is an ineffective way of bringing such pressure to bear.

3 Community and Conflict in the Aid Donor Community

3.1 DRAMATIS PERSONAE

In this chapter our focus will be on the organisations that spend the aid budget on behalf of governments. Sometimes these organisations are fully fledged ministries in their own right, as in the Netherlands; sometimes they are departments within the ministry of foreign affairs, as in Britain and the United States of America; sometimes they are quasi-autonomous government corporations, as in Denmark and Sweden. They are all, however, bureaucracies, and as such driven by imperatives other than the profit motive.[1] In this chapter we explore what imperatives they are driven by, and in the light of this explanation consider how competent they are to fill the hole in the international capital market identified in the first chapter.

First: who are 'they'? In Figure 3.1 we set out the organisation chart of a typical bilateral aid bureau, the British Overseas Development Administration (ODA), and of the largest multilateral development agency, the World Bank. We shall find it convenient to split their employees into four groups:

(1) *Administrators proper*: the people who manage the aid programme. As a rule, particularly in bilateral agencies, they lack any particular disciplinary specialisation.[2] In Britain and other bilateral donor countries they share a common career structure with other members of the administrative civil service.

```
                         Under Secretary          Assistant Secretary
                         level posts              level posts

                                                 ┌ Head, Eastern Africa
                                                 │ Development Divisionᵇ
                           ┌ Africaᵃ ────────────┤
                           │                     └ Head, Southern Africa
                           │                       Development Divisionᵃ

                           │                     ┌ Head, South-East Asia
                           │                     │ Development Divisionᵇ
                           │  Asia and───────────┤ Head, Caribbean
                           │  Oceaniaᵃ           │ Development Divisionᵇ
Permanent  Deputy          │                     └ Head, Pacific
Secretaryᵃ ˉ Secretaryᵃ ──┤                       Development Divisionᵇ

                           │  Establishments
                           ├  and Financeᵃ ───── Assistant Secretaries

                           │  Education
                           ├  and Investmentᵃ ── Assistant  Secretaries
                           ├ Internationalᵃ ──── Assistant Secretaries
                           │  Science and
                           ├  Technologyᵃ ─────── Assistant Secretaries

                           ├ Head, Economic ──┬ Head, Evaluation Unit or
                           │  Serviceᶜ        └ Senior Economic Advisersᶜ

                           │  Chief Education
                           ├  Adviserᶜ

                           ├ Chief Medical and
                           │  Health Services Adviserᶜ

                           └ Chief Natural
                             Resources Adviserᶜ
```

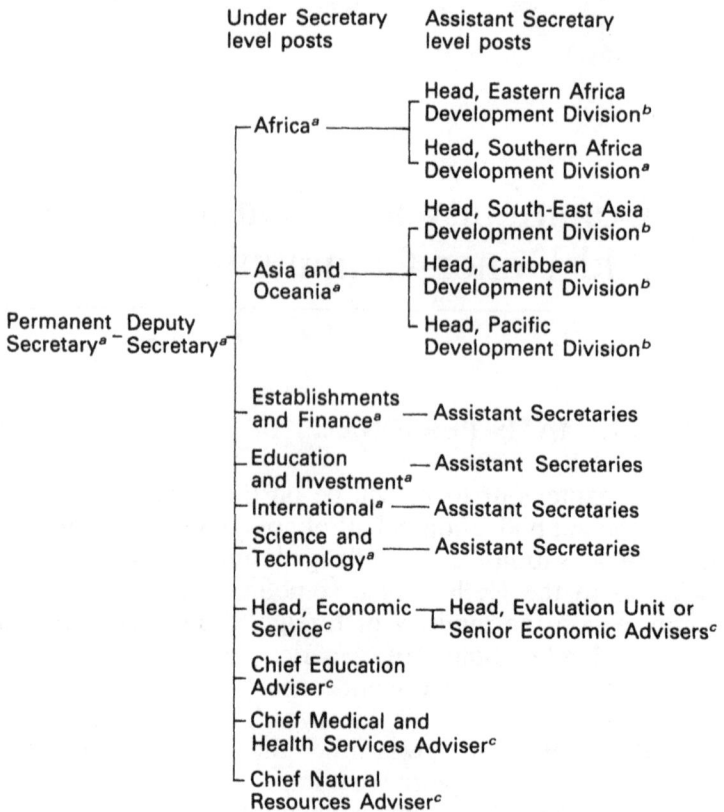

Figure 3.1(a): UK Overseas Development Administration: organisation chart, January 1986

Notes: ᵃ Administrators (headquarters).
        ᵇ Overseas staff.
        ᶜ Professional staff (headquarters).
Not all Assistant Secretary level posts are shown.

(2) *Technical advisers* from a wide range of development-related disciplines: engineers, economists, educationists, doctors, lawyers, accountants and so on. In many bilateral donor ministries these people too are career civil servants: for example, in Britain all the economists in the ODA are part of the Government Economic Service.

Vice Presidents

```
                                  ┌─ Financial Controller
                                  ├─ Pension Fund
                Senior Vice       │  Financial Policy,
             ┌─ President, ───────┴─ Planning and
             │  Finance              Budgeting
             │
             │                    ┌─ Cofinancing
             │                    ├─ Operations Policy
             │  Senior Vice       ├─ Energy and Industry
President ───┼─ President, ───────┼─ West Africa
             │  Operations        ├─ Eastern and Southern Africa
             │                    ├─ East Asia and Pacific
             │                    ├─ South Asia
             │                    ├─ Europe, Middle East and North Africa
             │                    ├─ Latin America and Caribbean
             │                    └─ Economics and Research
             │
             ├──────────────────────  Operations Evaluation*
             │
             │                    ┌─ Secretary
             └────────────────────┼─ Personal and Adminstration
                                  └─ External Relations
```

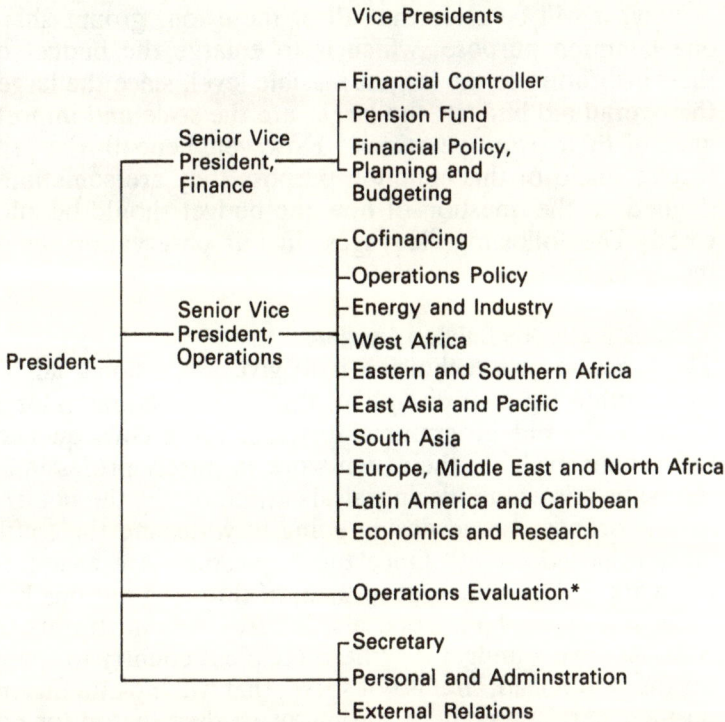

Figure 3.1(b): World Bank: headquarters organisation chart, January 1986

Note: *The Director-General, Operations Evaluation, reports directly to the President but is not formally classified as a Vice-President.

(3) *Staff working on projects overseas*, who will sometimes be permanent employees seconded from groups (1) and (2), but who will often be recruited on temporary contracts of two or three years.[3]

(4) *The evaluation unit*, whose core again consists of permanent employees on secondment but which often hires specialist help from outside the organisation on a short-term basis from universities, consulting firms, etc., partly for the sake of a specialist technical input and partly in order to give its assessments greater objectivity than an in-house review can provide.

Now, it will be clear that all of these four groups share one common purpose, which is to enlarge the budget of their institution to the largest feasible level, since the larger the overall aid budget, the larger are the scale and importance of their own operations.[4] However, beneath the protective shield of this common purpose they are sometimes divided on the question of how the budget should be allocated. The following cleavages, in our observation, commonly arise:

Administrator–technician tensions

The function of a technician is to give professional advice from within his own discipline: that of an administrator is to carry the aid programme forward. As a consequence, technicians evaluate their own work in purely professional terms: 'is this economic appraisal carried out by the book?', 'is this proposed road design going to withstand the traffic flow proposed for it?' Once those questions are answered the work is done; the cost to them of throwing out one bad proposal, or ten bad proposals, is zero. Administrators by contrast have a budget for 'their' recipient country to spend for the year ahead;[5] if it is not spent, that will look inefficient on their part unless there is some overriding reason for not doing so, such as civil war. In addition to this internal pressure they are subject to external pressure from businessmen who stand to gain if aid contracts go forward and from diplomats in recipient countries whose task would be eased by the release of funds for specific projects. They must, therefore, always be thinking in terms of moving the money which has been allocated to them: in a concessional aid agency because an underspend this year means less money from the Treasury next year, and in a quasi-commercial organisation such as IBRD because no money lent this year means no income in future years.[6]

The cost to administrators if a proposal is found to be technically or financially unviable, therefore, is not zero; their reaction is likely to be not 'let's forget about that bum project' but 'let's try again', that is, with a different technical specification. At the appraisal stage of the project cycle,[7] therefore, friction may arise if administrators are trying to get a project approved for overriding political or commercial reasons, whereas economists (for example) are trying to persuade them that it will never be viable in any technical specification. Cases of this kind of dispute are described later in the chapter.

There is a second issue, which we may describe as 'the exit problem'. All aid is ultimately intended, as the platitude has it, to 'help countries help themselves': that is, it sets up an institution or piece of equipment which after a defined period of time can be handed over to the recipient country as its sole financial responsibility. This is often difficult, especially in very poor countries with projects which do not generate their own cash-flow (e.g. rural health centres, integrated rural development) and which have heavy running costs. Now, the economist's operating principle is that a project should be implemented, and is therefore eligible for aid, if the discounted present value of net economic benefits of the project is positive; the mechanics of cost recovery are not his formal concern. However, they are of the very essence of the administrator's concern, since if costs cannot be recovered, the project will never be in a state to be handed over to the recipient government, and will be a chronic charge on the aid budget if it is to remain in being. There may be, of course, a very large gap between economic and financial values if, for example, the exchange rate is artificially pegged, the output of the project is subsidised or labour is paid more than its marginal cost. In such a situation the roles may be reversed, and technicians and economists may find themselves pushing for projects which administrators, because of anticipated 'hand-over' problems, wish to reject.

Home staff—overseas staff tensions
Administrators and technicians in donor countries, whether in Washington, The Hague or London, frequently find themselves aligned on the same side of the fence against field staff who are 'causing difficulties' by refusing or failing to carry out the programmes originally envisaged in the project agreement: frequently they typecast field staff as slow, analytically backward and behind the times. Field

staff, for their part, castigate head office for being 'out of touch' with an environment where the water and electricity frequently do not flow and the counterparts frequently do not come in to work, for denying them flexibility[8] and for demanding data, replies to telegrams and detailed reports on a scale which jeopardise their ability to do the actual work of development. Now, it is indeed true that administrators frequently, and wrongly, judge the success of a project in relation to its conformity with 'objectives' agreed at the planning stage which are frequently exposed as becoming increasingly irrelevant as the project progresses.[9] It is also true that expatriate communities in remote places often retreat into the values and habits practised in the Old Country in an age now vanished: the last stronghold of male *galanterie*, the steamed sultana sponge and the blue orlon pullover.[10] What is crucial here is that these cleavages of understanding between home and abroad can hamper and, in extreme cases, abort the progress of a project whose technical design is impeccable—unless, as frequently happens, the tension is diffused by making a scapegoat of the recipient.[11]

Operating staff—evaluation unit tensions

The problem here is more simple: no adult likes being marked out of ten, particularly if their future career is going to be influenced by the mark. This fact creates an opposition of interest between the evaluators and the evaluated, that is, the administrators on particular country desks and more particularly field operating staff, who on this issue find themselves on the same side of the fence. The conflict will normally concern, not so much whether evaluation is done, but *how* it is done: the evaluators will lay emphasis on methodological rigour, the computation of statistical measures of project performance and wide diffusion of results, whereas the evaluated will be more interested in quick feedback to management, with academic rigour, computation of numbers such as *ex post* rates of return and wide diffusion of results at a discount.[12] But there may also be conflict, in those agencies where not all projects are evaluated *ex post*, concerning which sample of projects is selected for evaluation.[13]

From the above it will be clear that there exist potential conflicts of interest between occupational groups within agencies which may affect the managerial efficiency of the agency. These are summarised in Figure 3.2.

In the light of this discussion, we now proceed more formally to investigate the decision-making process within donor agencies. This investigation will relate particularly, when we move down to the project level, to the identification and appraisal phases of the project cycle; the implementation phase concerns the recipient governments more intimately and is discussed in more detail in Chapter 4.

Administrators	Technical Advisors	Overseas project staff	Evaluation staff	
/////	Acceptability of projects which pass on financial but fail on social criteria (or vice versa)	Speed of implementation, need to tailor implementation to local political interests	Measures of statistical performance in evaluation reports	Administrators
	/////	Speed of implementation, need to tailor implementation to local political interests		Technical Advisers
		/////	Measures of statistical performance in evaluation reports	Overseas project staff
			/////	Evaluation staff

Figure 3.2: Areas of potential internal conflict within aid agencies

3.2 MACRO-LEVEL BARGAINING: THE DETERMINATION OF THE AID BUDGET

It is a not unreasonable supposition that most employees of aid agencies, in each of the four groups denoted above, would prefer, other things being equal, to be involved in the administration of a large aid programme than a small aid programme. The larger the aid programme, the greater are the individual's official responsibilities (at any level) and the greater his scope for creative policy initiatives, since those can seldom be implemented without money to put them into effect. When the aid budget is cut sharply, the cut invariably falls on the really exciting work—the design and appraisal of new projects—as there is no money left over from commitments made in previous years and the entire ministry has to devote its energies to the relatively tedious routine work of administering those commitments. The drop in morale of all staff when this happens, which I had the opportunity to observe personally as a member of the British Overseas Development Administration in the winter of 1979/80, is pitiful to behold.[14] Nobody who had the opportunity to compare the mood of British aid staff during the years of growing budgets in 1977/8 and during the years of contraction 2 years later will readily dissent from Niskanen's famous hypothesis that bureaucrats will have a common interest in attempting to maximise the relative size of their bureau.[15] The real point at issue, at this macro-level, is however not whether aid officials would prefer more aid to less but what other objectives they wish to pursue, and what constraints exist on their ability to pursue them.

These constraints are of three kinds: finance; pressure from other donors; and, in the case of bilateral aid agencies, pressure from the electorate.

The financial constraint differs somewhat according as the aid agency under discussion is bilateral or multilateral. In a bilateral agency the constraint is administered by the institution entrusted with control over public expenditure (in America, Congress; in Britain, and most other donor countries, the Treasury or Ministry of Finance). This gate-keeping institution has the job of cutting back the aid agency's initial bid for funds by as much as is required by the state of the economy. The overseas aid budget, in most countries,[16] is notoriously easy to cut in a recession because little of it is committed by statute and because those who will be hurt by the cut—the development lobby and the beneficiaries in developing countries—have little ability to vent their displeasure by depriving the government of votes. As the DAC (Development Assistance Committee) Chairman lamented in 1975,

A large proportion of central budget expenditure is pre-empted by recurrent costs (e.g. salaries) or payments whose amount is determined by long term legislation (e.g. social welfare payments) with the result that aid programmes, which mostly fall into neither of these 'incompressible' categories, are particularly vulnerable at times of budgetary stringency.[17]

For multilateral aid agencies such as the World Bank, which raise much of their money in the financial markets, the constraint on their expenditure is formally set not by a gatekeeper but by the amount they can borrow. However, to be able to give money out as 'aid', that is, on concessional terms, multilateral agencies need in addition to raise money by subscriptions from bilateral donors, such as the periodic replenishments of the World Bank's IDA.[18] These subscriptions are subject to annual review by gatekeepers in precisely the same manner as bilateral aid budgets: to this extent there is a family resemblance between the financial constraints encountered by the two kinds of agency.[19]

The constraint administered by the donor public operates in a far more subtle manner. Official aid to LDCs, as has often been pointed out, is very different from personal charity, and individual taxpayers have no immediate power to stop their government spending money on development aid, or to make it spend more. However, if they are unhappy with either the quantity or the quality of official aid then, as in the case of any publicly supplied service such as health or education, it is open to them to engage in political action—letters to newspapers, pressure on members of the legislature, lobbies of parliament—to try and adjust the quantity of aid supplied to the amount which they desire.

Dissatisfaction with the current aid programme, for example, can if sufficiently powerfully expressed influence the government either to increase the volume of its aid programme, or alternatively to change the composition and thus the 'quality' of the programme as a means of gaining political support. A formal model of how these factors on the 'demand side' of the market for aid may influence the size of aid budgets is set out in the appendix to this chapter.

Finally, a third pressure on the level of bilateral aid budgets must be mentioned, although it is stretching language to describe it as a constraint. This is the pressure which individual donors exert on *each other's* aid disbursements. A forum now exists, the Development Assistance Committee of OECD, in which every year each OECD donor's aid performance, measured not only by quantity but also by 'quality' measures such as interest rates, proportion of aid given on grant terms and share of aid given to least developed countries, is formally scrutinised by other members of the committee. Not only do norms for aid performance exist, in other words, but also an apparatus of social control to enforce them. These social controls cannot, of course, be made to bite by any apparatus of international law, and so they may be resisted by determined donors. None the less, it seems reasonable to suggest that they are sufficiently strong to cause substantial complementarities, akin to the 'Duesenberry' or 'bandwagon' effects of consumer theory,[20] between the policy of any one aid donor and the policies of OECD aid donors as a group. It is believed, for example, that Japan—a 'poor performer' for many years by OECD standards on the criteria of aid/GNP ratio and concessionality of its aid—was in the early 1970s persuaded to increase its overseas aid substantially purely as a result of pressures from other donors.[21]

3.3 MICRO-LEVEL BARGAINING: COUNTRY, SECTOR AND PROJECT ALLOCATION

Each year, therefore, an overall aid budget for the following year is negotiated by the donor agency, whose size will be dictated by the pressures described above. This budget now has to be apportioned between countries; within countries it must be split between economic sectors (e.g. between power generation and plantation agriculture) and within sectors it must be split between projects, for example the power generation budget for Kenya must be apportioned between hydropower, thermal power and traditional sources of energy such as wood fuel. How is this allocation of scarce aid resources between alternative uses accomplished?

Allocation by country

Let us first consider the split between countries. A large part of this decision, for all donors, is taken out of their hands by prior commitments. When Britain pledged itself in 1979 to contribute £100 million over 7 years towards the cost of the Victoria dam and power station in Sri Lanka, that decision immediately set a fairly hefty lower bound on the size of the British aid programme in Sri Lanka, not only in 1979 but in 1984 and 1985 as well. And even when there is no specific project commitment, both donors and recipients, as we shall see in the next chapter, are keen to negotiate the approximate size of aid flows three to four years in advance to facilitate their financial planning. As with other public sector budgets, therefore, so with aid programmes, Wildavsky's dictum holds good: this year's budget is determined by the size of last year's budget. And what determines last year's budget? As we have seen, a rather large literature has asserted that bilateral aid budgets, at least, are determined by considerations of 'donor interest' rather than 'recipient need': that is, that they represent investments in the maintenance of political and trading relationships developed in colonial times, or in building up new relationships, rather than redistributive gestures towards the poorest countries.[22] But this assertion over-simplifies enormously by implying that the two objectives are always separable. It is possible for Britain, for example, nearly all of whose colonial empire was in the countries now classified amongst the fifty poorest in the world, to claim quite legitimately that most of its aid programme goes to the poorest countries[23] and thus satisfies the 'recipient need' criterion, while at the same time admitting and indeed vaunting the proposition that its aid policy is an instrument of its foreign policy objectives.[24] There are other factors at work tending to make the OECD aid programmes more 'recipient need-centred' over time, in particular the growing share of Dutch and Scandinavian aid programmes which are particularly humanitarian in nature, and the tendency of disaster aid programmes, which are mainly needed in the poorest countries, to turn over time into programmes of rehabilitation by means of capital aid.[25] Initial aid allocations may have their origins in the requirements of 'foreign policy', as we saw in the last chapter, but with dramatic exceptions—such as the US aid programme to Israel, which is not a poor country—these requirements are often in themselves consistent with those requirements of a humanitarian allocation of aid. The one thing which country aid allocations are *not* determined by, broadly speaking, is 'effectiveness' in the sense of the ability of aid flows to achieve high rates of return or influence the rate of economic growth. Over the last 10 years at least, aid has been far more successful in Asia than in Africa on both criteria, but increasingly aid is being switched from Asia to Africa to deal with the 'crisis of sub-Saharan Africa.'[26] And within sub-Saharan Africa, aid is increasingly being moved from successful countries such as Botswana and the Ivory Coast to countries in difficulties such as Tanzania and Sudan.[27] In our view, this is as it should be, but defenders of the aid allocation process as it currently is should be aware that it is motivated more by hope than by experience.

Allocation by project and sector
The division of aid budgets by project *within* countries, however, is in principle determined by considerations of strict economic rationality. Country economic reports written by the aid agency's country desks and field staff identify promising sectors within each country for the aid agency to invest in, and a thorough process of technical and economic appraisal ensures that any projects nominated for aid by the recipient country show a surplus of social benefits over costs. This process of expert screening has indeed been

advanced by some aid agencies as an important reason for believing that aid projects may be able to supplement and even surpass the achievements of the private sector in developing countries.[28]

In reality the scope for economic rationality in allocating foreign aid resources is severely constrained. In the first place, large parts of the aid budget, in every agency, are never subjected to appraisal. *Small projects* are usually exempted from formal appraisal on the grounds that the expense and delay involved in analytical work of this kind is not justified in relation to the size of the expenditure involved.[29] *Projects on which the return is not easy to measure* are usually exempted from the formal rituals of cost–benefit analysis on the grounds that the uncertainties involved make the computation of a single figure for the project's economic rate of return meaningless. Two examples of great, and probably increasing, importance are technical assistance and programme aid, on which even the World Bank does not attempt to estimate *ex ante* rates of return. As an example of the former, consider a proposal to establish a training institute for agricultural extension, designed to help increase food output. Before this ultimate objective can be realised, the project must pass through many intermediate stages. The institution must be built. Satisfactory teachers must be recruited. Students must come forward who are willing to learn agricultural extension. They must assimilate their learning satisfactorily. They must find employment. They must be supplied with appropriate recommendations to extend. Farmers must be willing to adopt these in sufficient numbers. If they are, they must be able to sell their output at a remunerative price. All of these links in the chain must be forged if the objective of the project is to be realised; but each one of them is beset by so many uncertainties, and spread across such a long period of time, that most appraisal committees shrink back from an attempt to forecast the entire chain reaction and confine themselves, perhaps, to cost-effectiveness analysis on the first link in the chain. Broadly similar observations apply to programme aid: the ultimate objective being sought is nothing less than the structural transformation of the recipient economy, but the intervening steps—the specific imports which the programme finance is used to finance, the nature of the accompanying policy changes, and the resulting alterations in the pattern of investment in the recipient country—are not steps which aid agencies have been happy to try and forecast. The author is unaware of any attempt yet made to estimate the *ex ante* present value of a programme loan or grant. Even the World Bank's Structural Adjustment Loans—the most ambitious experiment in programme finance yet attempted—confine themselves to guesswork in the forecasts of project impact which they offer to recipient countries.[30] Finally, some parts of all aid programmes are not appraised properly *ex ante* because of sheer lack of time. A classical case of this problem is 'mixed credit': the provision of aid to a recipient government which is designed to persuade that government to place a contract with a firm from the donor government's country rather than with competing firms from other countries. Mixed credit is copiously provided by, amongst others, the aid ministries of Britain, France and Japan.[31] Although large sums are often involved,[32] the time available for the aid agency to appraise them is subject to the usual deadlines of the private business environment: it is not uncommon for the economists of the British ODA to receive proposals for mixed credit finance on a Tuesday, accompanied by a request that a decision be made by Friday, otherwise the firm making the proposal will not be able to make a competitive bid before the tender deadline. Under such circumstances all that anybody in the aid ministry can do, as a senior British administrator has described it, is give a 'snap judgement'.[33] As part of this judgement, the economic staff in ODA are required to perform a 'minimum test of developmental soundness'[34] on mixed credit projects, but given the shortage of time and data available to them, such tests have to be very minimal indeed: of the dozen or so I have seen, none runs to more than half a page.

A large part of every aid budget, therefore, is removed from the pressures of formal cost–benefit analysis: I estimate this proportion, for the British ODA in 1984 and 1985, to be about 40 per cent.[35] And even the part of the budget which is subjected to cost–benefit analysis is not necessarily subjected to an analysis which will adequately determine whether aid improves or worsens the allocation of resources. The fault does not lie with current manuals of cost–benefit analysis, which are elaborate and sophisticated, or with the highly trained people who use them. Rather it lies with the quality of the data with which they have to work, which as a broad generalisation deteriorates with the standard of living of the area for which data are required. The greater the need for aid, in other words, the greater is the risk of spending it badly out of sheer ignorance. For an example of the short-cuts to which project analysts are thus forced to resort, consider the following excerpt from the appraisal report for a road in highland Nepal.

In calculating the shadow wage rate,[36] we require information concerning the marginal product of labour in the rural area from which the labour force for the new road would come. For want of better data we have been forced to assume that the marginal product of labour in rural areas is half the average product.[37]

Even if data are available which correspond exactly to the magnitudes required by theoretical cost–benefit analysis, they may well be completely unreliable. Sometimes this is because of 'pure' uncertainty and sometimes because figures have been deliberately falsified by a contractor who hopes to undertake an aid project. In 1980 the ODA sanctioned aid money for an infrastructure development on the Turks and Caicos Islands on the basis of capital cost figures, supplied by the consultants, of $0.84 million and recurrent cost figures of $0.26 million, which were used in the appraisal; a few weeks later, after the project had been approved, the working estimates had been changed to $2.7 million capital cost and between $0.68 million and $0.95 million recurrent cost.[38]

Economic appraisal of aid money, then, may not be done, and if done it may not be trusted, because the data are known to be unreliable. This opens up very substantial scope for the taking of aid allocation decisions by criteria other than the level of the economic rate of return. One simple and powerful one is risk avoidance. The one circumstance most likely to damage an aid official's career, apart from rudeness to superiors or failure to answer letters, is manifest responsibility for pushing a project which turned out badly: a Mali Integrated Rural Development or a Tanganyika Groundnut Scheme.[39]

The motive to avoid incorrectly approving inappropriate projects ('type II errors', in statistical jargon) weighs heavily, therefore, on all officials in relation to every specific expenditure decision, whereas the motive to avoid falsely rejecting appropriate projects ('type I error')[40] weighs much less heavily; there is indeed a penalty (on administrators) for failing to spend the aid budget as a whole,[41] but none for throwing out an individual good idea. This bias in favour of avoiding type II error, united with administrators' need to spend the budget, has the consequence of making aid officials risk averse: inclined to give the benefit of the doubt to projects (such as power, transport and plantation agriculture) where the technology is known, large amounts of money can be moved rapidly and the risk of catastrophe is small, and to be very disinclined to take on projects such as integrated rural development and experimental energy projects where the technology is experimental, the possibility of failure is high, and the going generally harder, whatever the statistical expectation of the rate of return.[42] As a former Canadian official has written:

Just as the performance of the Agency itself is measured by its ability to spend the funds allocated to it, so too is the performance of its individual staff members ... There is no incentive to be innovative since innovative projects, as a rule, require more time to plan and implement than do run-of-the-mill activities. There is no pay-off for *innovation* when progress is measured by the quantity of disbursements.

CIDA officers have tended to be attached to those channels or projects where skills are minimised, rapid disbursement potential is maximised and Canadian involvement is longstanding. This contributes to the popularity of programme aid and to infrastructure projects in Bangladesh.[43]

As this writer implies, the logical implication of risk aversion is that aid officials should endeavour to spend as high as possible a proportion of their country budgets on programme aid, which can be spent very rapidly and which cannot 'fail' since no technique is available to trace its precise effects and hence to evaluate it.

The conclusion to which we are being forced is that the allocation of a country's aid budget between sectors and projects is very far from being a rational optimising process, in which the aid agency chooses between projects according to their expected economic rate of return. Rather, it is a sequential satisficing process which may be likened to a show-jumping trial. Projects originate, usually from the development plans of recipient governments, but sometimes from suggestions by exporters in the donor country.[44] They then have to try and jump over several 'fences', or feasibility tests. Formally these are technical appraisal, economic appraisal and financial appraisal, *accompanied* by background papers on commercial and political aspects of the proposal. However, the technical appraisal is often done against the constraint of regulations which require procurement of imports to be from the donor country.[45] And within this constraint it is often further abbreviated by the desire of both donor and recipient to seek a quick agreement—the donor because he has to spend his budget somehow, and the recipient because he is anxious for the political benefits of aid flows to come on-stream as soon as possible.[46] As a consequence, a project for aid finance usually comes before the decision-making body not in the form of a 'production function' or a set of technical options, but rather in the form of one technical option only.[47]

The economic appraisal, as we have seen, may not be done at all.[48] If it is done, and it conflicts with the financial appraisal, then this will put economists and administrators into conflict. If the financial appraisal is adverse but the economic appraisal positive, then as long as the project does not appear too risky, the economists are likely to seek methods to make the proposal financially viable, for example a system of user charges. If on the other hand the economic appraisal is adverse but the financial appraisal is positive then this presents a much more attractive prospect to the administrators, who need to spend their budget and will be heartened by the indications that the project can be handed over to the host government in a self-financing condition. Provided, once again, that the project does not look like a banana-skin on which they are likely to slip the administrators will then look for arguments to sell it to the decision-making committee.

Often, particularly in the case of a proposed programme loan or grant, such arguments will be derived from a presumption of political necessity; for example, in 1979 Britain gave balance-of-payments support grants to both Turkey and Jamaica, both of them middle-income countries, on the grounds that Western strategic interests required both those countries to remain in non-communist hands, and that financial help to enable their existing governments to weather the recession might facilitate that end.[49] However, a deadlock can also be resolved by reference to commercial arguments. We shall give two examples. In 1974 economists of the ODA were asked to advise on the desirability of providing aid to the Majes project in Peru, an ambitious scheme to tunnel water westwards from the eastern flank of the Andes to irrigate the deserts of the coastal plain. The World Bank and Inter-American Development Bank had both turned the project down, and the ODA's Economic Planning Staff, after its appraisal, advised likewise. However, ODA eventually overruled this advice and agreed to fund the project, following pressure from the Department of Trade and Industry and from a private firm—Tarmac Construction—which hoped to break into the Latin American civil engineering contracts market if the project went ahead. (It did, but subsequent ODA evaluation was to reveal that the overall impact of the project on British exports had been small[50] and the World Bank, in a report of 1979, blamed this project and other non-productive public-sector investments as major causes of the growing financial deficit and inflation in Peru.) Five years later the Minister for Overseas Development authorised the commitment of £1.2 million of aid money for Land Rovers for the Kenya Police, again in face of opposition from economists both in London and in the East African Development Division in Nairobi.[51] In this case the aid could not even be justified by the claim that it would enable a British company to break into a new market, since Land Rovers had been a familiar sight on Kenyan roads for nearly 40 years.

3.4 SUMMARY OF ARGUMENT

In this chapter we have argued:

(1) that the size of the overall aid budget is determined by bilateral bargaining between an aid minister, pushing for the largest possible aid budget, with all of his staff behind him, and the donor finance ministry. The outcome of negotiations is determined by the state of the domestic economy, and possibly also by pressures from other donor countries and from interest groups affected by the quality and quantity of aid;

(2) that the allocation of aid between countries is determined partly by historical commitments, partly by the emergence of special needs such as natural disaster, but scarcely at all by measured 'aid effectiveness';

(3) that the allocation of aid between projects and sectors is determined only to a relatively small degree by the 'technocratic' criterion of forecast economic rates of return. On some projects, a satisfactory economic rate of return is not even a necessary condition for 'the project's acceptance for aid financing, and it is never a sufficient condition. We have further argued that the types of project accepted for aid financing would reflect common administrative interests within, and political pressures on, the donor aid ministry. In particular, such projects would tend to be:
    (a) risk minimising (reflecting the common interest of all decision-making groups within the administration),
    (b) large and quick disbursing (reflecting administrators' desire to spend their budget),
    (c) intensive in imports from the donor (reflecting political constraints on the technical specification in which projects are embodied).

The last-named effects, to the extent to which they are believed to be inimical to development, may be thought of as resource allocation biases or 'substitution effects' to be set against the 'volume effect' of the overall aid flow. Other such biases will emerge from our examination of the recipient's side of the aid relationship in Chapter 4. But even if their existence is proved, and most of our evidence is only suggestive, that does not mean that they overwhelm the 'volume' or 'income' effect of the aid flow. Whether they do or not must be inferred from the empirical evidence to be advanced in the second part of this book.

APPENDIX. A FORMAL MODEL OF THE DETERMINATION OF BILATERAL AID DISBURSEMENTS

Demand

Of the three groups outside the donor government which may expect to gain some benefit from the disbursement of overseas aid—donor country taxpayers, recipient country governments and target groups in the recipient country—we would contend that only the first has any power to influence the variable with which we are concerned in this paper, namely the overall disbursement of overseas aid by a donor. It may be possible for the government of India or groups within that country, either by impassioned pleading or by establishing a reputation for being a 'good user' of aid, to increase the amount of British aid that it receives next year; but neither group tries to influence the total amount of aid that Britain gives, nor does a big increase in one or more country programmes have any necessary implications for the overall aid budget, since many aid agreements terminate every year and there is a large contingency margin.

We do not believe that taxpayers' demand for aid is influenced by its tax-price: surveys (for example T. S. Bowles, *Survey of Attitudes Towards Overseas Development*, London, HMSO, 1977) show that they are profoundly ignorant of what the tax-price is, and in any case there are a priori reasons for thinking that taxpayers' 'demand' for aid may be altruistic and therefore perversely related to its cost. Rather, all the available survey evidence suggests that it responds above all to two things: the taxpayer's perception of the donor country's ability to pay in relation to other countries[52] and his or her perception of the quality of his country's aid. The former can be fairly easily summarised in terms of national income in relation to the average of all donors; the latter is a multi-faceted concept[53] since the quality of aid can be variously seen in terms of equity, 'developmental', diplomatic and trade-creating criteria. We return to these difficulties later and for the moment write:

$$A_{it}^* = b_0 + b_1 \left(\frac{Y_i}{Y_w}\right)_t + b_2\theta_{it}; \qquad b_1 > 0, b_2 > 0 \qquad (3.1)$$

where:

A_{it}^*	= desired quantity of aid in country i in year t,
$(Y_i/Y_w)_t$	= level of per capital income in country in relation to per capita income of other OECD countries in year t,
θ_{it}	= indicator of aid "quality" in country i and year t.

Supply

As Wildavsky has pointed out (1964, also Heclo and Wildavsky, 1979), the principal influence on the budget for any spending agency in the current year is last year's budget. This is, if anything, even more true of aid than of other categories of public expenditure, since so much aid consists of money committed several years in advance for the support of projects, commitments which cannot be rescinded without serious offence to foreign governments. All that those seeking to influence the type and quality of foreign aid can therefore do, as one Treasury official put it to Wildavsky, is 'mess about at the margins'.[54] These marginal influences, however, as noted earlier, are multiple and in mutual conflict. First, there are the pressures exerted by the Treasury, or whichever ministry controls the aid agency's budget. Second, there are pressures from other donor countries; finally, there are pressures from the 'demand side', that is, from the donor country's electorate.

The job of the *Treasury* is to cut the aid ministry's initial spending bid back to whatever percentage is necessary to satisfy its targets for public-sector borrowing, interest rates and the money supply. On this view, the extent by which the aid agency's initial bid is cut back will depend on the state of the domestic economy. 'The state of the economy' can of course be diagnosed in a variety of ways, but a plausible initial hypothesis would be that finance ministers will seek to cut back on the volume of overseas aid particularly hard if *either* the domestic budget is in deficit or the domestic economy is in recession,[55] and that they will take a more liberal line at other times.

Other donor countries now influence the budget of individual national donors far more than they did, through the examination of each OECD aid donor's annual performance by other OECD members (see p. 58).

To sum up so far, it seems reasonable to suggest that the supply of foreign aid expenditures by a government in any year is heavily influenced by a constant representing last year's expenditures and that any increase or decrease in the value of this constant will be determined by: (a) the behaviour of the finance ministry, which will reflect the state of the domestic economy, (b) the aid-giving behaviour of the international community, and (c) an adjustment parameter reflecting the adjustment of 'supply' thus determined to the electoral 'demand' for aid. Formally:

$$A_{it} = b_3 A_{i,t-1} + b_4 U_{it} + b_5 B_{it} + b_6 \sum_{j \neq i} A_{j,t-1} + b_7 (A^*_{i,t-1} - A_{i,t-1})$$

$$(3.2)$$

$$b_3 > 0, b_4 < 0, b_5 < 0, b_6 > 0, 0 < b_7 < 1$$

where:

A_{it}	= actual aid disbursement by government of country i in year t,
A^*_{it}	= 'desired' quantity of aid in country i in year t, as defined on p. 71,
U_{it}	= unemployment in country i in year t,
B_{it}	= government budget deficit in country i in year t,
$\sum_{j \neq i} A_{j,t-1}$	aid disbursement in period t of all OECD countries [56] other than country i.

The nature of the 'adjustment parameter', b_7 of supply to 'desired supply', of course, has not yet been considered. This is because the heart of our disagreement with earlier authors lies in the nature of the adjustment mechanism. We close this section by considering this relationship.

The adjustment of supply to demand. The market for publicly-supplied services, as Breton (1974) has pointed out, is one in which consumers have very limited scope for expressing their wishes. If consumers wish, for whatever reason, to buy less bananas, then they can go ahead and do this, but if they want a reduction in the foreign aid budget then all that they can do *through the 'market'* is reduce their contributions to voluntary agencies, if they make any, and these, for various reasons, are not a perfect substitute for official aid.[57] Hence people for whom aid actually supplied (A_t, in the notation used above) is not equal to aid desired or 'demanded' (A_t^*), must resort to *political* action—lobbies, pressure on MPs, writing to newspapers and so on—if they want to effect an alteration in the amount of aid actually supplied.

However, the channels of communication and of influence do not just flow one way; it is, of course, open for government to try and influence public opinion, as well as for public opinion to try and influence the government. The degree of public ignorance about aid and its distribution, revealed in the previous section, makes the scope for such influence particularly great. Specifically, if a government is made aware that a gap has developed between the quantity of aid that it is providing and the quantity of aid that the electorate would like to see, then three 'market adjustment' strategies are open to it:

(1) It can behave in the conventional way, as a 'market follower', and adjust its aid disbursements upwards or downwards in any year according as the previous year's disbursements fell short of or exceeded the desired level. In this event coefficient b_7 will be significant and positive.

(2) It can behave as a market leader at the level of *quantity*, and by publicity and other means of persuasion it can try to persuade the public that its currently desired level of aid should be revised so as to approximate more closely to the level which it wishes to provide. In the language of Galbraith (1968) it can 'revise the sequence' so that the producer dictates to the consumer, rather than vice versa. In this event coefficient b_7 will be insignificant. The existing literature, by considering only 'supply-related' influences on the level of aid, has by implication assumed that this is the only available market adjustment strategy.

(3) It can behave as a market leader at the level of *quality*, and alter the composition of its aid without changing its volume. In this event coefficient b_7 will still be insignificant, but 'aid quality', rather than quantity, will respond to pressures on the demand side. That is, the quality parameter θ_i will be significantly associated with the residuals from the supply equation (3.2) *without the market adjustment term included.* By this means, according to hypothesis (3.1) on p. 69, it will also influence the desired quantity of aid. Indeed, chain reactions may develop, of two kinds. In the first hypothetical case, an improvement in the quality of aid may bring about greater public support for it, leading to a further improvement in the quantity *or the quality* of aid offered by a given donor. In the alternative situation, a deterioration in the quality of aid may reduce public support for it, leading to a deterioration in the quantity *or the quality* of aid offered by a given donor. It will be our contention that 'spirals' of both these types are observable in post-war Western experience.

At this point it becomes necessary to spell out what is meant by aid quality. It means the return or yield which is obtained on a given input of aid; but, to repeat, different interest groups expect a different sort of yield from governmental aid expenditures. In a recent paper (Mosley, 1982a) I have constructed three different indices of the 'quality of aid', each reflecting the values of a different interest group on the 'demand side' of the market for aid. The indices are set out in full in the appendix to Mosley (1985a), and the variables from which they are built up are set out in Table 3.1. Our assumption is that commercial interests will be principally interested in aid as a vehicle for export promotion, and hence appreciate devices such as aid tying, mixed credit and the giving of aid to fast-growing economies; that diplomatic interests will be mainly concerned to spread aid across as large a number of countries as possible; and that 'altruists' will be concerned to get aid to the poorest countries and the poorest people, and also to release aid from the restrictions which the commercial lobby would like to impose on it.

All of the three interest groups are represented in every country. But their relative strength differs according to historical circumstance. Countries with a colonial past, which have influence

Table 3.1: Alternative criteria of aid quality

Indicator of aid quality	1 Proportion of aid tied to purchases from donor countries	2 Proportion of aid provided as 'mixed credit'	3 Proportion of aid given to countries with growth of GDP, 1970–9, over 4 per cent	4 Total number of countries to which aid is provided	5 Proportion of total aid budget allocated to 'LDCs'	6 Proportion of total aid allocated to agriculture and social infrastructure projects
Interest group						
(i) Commercial interest in donor country	*	*	*			
(ii) Military and diplomatic interests in donor country				*		
(iii) 'Altruists': persons interested in redistribution to poorest countries and people in the Third World					*	*

The symbol * in a particular cell means that the index in that row is positively associated with the indicator in that column.

to lose as well as gain, are likely to give more weight to the pleading of 'military and diplomatic interests'; countries which have recently been in balance-of-payments trouble are likely to give more weight to the pressures of the commercial lobby than whose which have stayed in surplus without needing to use aid to subsidise exports. In constructing an overall aid quality index, θ, on p. 79 we adjust the weights given to aid quality indices (i), (ii) and (iii) to reflect these variations in countries' historical experience.

Empirical Tests

We have so far:

a demand equation,

$$A_{it}^* = b_0 + b_1 \left(\frac{Y_t}{Y_w} \right)^t + b_2 \theta_{it} \tag{3.1}$$

and a supply and market adjustment equation,

$$A_{it} = b_3 A_{i,t-1} + b_4 U_{it} + b_5 B_{it} + b_6 \sum_{j \neq i} A_{j,t-1} \tag{3.2}$$

$$+ b_7 (A_{i,t-1}^* - A_{i,t-1}).$$

Substituting (3.2) into (3.1),

$$A_{it} = b_3 A_{i,t-1} + b_4 U_{it} + b_5 B_{it} + b_6 \sum_{j \neq i} A_{j,t-1} \tag{3.3}$$

$$+ b_7 \left\{ \left[b_0 + b_1 \left(\frac{Y_t}{Y_w} \right)_{t-1} + b_2 \theta_{i,t-1} \right] - A_{i,t-1} \right\}$$

which simplifies to:

$$A_{it} = \text{constant} + b_4 U_{it} + b_5 B_{it} + b_6 \sum_{j \neq i} A_{j,t-1} \tag{3.4}$$

$$+ b_{10} A_{i,t-1} + b_8 \left(\frac{Y_t}{Y_w} \right)_{t-1} + b_9 \theta_{i,t-1}$$

where: constant $= b_0 b_7$

$$b_8 = b_7 b_1$$
$$b_9 = b_7 b_2$$
$$b_{10} = b_3 - b_7.$$

It will be appropriate to estimate this equation by ordinary least-squares if all the variables on the right-hand side are genuinely exogenous. However, if a donor chooses to adjust to the 'market' by varying the quality of its aid,[58] then the quality of aid will be endogenous, and a different estimation technique will be required. We therefore proceed in two stages. We begin by estimating an equation for aid quality:

$$\theta_t = b_{11} \left(A^*_{i,t-1} - A_{i,t-1} \right) \tag{3.5}$$

$$= b_{11} \left\{ \left[b_0 + b_1 \left(\frac{Y_t}{Y_w} \right)_{t-1} + b_2 \theta_{i,t-1} \right] - A_{i,t-1} \right\} \tag{3.6}$$

to see whether any significant response of aid quality to the difference between supply and 'demand' for aid can be discerned. If it can, we treat aid quality as endogenous and then proceed to estimate (3.4) by two-stage least squares. If it cannot, we treat aid quality as exogenous and estimate (3.4) by ordinary least squares.

The countries for which aid quality appears to be endogenous are the Netherlands, Canada, the UK and West Germany. For these countries equation (3.6) estimates for the period 1961–80 are as set out in Table 3.2. In general, aid quality is responsive to the level of aid disbursements; also, in Britain and West Germany, it is responsive to the donor's income *vis-à-vis* the OECD average. In these two countries, in other words, particularly in Britain, aid quality seemed to improve as the donor's relative economic position deteriorated. This could be because aid was shifted, in the recessions of 1974–5 and 1979–81, away from industry in developing countries which might compete with industry in donor countries, and towards agriculture, implying an increase in the value of our aid quality index. For all other donor countries, aid quality could not be significantly correlated with any of the possible explanatory variables and we therefore treat it as exogenous.

We now proceed to look at aid disbursements themselves and hence to estimate equation (3.4). In the case of the four countries mentioned above we use two-stage least squares, treating aid quality as endogenous and aid disbursements lagged 1 year as an instrumental variable. In the case of all others OECD donor countries we simply estimate equation (3.4) by ordinary least

Table 3.2: Countries for which aid quality is endogenous: empirical results for equation (3.6) for period 1961–80; dependent variable: aid quality index θ

	Constant	Regression coefficients on independent variables:			
		Income per head relative to OECD average $(Y_i/Y_w)_{t-1}$	Aid disburse-ments lagged one year $A_{i,t-1}$	Lagged value of aid quality index $\theta_{i,t-1}$	r^2
Netherlands	3.09	12.5	0.025*	0.11	0.7081
	(0.12)	(1.07	(2.23)	(0.44)	
United Kingdom	210	−249*	0.088*	0.062	0.6938
	(2.46)	(2.34)	(2.31)	(1.31)	
Canada	−12	20.4	0.78**	0.21	0.6793
	(0.49)	(0.78	(2.79)	(1.95)	
West Germany	31.6	−5.8*	0.46*	0.17	0.3482
	(0.94	(2.19)	2.43)	(1.03)	

Sources: see Table 3.4.
Figures in brackets beneath coefficients are Student's *t*-statistics.
*denotes significance at 5% level;
**denotes significance at 1% level.

squares. The equations are estimated in first differences in order to eliminate the automatic correlation which results from the fact that both the dependent variable and several of the independent variables such as unemployment and total aid disbursements are all subject to an upward drift over time. The results are set out in Table 3.3.

The following preliminary conclusions emerge from Table 3.3. On the supply side, aid disbursements by nearly all donors are significantly influenced in an upward direction by past dis-bursements ($A_{i,t-1}$; column 6) which tend of themselves to create commitments, and by other countries' disbursements ($\Sigma_{j\neq i}A_{j,t-1}$; column 7) which encourage, or shame, donors to keep up with the Jones's within the DAC. The exceptions to this general pattern are the United States, which has been running its aid programme down, against the general OECD trend but with considerable and irregular year-on-year variations in aid disbursements (so that there is no significant serial correlation between A_{it} and $A_{i,t-1}$) and Sweden, which has always pursued a rather generous aid policy irrespective of the OECD trend and which thus appears insensitive to the 'international demonstration effect' (so that there is no significant correlation between A_{it} and $\Sigma_{j \neq i, t} A_{j,t-1}$).

Also on the supply side, the regression coefficients on unemployment and the domestic budget deficit are in all cases of the expected sign, but they are significant—and then only just—in the UK, the United States and Japan only. International aid, it seems, is only mildly responsive to the state of the domestic economy.

On the demand side, the general picture is that a country's aid disbursements are in general elastic with respect to that country's income (Y_{it-1}/Y_{wt-1}; column 8) within OECD, but that the response of aid disbursements to aid quality (θ_{it-1}; column 9) is highly variable. Some countries (Netherlands, West Germany, Norway, Sweden and to a lesser degree the UK) exhibit a positive and significant response of aid disbursements to aid quality; thus we may infer that in these countries there was *both* a response of public demand to aid quality, and a response of government behaviour to public demand. In the other countries in the sample, namely the United States, Canada, France and Japan, the response coefficient is insignificant and in the latter two cases it is actually negative. Of these four, we have seen from Table 3.2 that in Canada the quality of government aid was apparently responsive to public pressure; in France, Japan and the US, however, it is possible to observe neither an influence of quality on the 'demand' for aid, nor an influence of the 'demand' for aid on quality.

In conclusion, we perceive three patterns of adjustment in the 'market' for international aid. In the first pattern (West Germany, Netherlands, Norway, Sweden) electorates are responsive to the quality of aid which their governments provide, and their governments respond to the pressures which they impose by altering the quantity of their aid. In the second pattern (Canada, UK) governments respond to such pressures from citizens by changing the quality, rather than the quantity, of their aid.[59] In the third and last pattern (France, Japan, US), governments do not respond

Table 3.3: Empirical results for equation (3.4): determinants of aid disbursements. Dependent variable - net official aid disbursement by government of country stated, in US$ millions (A_{it}). All variables in first differences.

Country	Period covered by analysis	Constant	State of domestic economy: Unemployment (U_{it})	State of domestic economy: Central government budget deficit (B_{it})	Past commitments $A_{i,t-1}$	International comparisons: Total OECD aid disbursements $\Sigma_{j\neq i}A_{j,t-1}$	International comparisons: Country's income relative to OECD average $(Y/Y_w)_{t-1}$	International comparisons: Aid 'quality' $\theta_{i,t-1}$	r^2	DW
(a) Countries for which aid and quality in endogenous: 2SLS estimation										
Canada	1961–80	-0.6 (1.18)	44.1 (1.22)	0.017 (0.60)		0.17* (3.18)		1.87 (0.41)	0.3886	2.0946
West Germany	1961–80	-0.8 (0.78)	-259 (0.60)	-0.30 (0.51)		0.13* (1.88)		21.4** (2.41)	0.4732	1.7167
Netherlands	1961–80	-1.0 (0.72)	-64 (0.30)	0.16 (0.43)		0.062** (2.51)		446* (1.90)	0.2885	1.9460
United Kingdom	1961–80	-0.2 (0.71)	-24* (3.65)	0.044 (0.51)		0.012 (0.73)		45.9* (1.70)	0.3206	1.7064
(b) Countries for which aid and quality is exogenous: OLS estimation										
France	1961–80	0.2 (0.42)	86.6 (0.82)	0.007 (0.44)	0.034 (0.23)	0.11** (3.42)	-110 (0.18)	-1.20 (0.13)	0.4922	1.3163
Japan	1961–80	-0.7* (2.40)	-56* (1.84)	0.0026 (0.39)	-0.025 (0.073)	0.16** (3.36)	276 (0.92)	-0.33 (0.050)	0.4855	1.4615
Norway	1964–80	-0.1 (1.30)	-13 (0.53)	-0.0011 (0.41)	0.94** (4.41)	0.09** (2.65)	80.7* (1.86)	0.45** (2.59)	0.4923	2.8899
Sweden	1964–80	-0.5 (1.28)	21 (0.51)	0.071 (0.45)	0.85** (3.22)	0.015 (1.06)	379* (1.81)	2.47** (2.71)	0.4900	3.2036
U.S.A.	1961–80	1.8** (2.63)	-287* (1.72)	-0.013* (1.87)	0.063 (0.45)	0.201** (4.52)	-121 (2.16)	1.53 (0.99)	0.3964	1.8202

For sources of data see Table 3.4.

Table 3.4: Variables and data sources

Symbol	Variable	Dimension	Source
A_{it}	Aid disbursements by country i in year t (net)	US $m	DAC *Annual Reports*
$A_{i,t-1}$	Aid disbursements by country i in year $t-1$ (net)	US $m	DAC *Annual Reports*
$\sum_{j \neq i}^{n} A_{j,t-1}$	Aid disbursements by all OECD countries other than country i in year $t-1$	US $m	DAC *Annual Reports*
Y_{it}	Income per capita in country i in year t	US $	OECD *Main Economic Indicators*
Y_{wt}	Average per capita income in OECD countries in year t	US $	OECD *Main Economic Indicators*
θ_{it}	Value of 'aid quality index' in country i in year t	Percentage	Mosley (1982a) Table 6
U_{it}	Unemployment in country i in year t	Percentage	OECD *Main Economic Indicators*
B_i	Central government budget deficit in country i in year t	US $m	IMF *International Financial Statistics*

to public pressure by altering the pattern of their aid, but rather by seeking to persuade the electorate to accept the pattern of aid which they have already decided to adopt. The implication of the existing literature is that only this last pattern of adjustment is worth considering; this preliminary study suggests, however, that it is not the only pattern of adjustment which exists, and that the aid-giving process is by no means as exclusively characterised by market leadership on the part of the state as that literature has implied. If the present approach is taken, and the quality and quantity of development aid are seen as jointly determined, a model results which explains the data better than simple 'supply-related' models.[60] For these reaons we put it forward as a first step towards a general explanation of the determination of aid expenditures.

NOTES

1. A bureaucracy is a 'non profit making organisation financed in whole or in part from a periodic appropriation or grant' (Niskanen, 1971, p. 8).
2. There is a tendency, however, for their ranks to become gradually permeated by economists from within the agency in search of quicker promotion.
3. Sometimes, after serving two or three contracts of this type, overseas staff will be offered security of tenure for a longer period, up to 10 years (British Corps of Specialists, German GTZ). But such security is characteristically limited to a very small proportion of overseas technical co-operation staff.
4. This proposition is given support on p. 56.
5. In Britain this is known as 'aid framework allocation' and is forecast on a 3-year rolling basis; *see* pp. 59–60.
6. For discussion of pressure to disburse in IBRD and IADB, *see* Tendler (1975), pp. 88–9.
7. The 'project cycle' is the sequence of operations through which a project passes: identification—planning—appraisal—implementation and monitoring—evaluation.
8. Often, of course, the flexibility desired by local project leaders is a euphemism for freedom to adapt the project to the requirements of local interests. On a project in Peru designed to give extension help to poor peasant farmers, I have seen a (British) technical assistance team leader successfully lobbied by large farmers to give help to them also. This led to the bizarre spectacle of British taxpayers' aid money being used to provide veterinary supplies to Peruvians who drove up to collect them in their Mercedes. The team leader saw this perversion of the objectives of aid as the price he had to pay to get the presence of an alien technical assistance team accepted in the town where the project headquarters were located.
9. As Rondinelli writes (1983, p. 79):

   in such situations the major criterion of success for many project managers turns on their ability to conform to plans or programmes designed in aid agency or national ministry headquarters, rather than on their ability to seize local opportunities in order to achieve a project's purposes or to modify goals to reflect changes or unanticipated conditions.

10. We refer, of course, to enclaves of British technical co-operation officers and their families. But traditionalism is not confined to these relics of the British Empire: Tendler, in her study of US aid, refers to: 'the slightly passé clothing of the aid employees and their wives, the lack of involvement in what was happening in their host country or home country, and a kind of folksiness associated with an earlier, smalltown America' (1975, p. 27).
11. This has become particularly common since it became fashionable to blame low productivity of projects on 'the policy environment' (i.e. policy-making blunders by the recipient).

12. *See* Gasper (1985), p. 9, who draws a distinction between the 'active' role of the project implementer and the 'deliberative' role of the analyst.
13. Practice varies: the World Bank issues project completion reports on all projects, though it now only subjects about half to independent audit; most other agencies only apply formal evaluation to between 10 and 50 per cent of their projects. *See* Mosley (1983) for a comparison of World Bank and ODA procedure.
14. In 1980 the ODA's Projects Committee, which allocates money for new projects, did not meet in the first half of the year, so severe had been the cuts in overall aid expenditure imposed by the Treasury the previous year.
15. Niskanen (1971), pp. 38 and 80.
16. The Scandinavian countries and possibly the Netherlands provide an exception to this generalisation.
17. OECD, *Development Assistance: Problems and Policies*, 1975 review, Paris 1976, p. 102.
18. International Development Association, the soft-loan arm of the World Bank, which provides credits to the poorest countries for an annual service charge of ¾ per cent. For a comprehensive in-house review of IDA, *see* World Bank (1982b).
19. In the case of the World Bank's IDA this became very clear in the autumn of 1984 when the United States Congress restricted its subscription to the seventh replenishment of IDA to two-thirds of the amount requested by the association. For details *see* Independent Group on British Aid (1986).
20. These effects (Duesenberry, 1949) consist of the influence on a given person's expenditure on particular items exerted by the consumption behaviour of other individuals within his reference group.
21. White (1974), p. 231.
22. *See* for example Griffin and Enos (1970), Hayter and Watson (1985), McKinley and Little (1978a, b, 1979); see also discussion on pp. 31–32 above.
23. In 1983 63 per cent of British aid went to the poorest fifty countries in the world, and its six largest bilateral aid programmes (India, Tanzania, Sudan, Kenya, Sri Lanka, Bangladesh, Pakistan) all went to countries within the group of the fifty poorest. *See* ODA, *British Overseas Aid 1984*, pp. 6–15.
24. The best symbol of this is the re-incorporation of the Overseas Development Administration into the Foreign and Commonwealth Office in 1979.
25. For a detailed development of these arguments *see* Mosley (1981b).
26. On the 'sub-Saharan crisis', and for a plea for increased (conditional) aid flows to deal with the problem, *see* World Bank (1981, Chapter 9).
27. *See* Chapter 8, p. 235 and footnote 7.
28. *See* Bridger and Winpenny (1983), Chapter 1.
29. In the British Overseas Development Administration only capital

projects of a value greater than £1.3 million are submitted to the
Projects Committee, and only these projects are subjected to full
technical and economic appraisal. Even some projects with value
over £1.3 million escape full appraisal if they are submitted under
the government's Aid–Trade Provision (*see* Chapter 7, p. 225).
30. For detailed discussion *see* Mosley (1985c), Table 3 and p. 60.
31. For substantial further discussion of mixed credit *see* Chapter 7.
32. In 1983 and 1984 Britain provided two grants of more than £15
    million under its mixed credit scheme, the Aid and Trade Provision:
    see Overseas Development Administration, *Annual Reports*, 1983
    and 1984.
33. R. M. Ainscow to the Overseas Development Sub-Committee of the
    House of Commons Foreign Affairs Committee, 27 April 1982;
    see House of Commons *Second Report from the Foreign Affairs
    Committee: Supply Estimates 1982–3* (HC 330 of 1981–2); Her Majes-
    ty's Stationery Office, July 1982, p. 36, paragraph 71.
34. *See* House of Commons, reference as for Note 33, for discussion of
    this test, in particular answer to question 7 on pp. 10 and 11.
35. The figure is estimated by working out the proportion of the budget
    which is (a) spent on projects of value less than £1.3m *or* (b) spent
    on ATP projects *or* (c) spent on programme aid *or* spent on projects
    in the education and technical assistance sector.
36. The analysts are using the Little–Mirrlees formula:

$$w^* = \text{SCF} \{c' - \frac{1}{S}(c - m)\}$$

where w^* = shadow wage rate.
      c' = worker's consumption in new employment.
      SCF = standard conversion factor reflecting relationship
             between domestic and world prices.
      S = imputed value of savings in terms of consumption.
      c = value of workers' consumption in previous (normally
             agricultural) employment.
      m = marginal produce of labour in previous employment.

The parameter which the authors are trying to calculate is *m* in the
above formula.
37. UK Overseas Development Administration: *Dharan–Dhankuta road,
    Nepal: ex ante appraisal*. South East Asia Development Division,
    Bangkok, 1976, p. 35. For additional evidence *see* Chambers (1983)
    who in footnote 1, p. 46 cites the case of an agricultural development
    project appraised by three different teams, who arrived at estimated
    ex ante rates of return of 19 per cent, 13 per cent and minus 2 per
    cent.
38. House of Commons: *Third Report from the Foreign Affairs Commit-
    tee, session 1980–1: Turks and Caicos Islands Hotel Development*
    (H.C. 26, Vol. II), paragraph 187.

39. The Tanganyika Groundnut Scheme is discussed in Chapter 2, p. 22. The Mali Integrated Rural Development Project had an estimated rate of return of 91 per cent at *ex ante* appraisal and of less than zero at *ex post* evaluation; for more detail *see* World Bank, *Seventh Annual Review of Project Performance Audit Results* (Washington, September 1981), statistical appendix.
40. On type II errors *see* Gasper (1985), p. 9.
41. *See* pp. 52–53.
42. The bias exerted against poverty-focused projects by the size of the administrative workload involved must not be understated. As Wiggins has argued, 'concern for the rural poor evaporates rapidly when overburdened administrators find themselves still emptying their in-trays at 7 p.m. on a Friday evening' (1985, p. 102).
43. Ehrhardt (1983), pp. 112, 125–6. Compare Tendler's judgement of the policy environment within US aid in the 1960s (1975, pp. 10–11):

    The special character of the foreign aid agency's task requires that the organisation has the proper atmosphere for groping without too much idea of what will result, for straying from tried and true solutions, and for struggling to escape from customary ways of thinking about things ... (However) in order to maintain credibility with Congress, public watchdog entities, and investors (in the case of the multilateral banks) the organisation could not admit that it often had to thrash around for solutions.

44. This is particularly often the case with mixed credit projects (*see* Chapter 7, pp. 225–227.
45. An estimated 37 per cent of OECD donors' aid in 1982–3 was tied to procurement in the source country: *see* Table 7.1. Source tying makes production in the recipient country more intensive than it would .otherwise be in goods imported from the host country, especially if source tying is accompanied by a restriction on the proportion of an aid transaction which the donor is prepared to finance in the form of local costs.
46. A 1981 review of rural roads by US aid found 'a failure to adequately consider alternative design standards' (Gasper, 1985, p. 14). Failure to conduct any systematic search between alternative technologies is also criticised by the recent IMF/IBRD study of aid effectiveness (Cassen *et al.*, 1986, p. 5) as perhaps the greatest remediable fault of aid donors' project selection procedures.
47. On the ubiquity of this problem in public sector spending decisions, *see* Jackson (1982), p. 192.
48. *See* pp. 61–62.
49. In the event both Turkey and Jamaica had by 1982 been taken over, in elections, by even more pro-Western and right-wing governments than those which were in power in 1979. The role of Western aid in this development is difficult to gauge.
50. James Moran: *Majes Irrigation Project, Peru: a Desk Study*. ODA Evaluation Unit, Report EV 115, 1979.
51. ODA, *British Overseas Aid 1984*, p. 8, and *Kenya Country Review 1983/4*, paragraph 4.3.6.

52. *See* for example the 1977 survey above quoted, where those respondents who believed that the UK was 'too poor' to give aid made it clear that they meant that it was too poor relative to other donors, who by implication should 'take up a greater share of the aid burden' (Bowles, 1978, p. 69). Y_w in equation (1) therefore stands for average income per capita in member countries of the OECD's Development Assistance Committee.
53. For full details of the calculation of experimental 'aid quality indices'' and of their value for DAC countries in the years 1960–79, *see* appendix to Mosley (1985a).
54. Quoted in Heclo and Wildavsky (1979), p. 22.
55. We take the level of unemployment as a measure of the extent to which the economy is in recession.
56. For reasons given above, we take the OECD countries as being the reference group for all countries belonging to that organisation.
57. Voluntary agencies give relatively more money for the relief of immediate disasters than official aid-giving bodies, and relatively less for long-term projects in agriculture and infrastructure. Indeed, their budgets and organisational capacity frequently are not on the scale necessary to mount projects of the latter type.
58. Strategy (3) on p. 72.
59. Most of the measured improvement in the quality of UK aid over 1960–81 is the consequence of an increase in the amount of aid which is given as an export subsidy. This will please the trading lobby but not, of course, the 'altruists' in the development lobby.
60. Squared correlation coefficients, which we can use as a measure of tracking performance, are as follows for the period 1961–79 in respect of the model with and without the 'demand-side' variable θ_i (the aid quality index) inserted:

	Without	With
Canada	0.31	0.39
France	0.45	0.49
West Germany	0.44	0.47
Japan	0.41	0.48
Netherlands	0.21	0.28
Norway	0.46	0.49
Sweden	0.41	0.49
United Kingdom	0.30	0.32
United States	0.38	0.39

4 On the Other Side of the River: Aid from the Recipient's Point of View

4.1 AID ALLOCATION AT THE MACRO-LEVEL

Seen from the offices of the Finance Ministry of Nepal or Tanzania, aid is something quite different from what it appears in Washington or Tokyo. For the donor, aid is an expenditure designed to further objectives of foreign and commercial policy; for the recipient, it is an inflow, designed to relieve a financial constraint. In the past a clear perception of the aid process has been made difficult by the tendency of many authors to portray one or other party as the sole controller of the manner in which aid is used.[1] To do this is, of course, as misleading as to represent a child as being made exclusively by the mother or by the father. In the previous chapter we considered the pressures operating on the donor side; this chapter looks at aid from the recipient's point of view.

Let us begin from the traditional neoclassical economist's way of seeing the choices open to the recipient government. In the poor country depicted in Figure 4.1, the possibilities of transforming income saved from current consumption (C_0) into future income (C_1) are represented by the line CD. The country can consume its entire current income, OC, in which case next period's consumption is zero; it can save its entire current income, in which next period's consumption possibilities are OD; or it can choose some combination of current and future consumption intermediate between OC and OD. In the example shown, the country's 'preferences' between future and current and

Consumption in
current period (C₀)

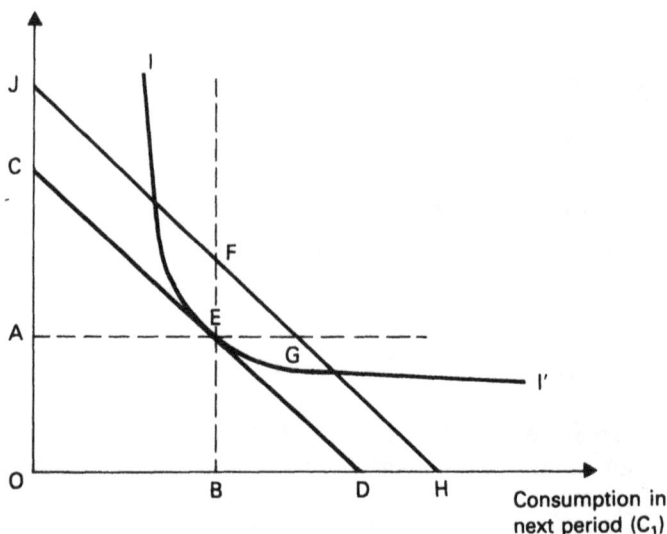

Figure 4.1: Present versus future consumption: aid allocation choices facing a recipient government

future consumption, as embodied in the savings decisions of government and private individuals, are embodied in the collective indifference curve or welfare function II', and the allocation of resources representing the highest possible value of this welfare function is the tangency between II' and the intertemporal transformation curve CD, at point E. Current consumption is OA, savings are AC, and next period's consumption possibilities are OB.

Let us now introduce an inflow of aid, to the value EF. What is done with this inflow depends on technical possibilities and on the government's choices, if we assume for the moment that all aid flows directly from government to government. Suppose that the country's consumption possibilities are expanded by the aid inflow from CD to JH. Assuming that the government has no wish to *reduce* either current or future consumption from their presently planned levels, the limits to choice are set by points F and G on the transformation curve *JH*. If all of the aid is allocated to current consumption (the assumption favoured by 'aid pessimists' of the left and right such as Griffin and Bauer)[2] we move to point *F*, and there is no increase in future consumption possibilities. If all of the aid is allocated to investment, and there is no shifting of present investment into consumption (the assumption favoured by 'aid optimists'), we move to point *G*, and there is no increase of current consumption, but an increase of *EG* in future consumption possibilities. Alternatively, of course, the government may settle at a point intermediate between *F* and *G*. It all depends on 'the shape of its preference function', that is, on the way in which it chooses to allocate the additional resources made available by aid between developmental and non-developmental purposes. It is possible, of course, for the donor to try and constrain the recipient's choice by tying his aid to specific capital investment projects, but to the extent that the recipient has already earmarked its own domestic resources for those capital projects, he is free to switch the resources released by aid into consumption expenditure, or for that matter into tax cuts or reductions of borrowing. This is the famous problem of 'fungibility'; it will quickly be apparent that the possibilities of switching aid money away from developmental purposes will be greater, the greater is the portion of the development budget which is financed from local resources. If aid is already paying for the entire development budget, then by definition there is no local development expenditure which can be switched into consumption or any other purpose, and fungibility will be zero. This is a commoner situation in very poor countries such as Nepal or Upper Volta than in middle-income countries, and, as a broad generalisation, the more prosperous the recipient country, the greater is the likelihood that the income effects of aid will be diluted by 'substitution effects' into unproductive government expenditure.

Uncertainty
In two respects the abstract model of Figure 4.1 oversimplifies even the macroeconomic picture. In the first place

the choice open to the recipient government is represented by the model as a choice between two certain alternatives portrayed by the transformation curves *CD* and *JH*. In real life the options open to the government, anywhere in the world but especially in a developing country, are anything but certain:

prices of primary exports may fluctuate up or down without warning; this may cause particular havoc for the budget forecasts of a country such as Ghana, Zambia or Bolivia which is heavily dependent on one export staple; *quantities* of all natural resource products may themselves change without warning on account of climate (for example the frost which killed off half the Brazilian coffee crop in 1976), disease (for example foot-and-mouth which, if it appears in one part of the Botswana national herd, makes exports from any part of the country impossible for a period) and still more mysterious biological circumstances (for example the sudden emigration of anchovies out of Pacific coastal waters, which forced a reduction in Peruvian exports of fishmeal in the early 1970s);[3]

data are themselves often not available (particularly in respect of the non-monetary sector of the economy, where bad communications and the illiteracy of respondents make the collection of information by conventional methods almost impossible). Even if the data are collected, they may not be available to decision makers because of shortages of skills and manpower in the central administration. As a visiting consultant in Ghana in the autumn of 1985 I was informed that no data on GDP, investment or foreign trade by categories had yet been collated for years beyond 1981. In such an environment the concept of 'governmental choice between different combinations and current and future consumption possibilities' clearly has only the haziest meaning;

finally, *political* uncertainties are of an entirely different order of magnitude in LDCs. In Asia, Latin America and Africa, and there only, change of government by *coup d'état* is common: within the last 5 years in sub-Saharan Africa alone there have been coups in Nigeria, Ghana,

Uganda, Sudan and Chad, and attempted coups in Kenya
and Liberia. This record of unpredictable and often viol-
ent change in government, projected into the future,
breeds insecurity, and also breeds strategies to protect
Third World governments against that insecurity, such as
diversion of aid money to support military expenditure
where that can be achieved.

These uncertainties react on one another: for example, a
sudden drop in price or volume of the principal export
may force austerity measures on the government—such as
reductions in food subsidies—which then increase its
exposure to overthrow.[4] What is critical to the present
discussion is that from the point of view of the recipient
government the major function of aid inflows from overseas
may be to *reduce these uncertainties themselves* rather than
to augment resources in a situation of certain knowledge.
This has two implications which are not apparent from the
simple two-period diagram of Figure 4.1. First, recipient
countries will have a *counter-cyclical* demand for aid: in
times of world recession, such as 1980–3, their need for
concessional resources (in particular programme aid for
balance-of-payments support) will rise sharply and without
warning. Unfortunately, it is precisely at such times when
donor countries are under most pressure to cut back on
domestic expenditure, particularly 'soft' items such as aid,[5]
and this has led to some painful conflicts of interest, in
particular the dispute over the seventh replenishment of
IDA in 1982.[6] Quite frequently, of course, recipient countries will seek 'emergency' bilateral aid in such conditions,
as Turkey and Jamaica did in 1979, in order to escape the
more unpleasant discipline of an IMF stand-by agreement;
the issue of the recipient government's choice between different forms of foreign resource inflow is taken up in Section
4.4 below.

A second implication of uncertainty is that those recipient
governments who want aid at all will want to contract for
it on a long-term basis, since this puts a bottom line on the
level of public revenue for several years ahead, and thus
makes one of the uncertain things within the budget more
certain. One of the most striking insights to emerge from

the survey of aid effectiveness commissioned by the IMF/ World Bank Development Committee was the affection which recipient governments evinced for donors, such as the Germans in relation to agricultural technical assistance in Kenya and the Danish government in relation to integrated rural development in Bangladesh, who were willing to stay with problems, and commit money, over a long period, and their irritation with donors who would only commit themselves a year or two ahead.[7] Here again, however, one encounters a conflict of interest between donor and recipient, since if all the donor's money is committed as far ahead as recipients would like, he cannot redirect aid money in response to sudden needs, or the desire to reward 'good performance' in specific countries. We shall return to this trade-off between flexibility and commitment in Chapter 8.

Fragmentation within central government

There remains a second unrealistic assumption within Figure 4.1 which we must correct, and this is the idea that in every developing country a unitary body called 'the government' makes binding and effective decisions about how aid shall be used. This idea departs from reality in three separate ways. First, not all of the public-sector budget is under central government control. In almost every developing country many of the functions of government are discharged not by government but by autonomous bodies variously known as statutory boards, parastatals and *quangos* (quasi-autonomous non-governmental agencies)—notably the functions of agricultural marketing, administering loans and encouraging regional development. These are, of course, functions critical to the development process. Very often autonomous agencies are set up in response to the promptings of some powerful interest group; this helps to explain the asymmetric relationship they frequently have with central government, which has responsibility for keeping them in being but little power to control their internal operations.[8] However, often they are set up at the behest of aid agencies themselves, on the presumption that government ministries will not prove effective implementing agencies, and that the critical function of aid effectiveness is better served by creating a new body which can cut through the red tape. By encouraging the creation of bodies such as the Damodar River Authority and the Basic Agricultural Services Programme, of course, the aid agencies weaken the very implementive capacity in central government whose debility they so often deplore. We shall return to that issue when we consider aid effectiveness in Chapter 5. For the present the critical matter is not the origin of these 'little republics'[9] but their consequence: in most developing countries a high proportion, often over half,[10] of public expenditures are incurred by autonomous agencies and hence are not included within the central government budget. As a consequence it is not possible for central government to exercise more than a limited leverage over the way in which money, in particular aid money, is used. In terms of the notation of Figure 4.1, it is not only the recipient government who decides where the country is going to end up between points *F* and *G* on that diagram; the autonomous agencies also play a large part.

Secondly, even within central government decisions about the use of aid are not centralised but are scattered between many ministries. Contracts for the disbursement of aid are simply signed between the foreign minister of the donor country and the relevant spending minister of the recipient country. Frequently, on account of weaknesses in financial control, the recipient country's treasury does not know for over a year what spending ministries have spent,[11] nor *a fortiori* what aid contracts they have entered into; the position is often further complicated because operating ministries, having obtained authority to incur expenditure under an aid agreement, do not bother to claim reimbursement from the finance ministry, which as a consequence fails to draw down aid money already committed.[12] The situation is improving, but more than 50 per cent of all developing countries do not have any central unit to monitor, much less centrally negotiate, the allocation of the country's aid inflow.[13] Those African countries which have such units only have had them, in most cases, since 1983 or 1984, when they were set up under prodding from the World

Bank.[14] In all the others the allocation of aid resources between projects by recipient governments remains, not a rational centralised decision but a classical case of what Braybrooke and Lindblom have called 'disjointed incrementalism'.[15]

If decision making is fragmented horizontally between departments of government, it is also fragmented vertically between different levels of the expenditure decision process: this is the third discrepancy between reality and the idea of the recipient government as a rational allocator of aid resources. In Sri Lanka, even development projects which have passed the tests of appraisal within the Ministry of Finance and cabinet approval, and have thus been included in the Public Investment Programme, will 'not necessarily be implemented according to schedule—or indeed at all— (unless) the Budget Division makes the necessary funds available'.[16] In Indonesia the finance minister has a special monetary committee which reviews the revenue situation before the beginning of each quarter, and frequently lops a large percentage off the agreed budget for the following quarter in the light of the latest information on the government's cash-flow.[17] 'Repetitive budgeting' of this sort is of course itself a response to the uncertainties described on pp. 87–89. But in its turn it creates further uncertainties, not least for aid agencies waiting to see whether money will in fact be voted for petrol for the water pumps which they have financed.

The aid agencies in their turn respond by making direct payments to suppliers in the recipient country, thereby bypassing the complex chain of authorisation through the finance ministry.[18] The consequence, of course, as in the case of the creation of new autonomous agencies to implement aid projects, is quicker implementation in the short term, but in the long term a further reduction in the finance ministry's control over its expenditure. It is not the least of the paradoxes of overseas aid that the agencies responsible for disbursing it have found it necessary, in order to disburse it efficiently, to undermine such control over decision-taking capacity as remains in the hands of Third World finance ministries.

4.2 ADMINISTRATIVE BIASES IN THE FUNCTIONAL ALLOCATION OF AID

(i) Choice of project and region

As we saw in Chapter 3,[19] aid donors do not devote much energy to the task of identifying suitable projects for financing: they leave the job to the recipient government. What projects will that government nominate? or, in terms of the notation of Figure 4.1, how will the portfolio of new projects *EG* negotiated between donor and recipient be divided between different sectors and regions?[20] Two factors, we shall argue, provide the key: domestic political pressures and the government's judgement concerning what the private sector will and will not take on.

Let us first remind ourselves that decision taking on aid is fragmented between many ministries and implementing agencies.[21] For each of these agencies aid is a potential instrument of power—it can pay for services which politicians' constituents desire; it can postpone highly unpopular price increases for those services; it can loosen crippling foreign-exchange constraints. Formally, the senior civil servants who assist in negotiating aid contracts are exempt from these pressures, but informally they often have powerful motives of their own for influencing the destination of aid money. Even if they do not themselves lose their jobs each time there is a change of governing political party, as occurs for example in Mexico, they are often heavily identified with their home regions and expected by this very extended family to deliver benefits to it as an obligation of their high office. Overseas aid projects, whose costs are normally borne by the budget of the central government ministry and not by the project beneficiaries, are an ideal instrument for delivering such benefits.

. It has been contended by Lipton (1977) and by Bates (1981, 1983), with reference to Asia and Africa respectively, that the power-base of Third World governments is essentially urban. Civil servants, industrial companies and their employees will all have an interest in policies which keep the urban standard of living up, in particular subsidies on the price of food and energy, protection of industry against imports, concentration of health, education and welfare services in the cities and fiscal exemptions for the urban middle class; in coalition, the argument runs, they form an interest group so strong that Third World governments— themselves composed of town dwellers—can nowhere stand up against them.[22] But if urban bias is to be sustained, this depends on a balancing act, since by their very nature underdeveloped countries have a large majority of their inhabitants living in rural areas.[23] This balancing act is achieved, according to Bates, partly by keeping the deprivations which rural people suffer as invisible as possible (e.g. farm-gate prices which are a small proportion of an export price of which they are unaware) and partly by compensating those collective deprivations with highly visible *selective* benefits, such as water schemes, health posts and agro-processing factories, each of which will redound to the credit of the legislator who claims the credit for providing them.[24] In providing these selective benefits, of course, overseas aid if it can be obtained has a critical part to play.

There are several reasons, apart from sheer convenience, why aid donors may be willing to accept the role of redressors of urban bias in which they are so often cast. Rural infrastructure and productive activities look egalitarian;[25] a dam, road, or drinking-water pump can be photographed and labelled 'a gift from the people of ...' as a sewer, telephone exchange or technical assistance transaction cannot; perhaps most important, they may well look unattractive to the private sector, in spite of being economically viable, so that there is a *prima facie* case for financing them out of aid money. The last point deserves expansion, as it takes us back to the central case for aid propounded in Chapter 1. The private sector, we there argued, will be averse to projects which (a) are risky, (b) have an extended pay-back period, or (c) have a negative expected *financial* but a positive *economic* rate of return, either because the benefits of the project cannot be recouped from beneficiaries or because market prices differ from shadow prices, and as a consequence market failure will prevail unless an outside agency intervenes. These characteristics apply, singly or in combination, to nearly all 'urban-bias redressing' projects. Most of agriculture and fishing, especially if the area is remote or the technique experimental, suffers from high risk; soil conservation, forestry and environmental improvement in general have a lengthy pay-back period; rural roads and water, in particular, suffer from a perennial problem of cost recovery; finally, it is largely agricultural projects which are subject to large discrepancies between economic and financial rates of return, because much of their output is exported, often at a disequilibrium exchange rate, and much of their cost structure is unskilled labour, whose wage may well lie far above the social marginal cost of labour. The characteristic aid project, therefore, is rural in its location and political orientation, even if the benefits from it are often captured by urban dwellers.[26]

This is illustrated by Table 4.1, which suggests that a majority of OECD aid commitments allocable by sector go either to purely rural or to mixed urban/rural users.

Table 4.1: Major bilateral donors: share of total aid flows by sector, 1983–4 average

Donor	Purely rural (Agriculture/ rural development/ rural infra- structure)	Mixed urban/ rural (education/ health)	Purely urban (urban infrastructure/ public administration)
United States	30.5	17.7	51.8
United Kingdom	39.6	16.7	43.7
Netherlands	46.8	20.2	33.0
Japan	44.1	10.6	45.3
West Germany	35.0	22.5	42.5
France	27.2	44.2	28.6
OECD average	34.5	22.2	43.3

Sources: OECD, *Twenty-five Years of Development Co-operation: a Review*, Paris 1985, Table 7, pp. 302–3.

(ii)   The Distribution of aid between capital and recurrent budgets

The preference of aid donors for transferring their aid in visible discrete lumps has further implications when we come to consider the allocation of recipient government budgets between 'recurrent' and 'development' expenditures. It is a commonplace even of journalistic reports on the Third World that many hospitals lack essential drugs, many water-pumps do not deliver water and many roads have crumbled back into mud, all of which imply that the maintenance, or recurrent, budget was not adequate to protect the original capital investment. It is also the case that most donors, for reasons already explored,[27] prefer to give aid for capital, rather than recurrent costs. A recent survey of the recurrent cost problem has indeed concluded that the problem is worst in those countries where, *inter alia*, there is 'a high level of external assistance from several sources'.[28] But mere association does not prove a causal link from aid inflows to subsequent financing difficulties: the problem needs a closer look.

It must first be stressed that political leaders in developing countries are under relentless pressure to announce and then to try and fulfil ambitious physical targets in development plans, which in their turn generate needs for capital spending, for aid, and ultimately for recurrent spending. Tanzania, for example, announced during 1971 the 'intention to meet various per capita targets for rural health centres, hospitals and doctors by 1980; a piped water supply within 400 metres of all Tanzanians by 1991; and universal primary education by 1989 (later revised to 1977)'.[29]

The fiscal implications of this massive expansion of social infrastructure were colossal; a World Bank team calculated in 1974 that meeting the stated targets would require new development expenditure of 275 million Tanzania shillings (at constant prices) per annum over the subsequent 15 years, which in turn would generate *new* recurrent expenditure of 90 million shillings per annum over the same period, implying that the real recurrent budget would have to quadruple between 1975 and 1990 simply to meet the governments' stated commitments in health, education and water alone.[30]

In all of this, the question of aid does not explicitly arise. However, it is only the expectation of foreign aid which allows the declaration of such targets in the first place, since in most very poor countries aid finances a large part, and in some the whole, of the development budget.[31] In most developing countries the development budget of each ministry is added up, financed and motivated separately from the recurrent budget. The recurrent budget, unlike the development budget, is financed almost entirely by domestic tax revenue, seldom by overseas aid grants, and never by borrowing; and is firmly in the hands of the Ministry of Finance, who have a strong incentive to keep it down. The opposite applies to the development budget. Finance officers in the spending ministries, with the targets of the plan hanging over their heads, will have every incentive to launch new development projects into being as quickly as possible; and country desks in donor countries' aid ministries, anxious to spend their own country budgets, will have little incentive to stop them. Both sets of officials, while clearly concerned in the abstract with the long-term success of projects, will in the real world have short-term horizons, and the politicians who stand behind them have even shorter ones. They know at the time that an agreement to commit aid funds is signed that the phase which is heavy in recurrent costs will be several years into the future, and that the responsibility for financing those recurrent costs will not in any case lie with them. Each party can also argue that the recurrent costs which its own individual projects will generate are small in relation to the total volume of resources available to the government.[32] And finally, if either party did wish in spite of these imperatives to make a conscientious forecast of the recurrent costs which its current pledges were generating, the data available to it would be desperately weak. There now exist World Bank estimates of the annual recurrent expenditures which a given capital expenditure is expected to generate in particular sectors; for example, in water development, annual recurrent costs are expected to be 20 per cent of original capital expenditure in constant prices.[33] However, in real life these 'r-coefficients', as they are known,[34] are likely to be as widely and unpredictably distributed around the sectoral norm as are estimates for that other notorious tool of development planning, the capital–output ratio. Technical failures in project design, a large pay award in the public sector, delays in the start-up of specific projects: any of these can cause the measured r-coefficient for a given sector to deviate (positively in the first two cases and negatively in the third) from the modal forecast. There may, but there will not necessarily, be an even number of cancelling errors across projects in a given sector. Given the unreliability of forecasts of r, therefore, few developing countries attempt the process of budgeting the stream of annual recurrent costs across future years.[35]

The consequences of this disjunction between recurrent and development expenditure decisions have varied between developing countries. In those where tax revenues have been buoyant, predictions of recurrent expenditure conservative, or dependence on foreign aid low, the problems have been minor. But in those which have recently experienced a rapid build-up of foreign aid commitments to build up the capital stock without any corresponding commitment to pay the ensuing recurrent costs, severe financial crises have recently developed, especially where the aid has flowed into sectors which are intensive in recurrent costs such as health, agriculture and rural development. A classical example of this type of country is Tanzania. In the water sector between 1974 and 1978, the change in annual recurrent expenditure was 1 per cent of development expenditure against the World Bank norm of 20 per cent;[36] throughout the rural sector the projects were imposed from above by the government with little local participation, with the result that villagers saw them as government's responsibility to maintain, and the consequence by 1982 was a budget deficit of 12 per cent of gross national product, with 35 per cent of recurrent expenditure of Tshs. 9.2 billion being directly attributable to commitments made by overseas aid donors.[37] In recent years, donors have shown awareness, not only in Tanzania, of the burden of recurrent cost which they have imposed on recipients: the principle of redirecting aid towards rehabilitation and maintenance is firmly enshrined in both 'Berg Reports' on sub-Saharan Africa,[38] and much development aid does now consist of spares and repairs, often as part of sectoral aid purchases. But these 'offshore' recurrent costs of development projects are only a small part of the total, and donors have generally been much more reluctant to finance local recurrent costs, particularly subsidies, wages and salaries.[39] The payment of such costs offers no commercial advantage, can appear economically regressive inasmuch as it subsidises 'consumption' rather than 'investment',[40] and presents the donor with the 'exit problem'[41] in its starkest form, since personnel costs are ordinarily open-ended commitments whose payment it can appear ungenerous to terminate once they have been assumed. It is therefore unrealistic to expect donors to go any further than they have already done in the direction of overcoming their bias against paying recurrent costs, in spite of the existence of an optimistic OECD guideline which advises them to do so.[42]

If aid is to avoid exacerbating the recurrent cost problem in recipient countries, action by the recipients themselves is needed, action first of all to forecast the recurrent implications of projects whose 'development' component comes to them at low or zero cost, and action secondly to refuse to take on even aid-financed projects whose recurrent revenue requirements cannot be provided for. The second recommendation runs so strongly counter to the interests of development budget makers in spending ministries that it may be thought naive. It has in fact been implemented, for example, by the government of Papua New Guinea, which refused an offer of British aid for a highway from Port Moresby to Lae on the grounds that the budget would not support the future stream of associated recurrent costs.[43] But the central point remains. Political and bureaucratic imperatives set up many diverse pressures which will cause the allocation of aid money, in the peculiarly fragmented environment of decisions surrounding that allocation, to deviate wildly from the economic optimum unless institutions, such as the budgetary planning board in Papua New Guinea, exist to override those imperatives. We now turn to a still more dramatic demonstration of this central point.

(iii) The multi-donor problem

The whole is less than the sum of its parts: the actions of
many individuals each taking rational decisions in isolation
may lead to an outcome which each was anxious to avoid.
This celebrated economic principle finds further application
in the field of overseas aid.[44] Twenty or more aid donors,
each supplying aid in competition to one developing
country, can produce results which are quite different from
those which would materialise if one donor supplied the
same quantity of aid, results which all the parties to the
transaction are willing to disown. The problems created by
multiplicity of donors are of three kinds: administrative
overload, proliferation of technologies, and mutually conflicting conditionalities. We consider these in sequence.

Administrative Overload
Peru, in 1984, received aid from twenty-two bilateral and
multilateral donors, Kenya from twenty-five, and India from
thirty-one.[45] In addition, these and other developing countries are hosts to a large number of private charities and
other non-governmental organisations, eighty in the case of
Kenya and several hundred in India.[46] Each of these donors,
in the interests of management efficiency and accountability
to its own taxpayers, wishes at the very least to apply an
economic, technical and financial appraisal to suggested
projects before they start; to engage in subsequent negotiations concerning location, technical specification, training
of counterpart staff, phasing of financial contributions and
very possibly aspects of the 'policy environment' such as
product prices, rail rates, subsidies and commercial policy;
to monitor progress• throughout the project, involving the
setting up of complex statistical-reporting systems; and to
evaluate the project at the end of disbursement and possibly
a few years afterwards as well. Even for a generously staffed
and highly trained organisation, which a very poor country
by the nature of the case does not possess, this is a great
deal of work. It is estimated that Upper Volta (now Burkina
Faso) received 350 separate aid missions in 1983, one for
every day of the year.[47] Each of these missions, characteristically, would stay a fortnight to three weeks, spend an

average of two to three hours with upwards of thirty people in the capital and upcountry, and demand large quantities of statistical data. In so doing it would suck a large quantity of such skilled manpower as the country possessed away from the routine managerial functions of government in order to be on parade for yet another team of strangers bearing gifts—or conditional promises thereof. As Carruthers writes,

(In East Africa) some of the most talented local personnel were tied up greeting, meeting and generally satisfying donor curiosity, whims, regulations and performance criteria. The care and attention given to visiting missions contrasted starkly with the cursory treatment given to the domestic annual budgeting process, which may account ... for shortfalls in recurrent allocations and sub-optimal project operating performance.[48]

Nor does the problem finish when the visiting missions are finally shepherded back to the airport, since in the course of their stay they will usually have asked for some local staff to be attached to their projects as counterparts to the expatriate technical co-operation officers; these people will, as we saw, have to be funded out of the domestic recurrent budget.[49] If that has to be cut for any reason, such as a macroeconomic stabilisation programme, each of the donors will scream if its own project is axed altogether; the consequence is pro rata cuts on every project, and a large number of projects limping along at half-cock, rather than a concentration of resources in areas of highest priority.

Some of these problems are, of course, problems of a large, multi-project aid programme rather than problems of multiplicity of donors. But multiplicity makes its own distinctive contributions to overload on the recipient's bureaucracy. Each donor has its own distinctive accounting system, its own procurement system for materials and consultants, its own reporting requirements, its own sensibilities, and its own view of the 'right policy environment' for its own projects, which may conflict with that of other donors. Keeping all your relatives happy at the Christmas party is a far more laborious job than simply placating Auntie Mary.

Technological Proliferation
Some of the costs associated with donor multiplicity do not
become apparent until long after donor personnel have
ceased to impose on the time of the recipient's civil service.
A particularly insidious example is proliferation of equipment, since for many donors aid is a vehicle for establishing
its own products more firmly in the markets of the Third
World, and each donor ties its aid to imports from the
country of origin. The results of this policy are that engineers of Kenya's Ministry of Water Development have to
wrestle with eighteen different varieties of water-pump.[50]
Indian farmers have to cope with five different makes of
tractor supplied by the UK alone (none of which, probably,
should be in use anyway),[51] and Bangladesh railways are
saddled with 'diesel locomotives from Japan, Canada and
the US; shunting locomotives from Hungary, West Germany and the United Kingdom; and freight wagons from
India, South Korea and the United Kingdom'.[52]
    The costs associated with this rag-bag of technologies are
of many different kinds: inability to reap economies of
scale in ordering equipment; delays which arise because
technicians trained on one type of equipment are not competent to mend or service other types; and, in extreme cases,
disruptions to service caused by complete incompatibility
between technologies, as when contractors to the German
aid ministry, hired to extend the municipal water supply of
Kisumu in Kenya originally laid down by the British, found
it necessary to rip out the original system in order to make
their own system work properly.[53] These costs, of course,
are supplementary to those imposed by bilateral source
tying itself.

Conflicting Conditionalities
A common response by donors to unsatisfactory performance of aid operations has been to try and assume
greater control over the success of those operations by
negotiating a 'policy environment' more favourable to the
success of the projects which they are financing.[54] However,
development policy is not yet a sufficiently objective science
for donors to be able to agree between themselves (let alone

with the recipient) concerning the appropriate alterations to be made to specific policy instruments. They may disagree on the relative weight to be put on efficiency and equity considerations, as when the World Bank, negotiating a system of charges for rural water supply in Kenya, requested a system of flat user-charges per gallon based on marginal cost, whereas the Swedish agency SIDA requested of the same ministry a quite different system whereby the charges per gallon should be graduated to the user's ability to pay.[55] Or they may simply disagree on the pace of adjustment in a given policy instrument, as when the IMF, in Jamaica in the years 1980–3, demanded a far quicker transition to an equilibrium exchange rate than did the World Bank.[56] 'Cross-conditionalities' of this kind can, at worst, paralyse the recipient's own decision-making capacity in relation to the relevant policy instrument, without any obvious countervailing gain.

Costs and Benefits of Co-ordination to the Recipient

If the multi-donor problem is indeed as serious for the recipient as has so far been implied, amounting even to 'institutional destruction' in the view of one observer,[57] it is pertinent to ask why recipient governments allow the problem to persist: why they do not deal with the administrative overload problem by taking more programme and less project aid, and why they do not deal with the technical proliferation problem by allocating specific donors to specific sectors? The answer is: up to a point they try, but beyond that point they do not perceive dependence on a single donor for a specific input to be in their interest, and such attempts as they make to stage-manage the allocation of aid to them by casting donors in particular roles are sometimes overridden by the donors themselves.

There is little doubt that central decision-taking units in recipient countries have been well aware of the multi-donor problem for a number of years, certainly since the upsurge of manpower-intensive rural development projects in the middle 1970s. They have requested, and in most cases secured, an increase in the share of programme aid in the total inflow;[58] where they were denied this, it was usually because the donor wished to retain more control over the end-use of aid money than is possible with balance-of-payments support.[59] They have also, in a minority of countries, instituted central units within the finance ministry to monitor and in some cases negotiate the flow of external aid into each government spending agency; many of these external aid divisions, however, were set up only in 1983 and 1984.[60] Individual spending ministries also, as a matter of comparative advantage, seek out donors to provide aid in those areas where they are known to specialise; it is normal for developing countries to import, on concessional terms where possible, a large part of their technical assistance in dairying from Holland and Switzerland, in sawmilling from Sweden and Finland and in car making from Japan. But not all, if they are wise. For one thing, diversification of aid flows by source, even if it leads to proliferation, is a powerful means of mitigating costs due to source tying, especially if a formal tendering competition can be set up between different bilateral donors.[61] For another, if one donor is paying for the entire development budget in a particular sub-sector, say rural roads or urban water supply, this gives that donor an undesirable stranglehold over all progress in that activity, and in particularly an ability to impose conditionality which the recipient ministry thinks undesirable, for example in relation to location or user charges. Quite separately from this, donors often approach recipient countries with firm requests to finance particular projects in the favoured budget or development plan which they fancy, regardless of any 'role' or sub-sector in which they have been 'cast' by recipient spending ministries or aid co-ordinating units.[62] When this happens it is a brave finance officer who will refuse a bird in the hand for the sake of two in the bush.

For these reasons it seems fair to describe prospects for reducing the costs of the multi-donor problem by means of country 'consultative groups' or 'round tables' as being limited.[63] It is beyond question that these groups, where they exist, provide the recipient country with a valuable opportunity to state both its overall needs for aid and its priorities to all donors at once, and donors, where they agree, to give their views on the policy environment that should exist in the recipient country.[64] But these exchanges of views will not of themselves solve the twin problems of administrative overload and technical proliferation, even if, on an optimistic assumption, the problems of cross-conditionality can be removed in advance of such meetings. There are limits to the reduction in the first problem—via a switch to programme aid—which donors will allow them, and there are limits to the reduction in the second problem which they will allow themselves. Recipients have indeed shown willingness to rationalise their purchasing policy and to curb some of the more luxuriant growths of inter-donor competition.[65] But they derive too much advantage by playing off one donor against another, in improving the terms of their aid and in evading those conditionalities which they wish to evade, to be willing to accept too great a concentration of aid through one or two inlets. And in keeping numerous channels of inflow open, donors for their own political and commercial reasons will often connive.[66]

(iv) Aid and the Recipient's Private Sector

Hitherto our discussion has centred on the effects of aid which operate through the public sector, both directly and indirectly through the various channels examined in this and the preceding chapter. However, even that majority of aid transactions which pass between one government and another are not confined in their effects to the public domain. They spill over into the private sector, in both a positive and a negative manner, and before concluding we must examine these spillovers.

In labelling these two types of spillover it is convenient to revert to the terminology of Myrdal and to refer to them as *spread* and *backwash* effects.[67] Spread effects are those which occur when aid manages to perform the function which the theory of Chapter 1 assigns to it, of filling a hole in the market and providing socially beneficial goods and services which the market cannot and will not deliver. An obvious example is infrastructure—transport facilities, electricity, telecommunications—which still account for the bulk of aid.[68] Private enterprise, especially in the least developed countries, seldom supplies these facilities, but without them the private sector could not function. However, in an increasing number of cases aid is actually channelled direct to the private sector, through development banks or through agricultural finance corporatiôns. Aid has even, on occasion, been used to bring a private sector into being, for example in Ghana, where the World Bank supported a 5-year project to develop a competitive road construction industry.[69] Finally, it must be stressed that a large proportion of programme aid, in particular from the World Bank, not only helps to release a foreign-exchange constraint facing the private sector but is explicitly premissed on the condition that the government will undertake policy actions which make life easier for that sector, for instance divestment of state assets or removal of quantitative restrictions on imports.[70]

This much is probably indisputable. Far more contentious are the backwash effects. The most eloquent advocate of the position that they are overwhelming is Bauer:

Aid ... enables governments to pursue policies which potently retard growth and exacerbate poverty ... (including) persecution of the most productive groups ... restraints on the activities of traders ... restrictions on the inflow of foreign capital, enterprise and skills; voluntary or compulsory purchase of foreign enterprises ... forced collectivisation, price policies which discourage food production; and generally, the imposition of economic controls which restrict external contacts and domestic mobility and so retard the spread of new ideas and methods.[71]

So far as the World Bank is concerned, and also those aid donors which line up with it,[72] the last two statements are, as we have just seen, the reverse of the truth, since much of their programme aid has been conditioned on the adoption of domestic policies which are the opposite of those described. In a broader sense, all aid to those regimes which practise 'restraints on the activities of traders (and) on the inflow of foreign capital' could be described as being supportive of those restraints, inasmuch as less aid might have hastened their demise and their replacement by a less *dirigiste* government; we shall, of course, never know. But a reading of the record does not support the proposition that an increase in the commitment of aid donors to a given country increases the restraints which the government of that country places on the private sector. Some leading examples may confirm this point. India has received large-scale aid inflows from the middle 1950s onwards, but the nationalisation of the central bank and the life insurance companies took place in 1955 and was the last act of its kind of any significance apart from the nationalisation of the commercial banks in 1969,[73] since which date a very substantial liberalisation of controls over foreign trade and industrial investment has occurred. Bangladesh has carried out substantial privatisation in the industrial sector and in agricultural input supply during the solitary decade of its existence, during which it has been heavily aided.[74] All in all, it is difficult to find support anywhere, particularly in recent years, for the second prong of Bauer's famous proposition that 'aid does not augment resources, it merely centralises power'.[75]

However, if the particular channel of 'backwash' nominated by Bauer appears to have little significance at the present time, this does not imply that no others exist. Our contention is that aid is more likely to influence private-sector activity, not overtly through acts of *dirigisme* but covertly through altering the prices and costs facing private businesses. This is particularly likely to happen in the case of non-tradable goods in remote areas for which the elasticity of supply is very low and for which, therefore, prices may be pushed up very sharply in the short term by the sudden injection of aid money. An example will illustrate. In 1976 the World Bank, assisted by several other donors, committed upwards of $100 million for an integrated rural development project in the Upper Region, Ghana's most remote and backward district. This involved a vast increase in the demand for factors of production, some of which (e.g. food, building materials) were difficult and wasteful to import, and others (e.g. unskilled labour, transport services) impossible. The price of these inputs was therefore forced up by the aid inflow,[76] not only, of course, for the aid project but for the entire private sector within the Upper Region. Similar cases could be cited for practically every aid-financed civil-engineering or rural development project in an underdeveloped rural area.[77] However, the price effects of aid on the recipient private sector are, of course, a sword which cuts with more than one edge, since the very purpose of aid is to cheapen the cost of the things it supplies: food, imported capital goods, training, management expertise. Nearly always these things are tradable, whereas by our argument above the inputs made more expensive by aid are non-tradable.[78] This puts additional weight behind the hypothesis stated on p. 102 above, that aid has, for better or worse, a tendency to open up the economy of the recipient, to bias it away from indigenous and towards imported sources of supply. Those who—mistakenly in our view— equate a more open economy with a move away from self-sufficiency[79] will regard this effect of aid as harmful.

4.3   AID AND RESOURCE ALLOCATION: PRELIMINARY HYPOTHESES

We are now in a position to put this chapter's analysis of the environment in which aid allocation decisions are taken on the recipient's side together with the previous chapter's discussion of the donor's side. We have found it convenient to divide the effects of aid on the recipient economy into two types: an *income* (or volume) effect reflecting what the aid would do if the structure of incentives were left unaffected by the aid inflow and a *substitution* (or relative price) effect which reflects precisely the changes which aid imposes on the structure of incentives. The tendency of most defences of aid until the present time has been to concentrate on the volume effects,[80] and the tendency of most attacks, whether from the left or the right,[81] has been to concentrate on the *negative* relative price effects, and then to assume, usually a priori, that these overwhelm the volume effects. As yet we are not in a position to quantify the effects of either kind: that will have to wait until the empirical third part of this book. However, the discussion of this and the previous chapter has enabled us to illustrate some of the relative price effects, or biases, which recipients and donors respectively impose on the allocation of aid. Sometimes these are mutually cancelling, but where they are not this generates a presumption that a bias away from the 'optimal' allocation of aid will operate. We shall now gather together a list of these presumed biases for testing in Part III. We have argued that *donors and recipients*, separately, are subject to a bias to seek quick agreement on the technical specification of aid projects (p. 65) and to under-fund the recurrent costs arising from capital aid (p. 96). We have argued that the practices of *donors* generate a bias towards large, risk-avoiding, import-intensive and capital-intensive projects (p. 64), and that there are no pressures within recipient administrations to counteract these biases. We have argued that the practices of *recipient* administrations generate a bias towards wasteful proliferation of technologies and, more controversially, towards rural projects which counteract the prevailing 'urban bias' (pp. 94–95). Finally, over and above these resource allocation effects operating within the public sector, we have argued that aid also has spillovers into the private sector (pp. 105–108), but that, contrary to the contention of Bauer and others, it is not at all clear which way these effects will operate.

These propositions are summarised in Table 4.2. If a plus sign appears against 'presumed eventual impact' in the third column of the table, the implication is that, on the evidence presented in the last two chapters, a resource-allocation effect of the type named will operate. However, the evidence we have so far assembled on the 'policy environment' of aid is suggestive and anecdotal: all that we have in Table 4.2 is a set of hypotheses, to be tested in due course against evidence on the leverage of aid on the variables it is supposed to influence.

Table 4.2 gives the a priori impression that the resource-allocation effects of aid are overwhelmingly negative. This is misleading. First, the biases in question do not *necessarily* represent a deviation from 'optimum resource allocation'; in particular, the rural bias of aid projects probably represents a corrective to price distortions which are endogenous to the political economy of most developing countries,[82] and the capital-intensive technology of many aid-financed

Table 4.2: Possible biases imposed by donor and recipient 'policy environment' on allocation of aid resources

Possible allocative bias towards:	Donor	Recipient	Presumed eventual effect	Supporting evidence on page
1 Limitation of technological choice, resulting from speed[c]	+	+	+	65
2 Capital—and import—intensity[c]	+	::	+	102, 108
3 Under-funding of recurrent costs	+	+	+	96–99
4 Risk aversion	+	::	+	64
5 Size	+	::	+	64
6 Technical proliferation[s]	::	+	+	102
7 Over-pricing of imports, resulting from tying[s]	+	–	?	66
8 Rural location, to offset 'urban bias'	::	+	+	94–95
9 Impact of aid on private-sector output	::	::	?	105–108

+ policy environment of donor or recipient, as stated, tends to bias allocation of resources in this direction;

– policy environment tends to bias allocation of resources in opposite direction;

:: direction of bias ambiguous;

c 'complementary' biases, which will probably be found together and may reinforce one another;

s 'substitute' biases, which will tend to counteract one another.

projects may be appropriate to the factor endowments of some developing countries.[83] Second, some of the biases may counteract one another; for example, multiple procurement of equipment from very many donors, even if it imposes its own costs, will offset the costs inflicted by source tying. Finally, the direction of influence of aid on the recipient private sector is thoroughly ambiguous. Hence, at this stage we do not even hold prior expectations concerning whether relative-price effects offset or reinforce the, by definition positive, volume effects of aid inflows. Let us now examine this question.

NOTES

1. Usually the donor; even the highly perceptive essay by Tendler (1975) falls into this trap.
2. *See* pp. 106–108.
3. For the detail of this episode, *see* Thorp and Bertram (1977).
4. On these mechanisms *see* Nelson (1984), pp. 992–1000.
5. *See* Chapter 3, p. 57.
6. The United States, the largest contributor, only paid in some two-thirds of its subscription, in part because of the worries of congressmen that expenditures of this type could not be justified in a recession.
7. Duncan and Mosley (1984), pp. 104–5 and 113; van Arkadie and de Wilde (1984), *passim*.
8. There is a long and honourable tradition of polemic by economists against the inefficiencies of statutory boards, particularly in crop marketing in East and West Africa. *See* for example Bates (1981, 1983), Bauer (1954), East Africa Royal Commission (United Kingdom, 1955, Chapter 7) and World Bank (1981).
9. *Republicacitas*: the Panamanian nickname for parastatals, which 'shows that they are seen as self-contained alternatives to the government within their areas': Caiden and Wildavsky (1974), p. 80.
10. In the early 1970s, 60 per cent in Chile, 65 per cent in Ecuador, 42 per cent in Nigeria and 50 per cent in Venezuela (Caiden and Wildavsky, 1974), p. 82.
11. For the Kenya case *see* Duncan and Mosley (1984), p. 81.
12. For the Kenya case *see* Leonard *et al.* (1983); also Duncan and Mosley (1984), pp. 63–5.
13. Cassen *et al.* (1986), p. 7/2.
14. Cassen *et al.* (1986), p. 7/2.
15. Braybrooke and Lindblom (1963), p. 128.
16. Veitch (1985), p. 10.

17. Caiden and Wildavsky (1974), p. 72.
18. For a description of arrangements of this kind (e.g. the World Bank's 'Procedure 3') *see* Duncan and Mosley (1984), pp. 120 and 133.
19. Pp. 60–64.
20. *EG* is the value of new aid-financed investment negotiated in a given time period. It does not necessarily correspond to the increase in investment during that time period since some of the aid may substitute for investment which the public or private sector would have carried out anyhow. *See* the discussion of 'fungibility' on pp. 85–87.
21. *See* pp. 85–87, also pp. 140–141 below.
22. *See* Bates (1983), Chapter 5; Lipton (1977) *passim*. There are of course exceptions to urban bias, both idealistic (for example Tanzania in the early 1970s) and grotesque (for example Cambodia under Pol Pot).
23. Bates (1983), p. 118.
24. Bates (1983), pp. 127–8.
25. The appearance may differ from the reality: *see* Chapter 7.
26. For example, the Victoria dam in Sri Lanka, £100m of which was financed by British overseas aid, was located in a rural area and widely represented as a poverty-focused project, but its principal function was to provide electricity for Colombo.
27. Capital costs are incurred over a short, self-limiting period; they have a higher import content; and their end-use is easier to monitor. For further discussion *see* pp. 94–95.
28. Howell (1985), p. 12.
29. TANU National Executive Committee, quoted in Kleemeier (1984), p. 193.
30. World Bank, *Tanzania: Fiscal Aspects of Decentralisation*, Eastern Africa Department, Washington DC, 1975, p. 51, cited in Kleemeier (1984), p. 193.
31. *See* Table 5.2 below.
32. See the essay by Heller and Aghevli in Howell (1985), p. 42.
33. See Kleemeier (1984), pp. 193–4.
34. *r* is the ratio of recurrent costs in year $n + 5$, $n + 6$ ... etc. to total initial capital cost, all measured in the price of year *n*. The term was invented by Heller (1975), and this paper sets out *r* coefficients for a number of specific sectors.
35. Heller and Aghevli, in Howell (1985), p. 39.
36. Kleemeier (1984), Table 4, p. 195; *See also* the case of Zambia, where the capital budget grew by 3.6 per cent annually from 1971 to 1980, but the recurrent budget declined by 3.8 per cent annually (*see* Carruthers, in Howell (1985), p. 51) and of Mali, which in December 1982 projected in its plan a ratio of planned development to recurrent expenditure of around 200 per cent (Stevens, in Howell (1985), p. 89).
37. R. Mushi 'Problems of budgetary forecasting in Tanzania', draft PhD thesis, Bath University, 1985, p. 150). I am grateful to Mr Mushi for allowing me to quote from the results of his calculations.

38. World Bank (1981), Chapter 9, pp. 126–127; World Bank (1984), pp. 25 and 38.
39. Howell, introduction to Howell (1985), p. 14.
40. In terms of Figure 4.1, it increases C_0 and makes no direct contribution to C_1.
41. See Chapter 3, p. 53.
42. OECD Development Assistance Committee, *Additional Guidelines on Aid for Maintenance*, Paris 1982, suggests that donors should consider with the recipient government the recurrent costs of subsidies and change their emphasis towards programme support rather than the initiation of new projects.
43. Cited by Heller and Aghevli, in Howell (1985), p. 40.
44. For example Keynes' Paradox of Thrift (each individual tries to save more, but in so doing lowers effective demand and thereby each individual's saving) and the Prisoner's Dilemma (e.g. all individuals elect to go without a public good, hoping others will pay, rather than have it and pay their share, with the result that it is not supplied). For development of the Prisoner's Dilemma in this context, see Lipton (1986).
45. Data from OECD, *Geographical Distribution of Financial Flows to Less Developed Countries 1980 to 1984*, Paris 1985, country tables.
46. Duncan and Mosley (1984), p. 18; Lipton and Toye (1984), Chapter 4.
47. Cassen *et al.* (1986), chapter 7.
48. Carruthers (1983), p. 49. Carruthers is writing specifically about aid to the irrigation sector; note the connection which he draws between the multi-donor problem and the shortfalls on the recurrent budget noted in the previous sub-section.
49. Some of them will be pulled away from other aid projects, again and again. Skilled local staff may often use their time sub-optimally on a series of short-term assignments as a consequence of competition between aid agencies.
50. Duncan and Mosley (1984), p. 121.
51. Lipton and Toye (1984), paragraph V.71.
52. Ehrhardt (1983), p. 85.
53. Duncan and Mosley (1984), p. 121.
54. This has happened in the private as well as in the public sector: many British firms of agricultural consultants have expanded their operations from project design into plantation management in order to try and ensure the success of the operations which they initiate.
55. Duncan and Mosley (1984), p. 123.
56. Details of this episode are provided in Killick (1984), Vol. II, pp. 115–63.
57. Morss (1984), p. 467.
58. *See* Table 1.3.
59. Tanzania, Guyana, Bolivia and (in the World Bank's case) Kenya are examples of countries currently being refused aid in programme form because many donors do not have sufficient trust in the 'policy

environment' in those countries to reward them with aid of this type.
60. This is true of Kenya, Malawi and Mali; *see* Cassen *et al.* (1986), paragraph 7.7.
61. Increasingly such tendering processes are being set up for major civil engineering and power contracts, especially by Latin American and South-East Asian governments; nominally the competition is between commercial firms, but since each commercial firm usually approaches its own aid agency for concessional money to make its bid more attractive it quickly turns into a competition between aid agencies to provide the best mixed credit terms. For further discussion *see* Chapter 7.
62. A case in point: the Machakos Integrated Rural Development Programme in Kenya was earmarked for German aid but was handed over to the EEC after strong representations from the latter donor.
63. 'Consultative groups' are organised by the World Bank and exist for South Korea, Philippines, Thailand, Bangladesh, Burma, India, Nepal, Pakistan, Sri Lanka, Colombia, Peru, Ghana, Kenya, Madagascar, Mauritius, Senegal, Somalia, Sudan, Uganda, Zaire, Zambia and the Caribbean countries as a group. Round Tables are organised by UNDP and exist for Benin, Burundi, Guinea, Lesotho, Malawi, Mali, Rwanda and nominally for Afghanistan and Laos. There also exists an inter-governmental consortium on aid to Indonesia (IGGI), organised by the Netherlands government.
64. In particular, in consultative groups the World Bank attempts to line donors up behind its prescription of freely floating exchange rates, reduction of subsidies and liberalisation of foreign trade.
65. For example the Kenya Ministry of Transport has reduced the number of suppliers of road graders, all of which are provided by overseas aid, from six to three.
66. An example will illustrate. Aid to the agricultural sector in Kenya in 1982 was already dispersed between fifteen donors. At this time the World Bank, in particular, was applying heavy pressure on the Kenya government to withdraw to a role of lender of last resort in the marketing of grain: the government was reluctant. At this precise moment the Japanese, not previously known as a donor to the sector, stepped in with an offer of aid for large bulk-storage facilities for maize grain, facilities which in the event of partial privatisation of maize marketing would have become irrelevant.
67. Myrdal (1957), pp. 26–33.
68. *See* Table 4.1 above.
69. World Bank (1981), Chapter 9. There are also cases where the stipulation by aid donors that civil engineering work should be done by the private sector brought into existence firms doing work which was previously handled by the government public works department; *see* Cassen *et al.* (1985), chapter 8.
70. Cassen *et al.* (1986), Chapter 4; Mosley (1985c), Table 2.
71. Bauer (1981), pp. 110–12.

72. The most important are Britain, West Germany and the USA.
73. Cassen *et al.* (1986), chapter 8.
74. Cassen *et al.* (1986), chapter 8.
75. Bauer (1981), p. 103.
76. Within 3 months in late 1976 the wage of unskilled labour rose from Cedis 2.50 to 4 per day, and the cost of lorry transport per ton-mile rose from Cedis 0.3 to 0.7 Mosley (1981a), pp. 221–222.
77. For further detail on the Upper Region case *see* Mosley (1981a).
78. If high transport costs did not act as a barrier against imports, the price rises described in the Upper Region could have been prevented by importation of the inputs in short supply.
79. For examples of this line of reasoning *see* Integrated Development Systems, *Foreign Aid and Development in Nepal* (Kathmandu, 1983); R. Sobhan, *The Crisis of External Dependence: the Political Economy of Foreign Aid to Bangladesh* (Dhaka, 1982); K. Griffin, *Underdevelopment in Spanish America (Allen & Unwin, 1968).*
80. For example: Brandt Commission (1980, 1983), Rosenstein-Rodan (1961).
81. Respectively: Griffin (1970) and Bauer (1981).
82. On endogenous factor-price distortions *see* Toye (1981).
83. *See* Pack (1976).

Part III
Aid Effectiveness: Evidence

5 Aid as Instrument of Development*

5.1 INTRODUCTION

In our introductory chapter we argued that the main theoretical case for aid rests on the presumption that the international capital market is full of 'holes' which only aid could 'fill': that is, beneficial projects which private capital could not or would not finance. We also drew attention to a counter-argument by Bauer alleging that, even if the presence of aid flows remedies market distortions in some areas, it creates them in others by reducing the supply of government 'effort' and by obstructing investment from the private sector. Using Myrdal's terminology (1957) there are potentially both 'spread' and 'backwash' effects from aid flows into the less developed economy. These effects are illustrated in Figure 5.1. There are, first, the direct effects of the aid disbursement, that is, the effects which can be traced directly to the project to which the aid money was nominally allocated, which are mostly of the 'spread' type. There are also indirect effects, on the recipient country's public and private sectors, which, following the analysis of Chapter 4, may be either of the 'spread' or of the 'backwash' type. The public sector may switch resources released by the inflow

---

* Much of the empirical research described in this chapter was done in conjunction with John Hudson and Sara Horrell in the summers of 1984 and 1985 and I am grateful for their permission to reproduce it here. There is a fuller report on our work in Mosley and Hudson (1984) and Mosley et al. (1986).

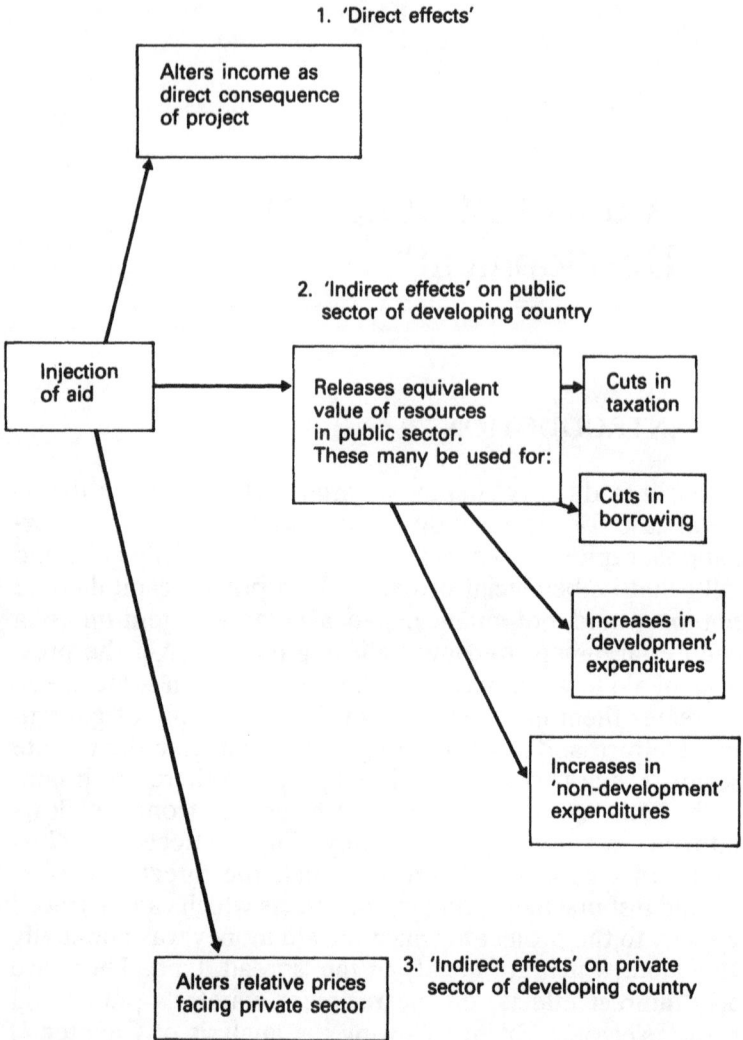

Figure 5.1: Channels through which aid inflows may affect the recipient economy

of aid into developmental forms of expenditure *or* (as Bauer predicts) into 'wasteful' ones (such as enlarging the army, paying off debts, reductions in taxation or reductions in borrowing). The private sector is both stimulated by the receipt of aid, through aid-financed orders and reductions in the price of aid-financed goods, and hampered through increases in the price of goods which are complementary with aid inflows, usually non-tradables such as cement, lorry transport and unskilled labour.[1] The crucial question for empirical analysis is which of these effects predominates.

5.2   EMPIRICAL TESTS (i): EVIDENCE FROM CROSS-SECTION DATA

The proof of the pudding is in the eating. Let us, initially, take the growth of GNP as a measure of 'development' (later on we shall widen the perspective), and let us begin by looking at a simple scatter of observations on aid flows and growth rates for all countries given a full listing in the 1984 *World Development Report*, averaged across the 10 years 1970–80. This is presented in Figure 5.2. It will immediately be seen that there is very little correlation.[2]

Our hypothesis is that this is due partly to non-aid influences on growth, and partly to inter-country differences in the way aid is used, as set out in the previous section. We are primarily concerned with the latter; let us, therefore, hold the former constant, and see how 'aid effectiveness' varies as the crucial measures of the indirect effects of aid—its influence on private investment, and its degree of 'leakage' into the recurrent budget—vary.[3] We shall first divide up Figure 5.2 into four quadrants, according to whether aid and growth were above or below the mean level for the period. We shall then compare 'high aid, high growth' countries and 'high aid, low growth' countries, with respect to the parameters mentioned above, holding approximately constant the effect of other significant influences on the rate of growth.

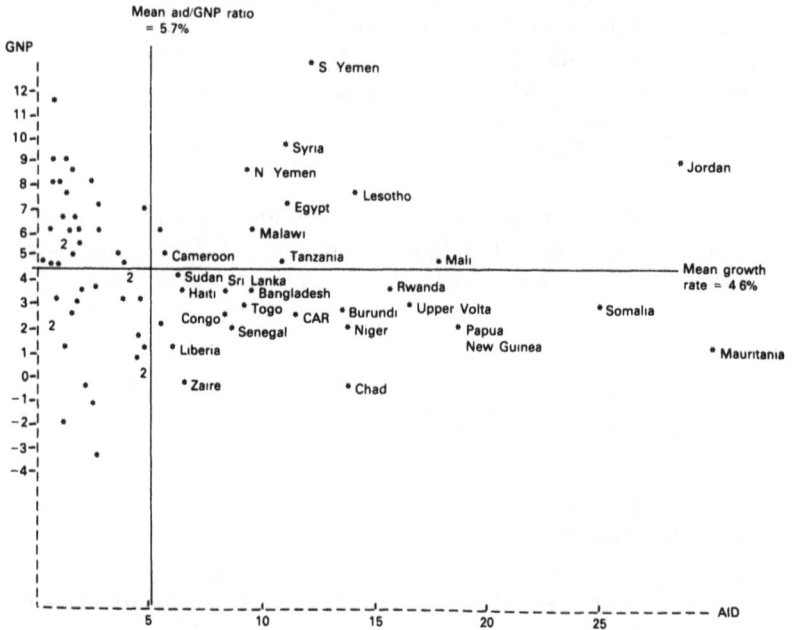

Figure 5.2: Scatter diagram for aid and growth of GNP, eighty less developed countries, 1970–80

Notes:
Definitions of variables:
GNP = annual average growth rate of GNP, 1970–80, for country stated. *Source:* World Bank, *World Development Report 1982*, Appendix Table 2.
AID = average ratio of overseas aid receipts (defined as 'total net ODA disbursements') to GNP, 1970–80, for country stated. *Source: OECD, Geographical Distribution of Financial Flows to Less Developed Countries,* successive issues from 1972 to 1982.
Only those recipient countries with more than the average ratio of aid to GNP are represented by name on the diagram.
For data arrays, see appendix to Chapter 6.

On the evidence which we shall be presenting in Table 5.3, pp. 132–133 below, the only non-aid influences on the growth rate of GDP in the 1970s which are significant across all samples of Third World countries are:

(i) the savings rate (as a proportion of GNP), and
(ii) the growth rate of export values.[4]

In other words, if we write:

S = savings as a proportion of national income,
b_1 = regression coefficient of savings on growth,
X = annual growth rate of export values,
b_2 = regression coefficient of export values on growth,

then for a proper selection of the two samples we require:

$$b_1S + b_2X = \text{approximately constant.} \qquad (5.1)$$

Table 5.1 shows, in the final column, estimates of the left-hand side of expression (5.1) for all the countries in Figure 5.2 with above-average levels of aid inflow. In order to satisfy the condition that they be 'approximately constant' let us impose the arbitrary requirement that for all members of the sample the value of $(b_1S + b_2X)$ should be within one standard deviation of its mean value.[4] If we delete all the countries in Table 5.1 which do not satisfy this condition, that is, in effect those countries in which exports and savings have an effect on growth which is less than 1 per cent or more than 3 per cent, we are left with the following samples:

'High aid, high growth' countries	'High aid, low growth' countries
Mali	Zaire
Egypt	Somalia
Malawi	Rwanda
Syria	Togo
Lesotho	Senegal
Yemen Arab Republic	Sri Lanka

Table 5.1: Countries with above average ratio of aid receipts to GNP, 1970–80: savings ratio and export growth

Country	(1) Average ratio of savings to GNP, 1970–80	(2) Savings ratio multiplied by estimated regression coefficient of savings on GNP growth, i.e. (1) × 0.096	(3) Annual rate of growth of export value, 1970–80	(4) Annual rate of growth of export value multiplied by estimated regression coefficient of export growth on GNP growth i.e. (3) × 0.257	(5) = (2) + (4) Estimated effect of export growth and savings rate on growth of GNP, 1970–80
High aid, high growth					
Mali[a]	6.8	0.6258	9.4	2.4158	3.0686
Tanzania	13.0	1.2480	−7.3	−1.8761	−0.6281
Egypt[a]	17.8	1.7088	−0.7	0.1799	1.8887
Jordan	−8.0	−0.7680	18.4	4.7288	3.9608
Malawi[a]	14.4	1.3824	5.7	1.4649	2.8473
Syria[a]	10.8	1.0368	6.8	1.7476	2.7844
Lesotho[a]	−37.3	−3.5808	18.0	4.6260	1.0452
Yemen Arab Rep.[a]	−0.3	−0.0288	9.6	2.4672	2.4384

High aid, low growth

Chad	1.2	0.1152	-4.0	-1.0280	-0.9128
Zaire[a]	17.2	1.6512	2.2	0.5654	2.2166
Somalia[a]	5.8	0.5568	5.5	1.4135	1.9703
Central African Rep.	13.5	1.2960	-1.1	-0.2827	1.0133
Niger	15.3	1.4688	12.8	3.2896	4.7584
Bangladesh	2.0	0.1920	-1.9	-0.4883	-0.2963
Sri Lanka[a]	19.0	1.8240	-2.4	-0.6168	1.2072
Upper Volta	-5.8	-0.5568	2.0	0.5140	-0.0428
Rwanda[a]	10.0	0.9600	3.5	0.8995	1.8595
Sudan	6.3	0.6048	-5.7	-1.4649	-0.8601
Togo[a]	15.6	1.4979	1.6	0.4112	1.9091
Senegal[a]	13.8	1.3248	1.2	0.3084	1.6332
Mauritania	15.4	1.4784	-1.1	-0.2827	1.1957
Liberia	34.6	3.3216	1.0	0.2570	3.5786

Sources: Ratio of savings to GNP, World Bank, *World Development Reports, 1978 to 1982*, appendix, Table 5, and for preceding years. United Nations *Handbook of National Accounts Statistics*. Growth rate of export values, World Bank, *World Development Report 1981*, Appendix Table 9. Regression coefficients in Columns (2) and (4) are from Table 5.3.
[a]: Country selected for statistical analysis in Table 5.2, i.e. countries for which $b_1S + b_2X$ is between 0.9 and 3.1 per cent (see text, p. 123).

Table 5.2: Countries with above average ratio of aid receipts to GNP, 1970–80: estimates of critical determinants of aid effectiveness

Country	Rate of return on capital: average of δ_1 and δ_2*	Share of aid inflows allocated to recurrent budget a_{14}* (per cent)	Relationship between aid inflows and private-sector capital investment a_{15}* (estimated regression coefficient)
High aid, high growth:			
Mali	27.6	..	..
Egypt	37.1	16.2	−0.05
Malawi	22.6	30.1[a]	0.22
Syria	54.0	11.8	0.26
Lesotho	61.3	26.0	0.02
Yemen Arab Rep.	35.4	..	0.91
Sub-sample average (unweighted)	39.6	21.0	0.27
High aid, low growth:			
Zaire	−0.7	39.2[b]	0.56
Somalia	..	48.3	..
Rwanda	34.9	28.5	0.22
Togo	13.3	30.2[a]	..
Senegal	16.0	17.6	..
Sri Lanka	29.6	19.5	0.05
Sub-sample average (unweighted)	18.6	30.6	0.28

* Notation is drawn from the Appendix to this chapter, pp. 142–148.
Sources: Return on capital is estimated as real increase in GDP measured at current prices, 1970–80, divided by investment at current prices over that period, both figures from World Bank, *World Development Report 1983*, Appendix Tables 2 and 5.

(Notes to table 5.2 continued)

Share of aid inflows allocated to recurrent budget is obtained from the following publications:

United Nations Development Programme (UNDP), Malawi, *Report on Development Assistance to Malawi*, miscellaneous years from 1972–82.

F. Bazy *et al.*, *Accumulation et Sous — Développement au Zaire 1960–1980*, Presses Universitaires de Louvain, 1982, annexe 10.

UNDP, Office of the Resident Representative in the Somali Democratic Republic, *Annual Report on Development Assistance 1970–80*.

UNDP, Office of the Resident Representative in the Arab Republic of Egypt, *Technical Assistance to the Arab Republic of Egypt*, annual from 1972.

UNDP, Office of the Resident Representative in Togo, *Rapport Annuel sur l'Assistance au Développement*, annual from 1970.

UNDP, Office of the Resident Representative in Rwanda, *Rapport Annuel sur l'Assistance au Développement*, annual from 1971.

UNDP, Office of the Resident Representative in Senegal, *Rapport Annuel sur l'Assistance au Développement en Senegal*, annual from 1971.

UNDP, Office of the Resident Representative in the Syrian Arab Republic, *Report on Development Assistance*, annual from 1981.

UNDP, Office of the Resident Representative in Sri Lanka, *Report on Development Assistance*, annual from 1970.

UNDP, Office of the Resident Representative in Mali, *Rapport Annual sur l'Assistance au Développement*, miscellaneous years from 1972–81.

UNDP, Office of the Resident Representative in Lesotho, *Report on Development Assistance*, annual from 1970.

UNDP, Office of the Resident Representative, Yemen Arab Republic, *Report on Development Assistance*, miscellaneous years from 1972–83.

Regression coefficient of aid inflows on private-sector investment is obtained by estimating the coefficient a_{15} in equation (5.14), p. 145 from the following sources:

Aid (average 1970–80) from OECD, *Geographical Distribution of Financial Flows to Less Developed Countries*, successive issues from 1972 to 1982.

Private-sector investment from IMF, *International Financial Statistics* and World Bank, *World Tables* (1st edn. 1976, 2nd edn. 1980, 3rd edn. 1983). In some cases private-sector investment has to be calculated as the difference between measured total capital formation and measured public-sector investment.

Now, let us see whether there are any systematic differences between these samples in terms of what appear a priori to be the critical determinants of aid effectiveness[5]—namely the marginal productivity of public and private capital, the share of aid allocated to the recurrent budget, and the extent to which aid 'crowds out', or alternatively supports, private-sector investment—which may be regarded as susceptible to government policy changes.

This is done in Table 5.2. The general finding is that the rate of return on capital is higher and the share of aid inflows allocated to the development budget are, on average, higher in 'high aid, high growth' countries than in 'high aid, low growth' countries, whereas the impact of aid inflows on private-sector capital investment is about the same in each group. It seems, therefore, that at least the first two of these three factors may have a part to play in explaining variations in 'aid effectiveness' between recipient countries.

We can try and take the analysis a little further by asking what lies behind the coefficients listed in Table 5.2. Behind the share of aid allocated to the recurrent budget lies a decision by the government concerning the proportion of recurrent expenditures which can*not* be financed from taxation. Frequently this decision is made at the last minute, and reflects factors which are not under its control, such as the extent to which a particular tax base has or has not responded to a change in taxation. However the choice of tax rates is the government's, as is also the choice of tax bases, for example, whether or not to impose a tax on land or other forms of wealth. We therefore suggest that those developing countries which finance recurrent expenditures out of aid are, in many cases, exercising a conscious and deliberate preference[6] for lower levels of taxation than those which would be feasible in the absence of aid.[7] A large literature now exists which attempts to measure the 'tax effort' of governments, that is, the extent to which they take advantage of their available taxable capacity. In a country where tax effort is rising, it is unlikely that aid resources are being switched into consumption; for such switching would reduce the amount of expenditure which has to be financed by local taxes and borrowing, which in turn would reduce rather than increase the level of tax effort. And indeed, if we use the measure of tax effort compiled by Tait, Grätz and Eichengreen (1979), it turns out that of the five countries in the 'high aid, high growth' sector of Figure 5.2 for which we have tax effort data, five exhibit rising tax effort and none falling tax effort between 1966–68 and 1972–76, whereas of the seven countries in the 'low aid, low growth' sector of that diagram for which we have data, six (Senegal, Sri Lanka, Zaire, Upper Volta, Burundi and Togo) show declining tax effort and one shows rising tax effort.[8] It may well be, therefore, that in some countries reluctance to raise taxes, or to collect the taxes that are due, forces the governments of those countries to drain some overseas aid into the recurrent budget, with damaging consequences for its measured effectiveness.

We consider next the measured impact of overseas aid inflows on the recipient country's private sector.[9] We note first that for a majority of countries this coefficient is significantly positive, therefore apparently contradicting the proposition put forward by Bauer and others that aid given to governments will tend to 'crowd out' enterprise and investment in the private sector of LDCs. Second, the impact of aid on private investment does not correlate in any significant way with the World Bank's measure of price distortion in developing countries,[10] and still less with the degree of state ownership in the economy.[11]

What is necessary if aid is to stimulate private investment is not a low degree of state intervention as such, but rather that its inflow not be accompanied by restrictions on private economic activity, and that it should, on balance, have the effect of lowering rather than raising the private sector's costs. If, as we surmise, the general effect of aid inflows is to lower the price of tradables and to raise the price of non-tradables, the application of this principle would dictate that aid agencies should avoid large projects in remote areas, which are likely to drive up dramatically the price of non-tradables such as labour and building materials in the local economy, possibly to a degree which will negate the beneficial influence of the reduction in the price of the tradable inputs provided by the aid project. It would also dictate that such agencies should avoid disbursing such aid money at a *speed* which leads to the creation of inflationary supply bottlenecks in the markets for non-tradables.[12] Finally it is desirable that the goods which aid reduces in price should not be locally produced: if they are, aid may simply spoil the market for local producers.[13]

5.3   EMPIRICAL TESTS (ii): COMPARISONS ACROSS TIME

Until now we have concentrated on differences in 'aid effectiveness' across countries. We now wish to consider whether 'aid effectiveness' has changed over time and what factors are responsible for those changes.

Various authors, including Griffin (1970), Papanek (1972, 1973, 1982) and Mosley (1980) have attempted to ascertain the effectiveness of aid from estimates of the single equation:

$$dY = a_{17} + a_{18}A + a_{19}S + a_{20}I_f \qquad (5.2)$$

where Y = national income;
$\quad\quad A$ = aid inflows;
$\quad\quad S$ = domestic saving;
$\quad\quad I_f$ = inflows of private capital from overseas;

with each of the variables measured as a proportion of national income in the recipient country over a period of one year, in order to control for the influence of country size and of price changes between periods. This is in essence a simple Harrod–Domar growth model, with investment divided into three components according to the source of finance: aid, commercial inflows from overseas, or domestic saving. It is perhaps too simple, inasmuch as it allows no role for changes in skills (i.e. in the stock of human capital) or in export volume and price (which may influence LDC income both directly and indirectly, by creating or removing a balance-of-payments constraint). In what follows, therefore, we shall work with an expanded version of (5.2) in which changes in the literacy rate and in export values enter the equation as additional independent variables:

$$dY = a_{17} + a_{18}A + a_{19}S + a_{20}I_f + a_{21}X + a_{22}L \qquad (5.2')$$

where all symbols have the meanings given to them in (5.2) and in addition

X = percentage annual rate of growth of export values
L = percentage annual rate of growth of literacy.[14]

We now turn to the specification of the model. The aid variable (A) is defined as the grant equivalent of gross aid inflows, as measured by the Development Assistance Committee of the OECD.[15] All the financial flow variables (aid, other financial flows and savings) are measured in percentages of recipient GNP to control for the effect of country size and price changes across time. We have experimented with a number of different lag-structures for aid and for 'other financial flows' (I_f);[16] the results to be presented in Table 5.3 below use the least arbitrary assumption for which we can obtain data, namely that all benefits from aid and 'other financial flows' were distributed across time in the same manner as the average of projects for which the World Bank reports information in its (1984) *Tenth Annual Review of Project Performance Audit Results*. This is as follows:

Year since aid first disbursed	Percentage of total project benefits accruing in year stated
0	3
1	18
2	24
3	18
4	13
5	9
6	8
7	6

Finally, we shall present results using three different estimation procedures: ordinary least squares, two-stage least squares with aid treated as endogenous, and the Cochrane–Orcutt iterative procedure to deal with problems of serial correlation of residuals.

The ordinary least squares estimates of equation (5.2') are set out in Table 5.3. They suggest, fairly reliably,[17] that when other determinants of growth are taken into account aid was a significant influence on growth neither in the 1960s nor in the 1970s if the group of LDCs is taken as a whole. For what it is worth, the multiple regression coefficient of aid on growth, a_{18}, is strongly negative and almost

Table 5.3: Results of regression analysis relating GNP growth to aid, savings and other financial flows in 67 less developed countries, 1960–70, 1970–80 and 1980–3

Sample		Regression coefficients on independent variables (Student's t-statistics in brackets)						R^2	D.W.
		Constant	Aid (as percentage of recipient GNP)	Other financial flows from overseas (as percentage of recipient GNP)	Savings (as percentage of recipient GNP)	Growth rate of export values (annual average over period stated)	Growth in adult literacy rate (annual average over period stated)		
All developing countries in sample ($n=67$)	1960–70	3.31** (4.78)	−0.04 (1.72)	−0.009 (0.67)	0.03 (0.97)	0.15** (3.67)	0.08* (2.11)	0.30	1.74
	1970–80	2.45** (2.67)	0.024 (0.21)	−0.082 (1.6)	0.09* (2.11)	0.23** (4.87)	0.006 (0.16)	0.36	1.37
	1980–3	0.47 (0.14)	0.13 (0.80)	−0.04 (0.33)	0.07 (0.47)	0.15 (1.28)		0.02	1.6
Poorest countries only: ($n=23$)	1960–70	2.01 (1.07)	−0.06* (1.65)	0.71** (2.80)	0.68 (0.42)	0.18* (2.21)	0.06 (1.01)	0.26	1.34
	1970–80	2.91* (1.86)	−0.054 (0.33)	0.137 (0.23)	−7.31 (1.28)	0.17* (1.59)	7.36 (1.29)	0.07	1.20
	1980–3	6.09 (1.16)	−0.049 (0.17)	−1.55 (1.69)	−0.005 (0.02)	−0.08 (0.23)		0.16	0.81

Middle income countries (n=44)	1960–70	3.73** (4.53)	−0.05 (0.98)	−0.008 (0.55)	0.019 (0.51)	0.14** (2.79)	0.09 (1.42)	0.22	1.37
	1970–80	1.57 (1.28)	0.41* (2.19)	−0.11* (2.14)	0.11* (2.29)	0.22** (3.73)	0.011 (0.30)	0.35	1.50
	1980–3	−4.15 (−1.01)	0.30 (1.49)	−0.04 (−0.36)	0.25 (1.41)	−0.06 (0.46)		0.11	2.01
Africa only (n=28)	1960–70	1.28 (1.08)	0.015 (0.35)	−0.024 (0.50)	0.073 (1.20)	0.109 (0.76)	0.13* (2.04)	0.22	2.37
	1970–80	2.32 (1.21)	−0.027 (0.13)	−0.20 (1.94)	0.26* (1.82)	0.19 (1.50)	−0.15 (1.16)	0.24	1.31
	1980–3	2.50 (0.41)	0.05 (0.21)	0.042 (0.30)	−0.21 (1.04)	0.15 (0.70)		0.05	1.64
Asia only (n=18)	1960–70	1.69 (1.21)	0.099 (1.31)	2.90** (3.43)	0.13* (2.04)	0.02 (0.36)	−0.007 (0.08)	0.63	1.55
	1970–80	1.86 (1.27)	1.35 (1.62)	0.28 (0.60)	0.06 (1.03)	0.19* (2.11)	0.078 (1.37)	0.55	1.98
	1980–3	−7.86 (1.63)	0.67* (2.49)	0.44 (1.12)	0.44* (2.19)	−0.05 (0.38)		0.50	1.06
Latin America and Caribbean only (n=21)	1960–70	1.39 (0.56)	0.07 (0.30)	−0.01 (0.98)	0.16 (1.08)	0.19* (1.82)	0.058 (0.58)	0.14	1.50
	1970–80	2.50 (0.79)	1.01 (1.19)	−0.02 (0.18)	0.10 (0.99)	0.08 (0.05)	−0.64* (1.77)	0.07	1.74
	1980–3	−15.2 (−2.01)	1.97 (1.51)	−0.09 (−0.32)	0.76 (2.25)	−0.19 (−0.52)		0.11	1.52

(Sources and notes follow on p. 134)

Sources and definitions: Aid as percentage of recipient GNP. This is defined as the grant equivalent of gross ODA, as measured by OECD, *Geographical Distribution of Financial Flows to Less Developed Countries*, Paris: various issues from 1960 to 1984. The raw data (given in Appendix 1, below) are subjected to a lagging process to simulate the actual time of impact of aid flows. Thus it is assumed that of a given year's aid flows:

3% takes effect in that same year
18% takes effect in the following year
24% takes effect in the second year after disbursement
18% takes effect in the third year after disbursement
13% takes effect in the fourth year after disbursement
9% takes effect in the fifth year after disbursement
8% takes effect in the sixth year after disbursement
6% takes effect in the seventh year after disbursement

This lag structure is derived from an examination of gestation periods for the World Bank-financed projects listed in World Bank, *Tenth Annual Review of Project Performance Audit Results* (Washington, 1984).

Other financial flows. These consist of export credits to governments of developing countries by banks and other private institutions, plus private portfolio and direct investment in those countries. Source: OECD, *Geographical Distribution of Financial Flows to Less Developed Countries*, Paris: various issues from 1960 to 1984. The raw data (given in Appendix 1 below) are subjected to a lagging process to simulate the actual time of impact of these flows. The lag structure used is the same as that given for aid in the previous note.

Savings as a percentage of recipient GNP, public and private sector combined. From United Nations. *Yearbook of National Accounts Statistics*, various issues.

Growth rate of export values. From World Bank, *World Development Report 1985*, Table 8, 'Growth of merchandise trade'.

Growth of adult literacy rates. From World Bank, *World Development Report 1985*, Table 23, 'Education' and 'UNESCO, *Statistical Yearbook 1976 and 1980*.

No usable data on the development of literacy from 1980-3 are available, hence this variable is excluded from the regression set for that period. *Growth of GNP.* From World Bank, *World Bank Development Report 1985*, Table 2. 'Growth of Production'.

Note: Ordinary least squares analysis. Dependent variable: growth rate of real GNP (% per annum). Figures in brackets beneath coefficents are student's t-statistics; * denotes significance of a coefficient at 5% level, ** denotes significance at 1% level.

significant in the 1960s, positive but altogether insignificant in the 1970s, and negative and insignificant again in the 1980s; but it is never wise to make too much play with insignificant statistics. The best conclusion, we believe, is that aid *in the aggregate* has no demonstrable effect on economic growth in recipient countries in any of the three periods. These results, we must note in passing, conflict with those recorded by Papanek (1972, 1973) which suggest a positive and significant influence for aid in the 1960s, indeed that aid: 'has a more significant influence on growth than savings or the other forms of foreign resource inflows'.[18]

It is possible that the discrepancy arises because we have used different data sets, and in the hope of providing a firm base for future research in this area the data set used by ourselves is reproduced in Appendix 1 to Chapter 6. Differences in response pattern between continents are not of any great importance, except for the period 1980–3, when aid emerges as a positive and significant influence in Asia only. If, however, the sample is split between the fourteen poorest countries and the rest, with the cut-off point being an average per capita income of US$ 300 in 1981, the middle-income country group shows higher effectiveness throughout all three periods, with a significant coefficient in the 1970s. The growth rate of exports is the only independent variable which retains significance throughout the twenty-year period 1960–80; the growth in literacy rate, also, is significant for the 1960s and the savings rate for the 1970s.

Before we proceed to interpret these results it is important to ascertain whether they are sensitive to changes in the method of estimation. First, there is a case for regarding aid levels as being *determined by*, as well as *determining*, the economic conditions of the recipient country and hence for estimating (5.2') by two-stage least-square analysis treating aid as endogenous;[19] second, the Durbin–Watson statistics reported in Table 5.3 suggest the presence of serial correlation of residuals in some of the equations, which may make the measured *a*-coefficients in Table 5.3 unreliable estimates of the true values. Table 5.4 shows, however, that under both two-stage least squares and the Cochrane–Orcutt

Table 5.4: Results of regression analysis relating GNP growth to aid, savings and other financial flows in sixty-seven less developed countries, 1960–80 and 1980–3: Two-stage least squares and Cochrane–Orcutt iterative methods. Dependent variable: growth rate of real GNP (% per annum)

Sample: All developing countries in sample (n=67)	Constant	Regression coefficients on independent variables:					Standard error of regression
		Aid (as percentage of recipient GNP)	Other financial flows from overseas (as percentage of recipient GNP)	Savings (as percentage of recipient GNP)	Growth rate of export values (annual average over periods stated)	Growth in adult literacy rate (annual average over periods stated)	
(a) Two-stage least squares analysis							
1960–70	11.1* (2.04)	−0.66 (1.72)	0.03 (0.52)	−0.32 (1.25)	0.48 (1.86)	0.005 (0.03)	6.07
1970–80	−23.2 (1.07)	3.27 (1.21)	−0.44 (1.12)	1.04 (1.28)	−0.01 (0.02)	−0.40 (0.89)	12.81
							R^2
(b) Cochrane–Orcutt iterative method							
1960–70	1.94* (2.53)	0.02 (0.76)	0.024 (0.19)	0.084* (2.33)	0.16** (3.62)	0.11 (2.03)	0.35
1970–80	2.89** (3.08)	0.17 (1.43)	−0.17* (2.43)	0.084 (2.00)	0.16** (2.98)	0.008 (0.20)	0.27
1980–3	−0.41 (0.10)	−0.16 (0.86)	−0.04 (0.32)	0.08 (0.46)	0.13 (0.99)		0.04

Sources for all data: As Table 5.4. Note: no data on growth of literacy rates available for 1980s.

iterative method of estimation, which corrects for serial correlation in the residuals, aid flows remain, in the aggregate, insignificant as a determinant of GNP growth.

To understand what is going on, let us now refer back to the analysis of the previous section. If aid is having no impact on growth overall, this suggests that the different influences on aid effectiveness which we have examined—the share of aid allocated to recurrent budget, the 'crowding out' or 'crowding in' effect of aid on private investment, the return on private-sector capital investment and the return on public-sector capital investment—are cancelling each other out. Let us now examine what has happened over time to each of those parameters.

On the proportion of aid allocated to the recurrent budget, we have no usable information, since during the 1960s OECD published no data on the allocation of aid by function, and the UNDP manuals used in the compilation of Table 5.2 did not exist for most developing countries.[20] The rates of return on capital in the public and private sectors have declined, as is made clear by the data of Table 5.5; the World Bank have blamed this on factors extraneous to the aid process such as the oil crisis,[21] but it seems clear also that the multiplication of the number of donors[22] and the attempt of each one of them to switch their aid from 'easy' projects such as power and infrastructure to 'difficult' projects such as integrated rural development[23] have raised the cost of implementing aid projects and led to a decline in the general rate of return on capital in the Third World between the 1960s and the 1970s.

Against this, however, the 'crowding-out' effect of aid on private-sector capital investment, which is strong and significant across our sample of recipient countries in the 1960s, disappears altogether, that is, becomes statistically insignificant, in the 1970s. This is superficially rather surprising, since the 1970s, as we have seen, was the decade of large rural development projects which raised the cost of non-traded inputs to the private sector. But it also saw three developments which counteracted this tendency, and increased the beneficial external effects of aid on the private sector. First, the probability of expropriation of private-

Table 5.5: Eighty less developed countries: estimates of critical determinants of 'aid effectiveness', 1960s and 1970s compared

Period	Return on investment (%)	Relationship between aid inflows and private-sector capital investment, a_{15} (estimated regression coefficient; t-statistics in brackets)
1960–70	26.8	−1.84** (3.83)
1970–80	20.5	−0.10 (0.86)

Source: Return on investment: World Bank *World Development Report, 1983*, Table 3.8, p. 38. Relationship between aid inflows and capital investment in private sector—as for final column of Table 5.3. The coefficient a_{15} in the final column is obtained by estimating the relationship: private sector investment = constant + a_{15} (aid/GNP) + a_{16} (private-sector investment lagged 1 year) across the sample of countries specified in World Bank, *World Development Report 1983*, Table 6.1, p. 60.

sector assets diminished; the number of countries experiencing acts of nationalisation without compensation in the 1970s declined to five by comparison with nine in the 1960s.[24] Hence the mechanism invoked by Bauer, in which overseas aid is used to buttress the power of a regime which then restricts the inflow of private capital, has probably become weaker between the two decades. Second, in the 1970s a far greater share of aid came to be disbursed in the form of 'programme grants' or 'import support aid', much of which was explicitly designed to break balance-of-payments constraints facing the private sector.[25] Third and last, in the 1970s a far greater share of aid came to be disbursed in official aid to agricultural credit agencies and development banks which then on-lent to the private sector.[26] These factors between them seem to have deprived official aid of whatever ability it once had to 'crowd out' private investment. This factor worked in the opposite direction to, and seems to have helped to cancel out, the undoubted negative effects on aid effectiveness of the decline in the rate of return.

5.4 CONCLUSIONS: THE 'MACRO–MICRO PARADOX'

The main empirical result of this chapter, therefore, is a negative one, namely that there appears to be no statistically significant correlation in *any* post-war period, either positive or negative, between inflows of development aid and the growth rate of GNP in developing countries when other causal influences on growth are taken into account. Theoretically, the model which we have developed draws attention to reasons why this should be the case, including the possibility of leakages into non-productive expenditure in the public sector and of the transmission of negative price effects to the private sector. The model assumes utility maximisation in the public sector, but this allows room for an enormous variety of behaviours in the use of aid money according to the preferences which public-sector decision makers demonstrate between tax reduction, expansion of 'productive' expenditures, expansion of 'non-productive' expenditures and other objectives of government policy.

All this will make depressing reading for those who are familiar with the reports of development agencies on individual projects, nearly all of which report a very high preponderance of 'successful' over 'unsuccessful' projects and a conviction that, on balance, overseas aid is an efficient instrument for generating growth in developing countries. For example, the World Bank reports average *ex post* rates of return over ten per cent in every continent and almost every economic sector over the twenty-year period 1961–81,[27] and a recent comprehensive report on the effectiveness of overseas aid squarely concludes that '*the great majority of aid succeeds in its developmental objectives*. The answer to the question "does aid work?" is "Most of it, yes; however ... "'[28] These conclusions are simply not consistent with the bleak macro-level results reported in Table 5.3, and it is important to understand why.

There are three potential explanations for the 'micro–macro paradox': inaccurate measurement, fungibility within the public sector, and negative side-effects, or 'backwash effects' of aid on the investment and output of the private sector. On the evidence of Tables 5.2 and 5.5 above there is, at least in the 1970s, no significant effect either way of aid on private-sector investment in recipient countries: the 'backwash' effects of aid on the private sector, such as they are, appear to be cancelled out by the 'spread' effects. The data on project impact collected by the World Bank relate only to some 20 per cent, or less, of total concessional aid disbursements and are collected at an arbitrary 'project termination' date when aid money is withdrawn;[29] likewise the GDP data used to compute Table 5.3 are based on data which can scarcely be called reliable.[30] It is possible therefore that the World Bank figures overstate the true average return on all aid-financed projects—in other words that the micro-results are worse than they look—or that the Bank's figures understate the growth rate of those countries (mostly least developed) which receive a great deal of aid—in other words that the macro-results are better than they look. Neither of these possibilities can be ruled out, but there is a lack of evidence in support of either. There is no comprehensive measurement of *ex post* rates of return on aid projects in any agency other than the World Bank, but those aid agencies which do measure rates of return on some projects—notably US AID, the Inter-America Development Bank, and the UK Overseas Development Administration—report results little different from, and certainly no lower than, the World Bank figures reported earlier.[31] Likewise it is perfectly possible that the GDP growth figures quoted in the *World Development Report* are understated—in particular because of inadequate coverage of the 'informal' and non-monetary sectors—but it is hard to see why the degree of this understatement might be greater in Somalia, for example, where aid in the period 1980–3 was 37 per cent of GDP, than in Ethiopia, where it was 5 per cent. Hence it is hard to find biases in either the macro- or the micro-data on aid effectiveness which would explain the split between the two measures. For such an explanation we are therefore thrown back on the ancient problem of *fungibility*, or switching of aid money into uses which are in some sense unproductive.

Some evidence on the importance of fungibility in aid effectiveness is given by Figure 5.2 above, which shows that countries which explicitly allocated a large proportion of aid inflows to the recurrent budget were countries where aid, *ceteris paribus*, was relatively ineffective. However, this only touches the surface of the problem, which as we saw in Chapter 4 is not so much the *direct* use of aid funds on unproductive purposes, as the diversion of government monies *which would otherwise have been spent* on productive investment into unproductive uses. The way in which government resources would have been spent in an alternative, hypothetical state of the world is not something which can ever be measured with scientific certainty; hence the muddled and inconclusive state of the debate. But some generalisations are possible. First, the larger the share of the development budget which is financed by aid, the smaller is the scope for switching. In countries such as Bangladesh, Somalia or Nepal where virtually the whole of the development budget is paid for by overseas aid donors, there is no scope for switching. The government uses its entire income, in these countries, for recurrent services and is too poor to budget any domestically generated money for development activities, hence there is nothing for aid to drive out. Second, by the argument of p. 128, if a decline in tax effort or an increase in the ratio of recurrent expenditure to national income regularly accompanies an increase in the share of aid inflows to national income, this implies that some aid is serving purely to facilitate tax cuts or increases in the recurrent budget, particularly if the share of development expenditure in national income is not rising at the same time. We observed quite widespread evidence of such behaviour by Third World governments in Chapter 4. Tentatively, therefore, we conclude that in some countries aid is 'ineffective' because it leads, directly and indirectly, to diversion of public-investment resources into consumption, and that these effects cancel out its beneficial impact in other countries, leaving the neutral overall effect which is observed in Table 5.3.

What is to be done about this unsatisfactory state of

affairs? If the reader will turn back to Figure 5.2 and put his or her hand over the top-left and bottom-right quadrants of that diagram, he will see that, statistically, aid could be made to look an 'effective' instrument of development simply by taking it away from those countries in which high aid is associated with low growth, or vice versa. Donors are unlikely to do this, on the grounds that aid serves many purposes other than the purely developmental, and that all of those other purposes are likely to be hindered by a sudden unprovoked withdrawal of aid funds.[32] However, they may well choose to shift incremental aid resources towards those countries which appear to 'use it well', and they may also try and increase *leverage* in the effectiveness of their aid, particularly their programme aid, by making their disbursement of it conditional on the adoption by the recipient of policy actions which are thought to be likely to raise the rate of growth of GDP and other indicators of development. This kind of strategy has been used with increasing vigour by some aid donors in recent years, and we shall examine the prospects for it, in the light of their experience, in Chapter 8.

APPENDIX.   THE PATHWAYS OF AID IMPACT: A MATHEMATICAL MODEL

Our point of departure is that the government of a developing country will attempt to maximise its own welfare in the face of budgetary constraints, and will use aid inflows from overseas as an instrument in the pursuit of that objective.

In this chapter, on the basis of their own published pronouncements,[33] we see them as taking a less ambitious perspective, and confining themselves, as the governments of advanced countries have recently found themselves obliged to do, to trying to steer certain 'intermediate targets' of policy as close as possible to their desired values. These intermediate targets, on the evidence of the public pronouncements reviewed above, appear to be government expenditure, tax revenues and public borrowing. For later reference we shall wish to distinguish between three categories of government expenditure: capital expenditure proper, recurrent expenditure which nevertheless contributes to the development of the country (e.g. expenditure on education, health and social services) and recurrent expenditure which makes no such direct economic contribution and serves instead a purely political function (e.g. expenditure on national defence, law and order and subsidies).

We therefore write the government welfare function as:

$$U = f(I_g, G_d, G_{nd}, B, T) \tag{5.3}$$

where:

U	=	welfare of public-sector decision makers;
I_g	=	government capital expenditure;
G_d	=	'developmental' recurrent expenditure by government;
G_{nd}	=	'non-developmental' recurrent expenditure by government;
B	=	public borrowing (from both domestic and overseas sources);
T	=	tax revenue.

For simplicity we shall define the welfare function U as a 'loss function' which is quadratic in deviations of the various 'intermediate targets' from their desired values: the further they stray from their targets, the lower is the level of government utility:

$$\begin{aligned} U = {} & -(a_1/2)\,(I_g^* - I_g)^2 \\ & - (a_2/2)(T - T^*)^2 - (a_3/2)\,(G_d - G_d^*)^2 \\ & -(a_4/2)\,(G_{nd} - G_{nd}^*)^2 - (a_5/2)\,(B - B^*)^2 \end{aligned} \tag{5.4}$$

where asterisks denote desired values of intermediate targets and the coefficients $a_1 \ldots a_5$ are fixed numbers.

We assume that the authorities derive the desired values of targets I_g^*, T^* and so on from observable macroeconomic data according to the following relationships:

$$I^*{}_g = a_6 Y_{t-1} + a_7 I_p \tag{5.5}$$

$$T^* = a_8 Y_t + a_9 M_{t-1} \tag{5.6}$$

$$G_d^* = a_{10} Y_t \tag{5.7}$$

$$G_{nd}^* = a_{11}G_{nd,t-1} + a_{12}Z \qquad (5.8)$$

$$B^* = 0 \qquad (5.9)$$

where Y is national income, I_p is investment expenditure by the private sector, M_{t-1} is lagged imports, Z is a 'wartime dummy' variable and the coefficients $a_6 \ldots a_{12}$ are fixed numbers. The rationale behind these specifications is as follows. The target level of government investment I_g^* is derived from a target rate of growth of the economy, an assumption about the current period's level of private investment and an assumption about the capital–output ratio; public investment is planned to supply the 'residual' needed to drive the actual growth rate up to its target level. The target level of tax revenue T^* is derived from estimates of the two main bases for taxation, namely total monetary income and overseas trade. The desired level of 'developmental' government expenditure G_d^* is planned to grow in proportion to current income. 'Non-developmental' government expenditure G_{nd}^* consists in normal years of a standard increment on the last period's value of the same variable, but takes a sharp upward jump in years when the country is at war. Finally we assume that *ex ante* the target for public borrowing, from both domestic and overseas, is zero.

We now turn to the constraints. The first of these is budgetary: all government expenditure must, one way or another, be financed. The simplest way of formulating the constraint would be to specify that all outflows from the exchequer must be balanced by inflows, that is:

$$T + B + A = I_g + G_d + G_{nd} \qquad (5.10)$$

However, in most developing countries it is extremely uncommon for recurrent government expenditure $(G_d + G_{nd})$ to be financed from borrowing.[34] We thus posit that all such expenditure derives from tax revenue plus aid receipts alone:

$$G_d + G_{nd} = a_{13}T + a_{14}A \qquad (5.11)$$

thus,

$$I_g = B + (1 - a_{13})T + (1 - a_{14})A. \qquad (5.12)$$

The second constraint consists of the, as yet unexplored, effects of aid, through the price system, on private investment, I_p: the effects in the bottom part of Figure 5.1. As noted earlier, these effects cut two ways. Aid inflows act so as to reduce the price of those goods and services which are supplied by the project, and counteract this by driving up the prices of those goods and services for which demand is augmented by the project. In general the former are 'tradable' (tractors, telecommunications equipment, consultancy services) and the latter are 'non-tradable' (cement, unskilled labour): indeed, aid is very frequently tied to exports of goods and services from the donor country. Call the former 'A goods' and their price p_a, and call the latter 'B goods' and their price p_b. Now the overall 'price effect' of aid on the private sector, if there are m A goods and n B goods, is

$$\frac{dI_p}{dA} = \sum_{a=1}^{m} \frac{\partial I_p}{\partial P_a} \frac{\partial P_a}{\partial A} + \sum_{b=1}^{n} \frac{\partial I_p}{\partial P_b} \frac{\partial P_b}{\partial A}. \tag{5.13}$$

It will be obvious that this effect depends, first, on the *size* of $\partial P_a/\partial A$ relative to $\partial P_b/\partial A$ and second, on the relative *impact* of these two terms on private sector output. That relative impact will in turn depend, partly on how far the price change in question spreads through the economy (which is related to the amount of 'distortion' in the market in question) and partly on whether the price which is changing is an input to other producers or an article of final demand. If, therefore, we write the relationship of private investment to aid as:

$$I_p = a_{15}A_t + a_{16}I_{p,t-1} \tag{5.14}$$

there are three factors which will influence the sign and magnitude of a_{15}: the mix of initial price changes administered by the aid package, the relative extent to which changes in the price of 'A goods' and 'B goods' ramify through the economy and their overall impact on input costs.[35]

Finally, there is the relationship of income, Y_t, to its determinants to be considered. Write the aggregate production function as:

$$Y = h(K_p, K_g, L) \tag{5.15}$$

where K_p is the private-sector capital stock, K_g is the government capital stock and L is the labour supply.

We now proceed to optimise the government's presumed loss function (5.4) subject to the constraints of finance ((5.11), (5.12)) and the linkage between aid and private-sector investment (5.13). This gives the following first-order conditions:

$$\frac{\partial U}{\partial I_g} = -a_1(I_g - I_g^*) + \lambda_1 = 0 \tag{5.16}$$

$$\frac{\partial U}{\partial G_{nd}} = -a_4(G_{nd} - G_{nd}^*) + \lambda_2 = 0 \tag{5.17}$$

$$\frac{\partial U}{\partial G_d} = -a_3(G_d - G_d^*) + \lambda_2 = 0 \tag{5.18}$$

$$\frac{\partial U}{\partial T} = -a_2(T - T^*) - \lambda_1(1 - a_{13}) - \lambda_2 a_{13} = 0 \tag{5.19}$$

$$\frac{\partial U}{\partial B} = -a_5(B - B^*) - \lambda_1 = 0 \tag{5.20}$$

$$\frac{\partial U}{\partial \lambda_1} = I_g - B - (1 - a_{13})T - (1 - a_{14})A_t = 0 \tag{5.21}$$

$$\frac{\partial U}{\partial \lambda_2} = G_d + G_{nd} - a_{13}T - a_{14}A_t = 0 \tag{5.22}$$

$$\frac{\partial U}{\partial \lambda_3} = I_p - a_{15}A_t - a_{16}I_{p,t-1} = 0 \tag{5.23}$$

where λ_1, λ_2 and λ_3 are the Lagrange multipliers attaching to the constraints (5.12) (5.11) and (5.14) respectively.

Our ultimate objective is to find out how the variables in this system, and in particular income, Y_t, will respond when the equilibrium depicted by equations (5.16) to (5.23) is disturbed by a change in the exogenous variable aid, A_t. We thus proceed to calculate the reduced form of the model. First, from (5.16):

$$\lambda_1 = a_1(I_g - I_g^*) \tag{5.24}$$

whence, substituting for I_g^* from (5.5):

$$I_g = \left(\frac{\lambda_1}{a_1}\right) + a_6 Y_{t-1} + a_7 I_p \tag{5.25}$$

Further, from (5.18):

$$\lambda_2 = a_3(G_d - G_d^*) \tag{5.26}$$

whence, substituting for G_d^* from (5.7):

$$G_d = \left(\frac{\lambda_2}{a_3}\right) + a_{10}Y_t \tag{5.27}$$

Now, from (5.20):

$$\lambda_1 = -a_5(B - B^*). \tag{5.28}$$

But, recalling:

$$B^* = 0 \tag{5.9}$$

(5.28) can be written as:

$$\lambda_1 = -a_5 B. \tag{5.29}$$

Finally, from (5.17)

$$\lambda_2 = a_4(G_{nd} - G_{nd}^*) \tag{5.30}$$

whence, substituting for G_{nd}^* from (5.8):

$$\lambda_2 = a_4 G_{nd} - a_4 a_{11} G_{nd,t-1} - a_4 a_{12} Z. \tag{5.31}$$

Now, differentiating (5.15)

$$dY = \frac{\partial h}{\partial K_p}dK_p + \frac{\partial h}{\partial K_g}dK_g + \frac{\partial h}{\partial L}dL \tag{5.32}$$

which, since investment is equivalent to the change in the capital stock, can be written

$$dY = \frac{\partial h}{\partial K_p}I_p + \frac{\partial h}{\partial K_g}I_g + \frac{\partial h}{\partial L}dL. \tag{5.33}$$

Now, denoting the above partial derivatives by δ_1, δ_2 and δ_3 respectively, (5.33) can be written as:

$$dY = \delta_1 I_p + \delta_2 I_g + \delta_3 dL. \tag{5.34}$$

Substituting (5.14), (5.25), (5.29) and (5.12) into (5.34) we eventually derive the reduced-form equation for income:

$$dY = \delta_1 a_{15} A_t + \delta_1 a_{16} I_{p,t-1} + \delta_2 \frac{1}{\pi}\left[(1-a_{13})\left(\frac{a_5}{a_1}\right)T + \left(\frac{a_5}{a_1}\right)\right.$$

$$\left.(1-a_{14})A_t + a_6 Y_{t-1} + a_7 a_{15} A_t + a_7 a_{16} I_{p,t-1}\right] + \delta_3 dL$$

(5.35)

where $\pi = \left[1 + \left(\dfrac{a_5}{a_1}\right)\right].$

Differentiating (5.35) with respect to A_t, we obtain an expression for the instantaneous rate of change of income with respect to aid when other variables are held constant, that is, the 'effectiveness' of aid:

$$\frac{\partial(dY)}{\partial A_t} = \delta_1 a_{15} + \frac{\delta_2}{\pi}\left(\frac{a_5}{a_1}\right)(1-a_{14}) + \frac{\delta_2}{\pi} a_7 a_{15}. \qquad (5.36)$$

This is the relationship which is discussed in Sections 5.2 and 5.3. It suggests that the 'effectiveness' of aid is determined by the three parameters of the government welfare function, a_1, a_5 and a_7; the two parameters of the constraint, a_{14} and a_{15}; and the two parameters of the aggregate production function, δ_1 and δ_2.

NOTES

1. It may also, of course, be hampered by any acts of expropriation of private companies which accompany the inflow of aid, as Bauer predicts (*see* Chapter 1, Note 22).
2. The regression equation (across all of the eighty countries for which data are given in Appendix 1 to Chapter 6) was:

growth of GNP = $\underset{(8.68)}{4.50^{**}} - \underset{(0.68)}{0.004} \frac{(aid)}{(GNP)}$; $r^2 = 0.01$.

3. For a formal model suggesting that these are the crucial determinants of 'air effectiveness', *see* the appendix to this chapter.
4. The mean combined effect of savings and export growth on the growth of GDP is 1.95 per cent, and the standard deviation 1.19 per cent, hence we include in our sample all countries for which ($b_1 S$ +

b_2X)is in the range 0.80 to 3.14 per cent.
5. *See* Appendix below, pp. 142–148.
6. This preference can also be exercised by using aid money for investment projects which had been earmarked for finance out of domestic revenue, as portrayed in Figure 5.1.
7. In the language of the appendix to this chapter this 'preference' for low taxation is measured by the coefficient a_2. There is clearly a complementarity between a_2 and the share of aid allocated to recurrent expenditure a_{14}.
8. For further development of this argument *see* Mosley (1980), pp. 86–8.
9. This effect is measured in the appendix to this chapter by the coefficient a_{15}.
10. The estimated statistical relationship was as follows:

$$a_{15} = -5.85 - 2.59 \text{ (index of price distortions)};$$
$$(0.79)$$

$$r^2 = 0.02; \text{ number of observations} = 31$$

where a_{15} = estimated value of coefficient a_{15} as recorded in Table 5.3, and index of price distortions is the index recorded in World Bank, *World Development Report 1983*, Table 6.1. The sign of this coefficient is perverse, but insignificant in any case.
11. The estimated statistical relationship is:

$$a_{15} = -2.62 + 0.15 \left(\frac{\text{government consumption}}{\text{GDP}} \right);$$
$$(0.52)$$

number of observations = 31, where a_{15} = estimated value of coefficient a_{15} as recorded in Table 5.2, and government consumption is the value recorded in World Bank, *World Tables*, 3 vols. (1976, 1980, 1983).
12. As in the case of the Upper Region Development Project: *see* Chapter 4, p. 107.
13. A classical example of this type of effect is food aid, which provides short-term benefits to consumers at the cost of a reduction in the price of food and hence a reduction in the incentive to local food producers. *See* Sandilands and Dudley (1975).
14. This equation can also be interpreted as a long-run form of equation (5.35), the reduced form of the model of the appendix. The variable I_p (private investment) in the reduced form is divided, in the estimating equation (5.2') into savings (S) and non-concessional foreign capital inflows (I_f); the growth of labour supply (dL in the reduced form) is represented in (5.2') by the growth in literacy rates, on the grounds that in most LDCs it is not the growth of the absolute supply of labour, but the development of skills, which forms the real constraint on production; foreign aid appears in the estimating equation unaltered; finally, the change in export values, X, is inserted

into the estimating equation as a proxy variable for the constraint of world demand.

15. The grant equivalent is a measure which reduces international transactions of varying degrees of concessionality (in relation to the interest rate, the term of the loan and the grace period) to their estimated grant value. For details of its computation *see* OECD, *Geographical Distribution of Financial Flows to Less Developed Countries 1980–83* (Paris, 1984), p. 280, paragraph A.3. This is the most appropriate measure of aid on the presumption that it is relieving a savings constraint; for experiments with alternative measures of aid, however, (giving very similar results) *see* Mosley and Hudson (1984), Table 4b.

16. For the details of these *see* Mosley and Hudson (1984), Appendix 2, pp. 44–6.

17. The implications of using alternative estimation techniques are reported in Table 5.4, of reverting to Papanek's original specification in Note 18, and of using alternative measures of development (life expectancy and infant mortality) as dependent variables in Mosley and Hudson (1984), pp. 41 and 42. In none of these alternative specifications is the coefficient on aid statistically significant.

18. Papanek (1973), p. 129. Obvious sources of discrepancy between our results and his are the following:

    (a) use of a different definition of 'aid' as the independent variable in the regression equation;

    (b) use of a different lag-structure;

    (c) use of a different set of independent variables alongside aid flows in the estimating equation.

We have cited on p. 130–131 our reasons for wishing to specify the equation in the way that we have. However, *even if* we adopt the specification used by Papanek (aid defined as net ODA; no lags in the equation; and other financial flows and savings as the only additional independent variables in the estimating equation apart from aid) the aid variable on the data cited in Appendix 1 remains insignificant:

$$1960\text{–}70: \text{growth} = \underset{(4.79)}{4.61^{**}} - \underset{(0.09)}{0.01}\left(\frac{\text{aid}}{\text{GNP}}\right) + \underset{(0.26)}{0.07}\left(\frac{\text{other financial flows}}{\text{GNP}}\right)$$

$$+ \underset{(0.90)}{0.04}\left(\frac{\text{savings}}{\text{GNP}}\right); \quad r^2 = 0.02;$$

$$1970\text{–}80: \text{growth} = \underset{(2.29)}{2.54} - \underset{(1.72)}{0.15}\left(\frac{\text{aid}}{\text{GNP}}\right) + \underset{(1.77)}{0.09}\left(\frac{\text{other financial flows}}{\text{GNP}}\right)$$

$$+ 0.12^{**} \left(\frac{\text{savings}}{\text{GNP}}\right); \qquad r^2 = 0.10;$$
$$(2.82)$$

contrary to Papanek's statement that aid is a consistently positive and significant influence on the growth of GNP.

19. In fact the case for regarding aid as determined by *levels* of income in recipient countries is much stronger than the case for regarding it as determined by the *growth rate* of income in the recipient; there is little evidence that donors give more aid to slow-growing underdeveloped countries. Hence we have presented the OLS estimates as the main results, and the 2 SLS estimates as auxiliary data which confirm those main results.

20. Informed guesswork suggests that the proportion of aid allocated to the recurrent budget of recipient countries was high at the beginning of the 1960s, in the immediate aftermath of decolonisation, and low at the end of the 1970s, in the wake of the oil crisis, but that there was no significant difference in a_{14} between the 1960s as a whole and the 1970s as a whole. But we cannot give this belief any statistical support.

21. Specifically, they have blamed it on many causes: 'the recession in world trade, oil price shocks, strains in the financial system, lower returns on capital locked in ageing industry, ineffective macro-economic policies that postponed rather than promoted adjustments, and more capital-intensive investment' (World Bank (1983), p. 43).

22. *See* discussion in Chapter 4 above, pp. 100–105. The number of bilateral and multilateral donors giving aid to some of the largest aid recipients, according to successive issues of the OECD's *Geographical Distribution of Financial Flows*, is as follows:

	1961	1981
India	13	29
Indonesia	9	27
Sri Lanka	8	28
Ethiopia	9	30
Kenya	6	28
Tanzania	8	32
Mali	3	22
Peru	8	26
Yemen Arab Republic	3	21

This classification excludes donors from centrally planned economies and treats the Arab OPEC agencies, for reasons of data limitations, as one donor.

23. For data on these, *see* Morris and Gwyer (1983) and Mosley (1981a).

24. The nine in the 1960s were Peru, People's Democratic Republic of Yemen, Chile, Tanzania, Somalia, Algeria, Guinea, Grenada, Libya;

the five in the 1970s were Ethiopia, Jamaica, Ghana, Nicaragua, Iran. Source: *Keesing's Contemporary Archives*, augmented by *Africa Contemporary Record*.

25. Loans and grants from official aid agencies for import support, *excluding* food aid, rose from an estimated average of 9 per cent in the years 1960–70 to 18.2 per cent in the years 1971–80. OECD, *Development Assistance* (Annual Report of the Development Assistance Committee), successive issues, Table B4, 'ODA Commitments by purpose'.

26. Loans and grants from official aid agencies to development banks in recipient countries (we exclude *regional* development banks such as the Asian Development Bank) rose from a negligible amount in 1970 and the preceding years to an annual average of $251 m (2 per cent of the total aid flow) in the years 1975–80. OECD *Development Assistance* (Annual Report of the Development Assistance Committee), successive issues, Table B6. 'Sector allocation of bilateral ODA commitments'.

27. The figures calculated *ex post* economic rates of return for individual sectors and continents are as set out on page 153.

28. Cassen *et al.* (1986), Chapter 1, paragraph 1.19.

29. In recent years the World Bank has made a strenuous attempt to find out what happens to the projects which it finances after aid money is withdrawn. For a pessimistic first report on the performance of a sample of projects which Bank staff revisited after several years after the withdrawal of external finance, *see* World Bank, *Sustainability of Projects: First Review of Experience*, Operations Evaluation Department, Report no. 5718, June 1985.

30. *See*, in particular, World Bank (1981) unnumbered table, p. 187, which provides estimates of GDP for certain African countries compiled from different sources; for example, the growth rate of Upper Volta in the 1970s is given as 0.7 per cent according to UNCTAD data and as 3.9 per cent according to French Government data, and the highest available estimate for GNP growth for African countries as a whole is more than twice the lowest available estimate.

31. *See* Cassen *et al.* (1986), Chapter 5.

32. In particular the application of this 'efficiency' criterion would dictate a withdrawal of aid from sub-Saharan Africa, where the most serious development problems are concentrated, into the fast-growing countries of South-East Asia.

33. We examined a number of published development plans to see what targets were expressed in quantitative terms. They were as follows:

Kenya: balance of payments, government revenue (development and recurrent), public borrowing (*Development Plan 1984–8*, Chapter 3).

Lesotho: balance of payments, 'vulnerability to external economic and political pressures'; public borrowing (*Third Five-Year Development Plan 1980–5*, Chapter 3, p. 45).

(*note continues on p. 154*)

27. The calculated average *ex post* economic rates of return for individual sectors and continents are as follows:

Economic sector	Geographic region						Total	No. of credits
	East Africa	West Africa	Europe Middle East, N. Africa	Latin America & Caribbean	East Asia and Pacific	South Asia		
Transport	14.5	20.1	18.6	22.6	21.9	22.2	20.0	185
Agriculture	9.7	15.4	18.0	12.7	21.7	27.2	16.8	221
Power	14.0	12.7	15.8	11.7	13.2	30.0	13.5	62
Industry	3.0	—	16.3	13.6	25.0	14.3	14.6	21
Telecommunications	14.0	—	26.0	18.0	19.1	19.9	19.9	28
Water	9.1	9.9	10.0	6.7	5.0	—	8.4	21
Total	11.7	17.4	17.6	15.8	20.1	23.2	17.3	538
No. of projects	78	92	85	138	92	53	538	

Source: World Bank: *Ninth Annual Review of Project Performance Audit Results*, Operations Evaluation Department, 1983.

India   economic growth, employment, public expenditure, government revenue, income distribution (*Third Five Year Plan*, Chapter 1, pp. 11–17).

Taiwan: economic growth, government spending, income distribution, changes in economic structure, balance of payments (*Fourth Five Year Plan*, Chapter 1, pp. 1–9).

Zambia: diversification of economic structure, income distribution, public expenditure, tax revenues, localisation of personnel (*Third National Development Plan 1979–83*, Chapter 2, pp. 21–2).

34. For examples of the Kenya government's reluctance to borrow even over a very short period for recurrent expenditure, *see* Holtham and Hazlewood (1976), pp. 89 and 167.

35. This argument is further developed in Mosley *et al.* (1986). It will readily be seen that the impact of aid on private-sector output does not depend in any systematic way on the number of distortions in the economy as suggested, for example, by the World Bank (1983), Chapter 6. Distortions do enter the picture, but the critical variable is not the *absolute* amount of distortion, but rather the *relative* amounts of distortion in the markets for what we have called 'A goods' and 'B goods'. This argument is given statistical support in Note 10 above.

6 Aid as Redistributive Tool

6.1 INTRODUCTION

Growth does not necessarily bring with it a reduction in poverty. In the Third World as a whole, growth in 'low-income economies' has actually been higher than in 'industrial market economies' over the period 1965–83,[1] but very many people have not benefited from this growth, and the number of people living in conditions of absolute poverty remains at around a thousand million.[2] To ask whether aid relieves poverty, therefore, is a different question from the question considered in the previous chapter. There is little doubt that this is, moreover, the question which those who finance aid transactions see as the more important test of the effectiveness of aid. Of the persons interviewed in the British Government's 1978 survey of attitudes to overseas aid, 42 per cent of those who supported the basic idea of Britain giving help to poorer countries gave as a reason for that belief the desire to assist very poor people (as against 8 per cent who cited motives of conscience, 4 per cent who felt that 'we would benefit by trade' and 3 per cent who felt that 'it would improve our political relations with other countries').[3]

To most respondents, aid is simply an international analogue to the income redistribution processes which the welfare state achieves within a developed country. And the test-question for such a process is not 'is it effectively used?' but simply, 'does it reach the right people?' The purpose of this chapter is to find out whether or not it does so.

Any assessment of the redistributive ability of aid must begin by defining the lower-income groups whom aid is meant to assist. This is a matter of personal ethical judgement, and also of endless controversy. For some, it will be sufficient that a given donor's aid programme should be directed towards the *poorest countries*; others will require that most of that programme go to the poorest people *within* developing countries, say the poorest 40 per cent;[4] others will agree with this general principle but adopt a stricter definition of 'the poorest', say the poorest 10 per cent; others still will define the poorest not in terms of income but in terms of assets (e.g. the landless) or in terms of presumed economic vulnerability (e.g. rural women and children). Improvements in the welfare of 'poor people' on one observer's definition may therefore be perfectly consistent with declines in the welfare of 'poor people' on another observer's definition;[5] for example, aid may be given to poor farmers who then buy up the land of still poorer farmers, or aid may be given to poor male farmers in the form of help with cash-crop activities which, when expanded, use up the space available for food crops, which are often grown by women.[6] Unlike the assessment of the impact of aid on growth, therefore, the assessment of its impact on income distribution is essentially subjective, and the best that one can hope to do is to present measures of distributional impact based on different criteria and invite the reader to choose the measure which he or she thinks most consistent with his or her own values.

It will be obvious that an attempt to direct aid towards a specific target group presents political difficulties over and above those associated with giving it to a ministry, development bank or agricultural producer co-operative, inasmuch as it involves exclusion of non-target group members or transfer of assets from rich to poor (e.g. land reform). These difficulties are compounded by the fact that the poor are very seldom 'a single class having a clear perception of its common interests and of how to act in order to secure them',[7] and by the fact that they are often far removed, by distance and by poverty itself, from ability to benefit from the services which the government makes available.[8] Redistribution of income between nations by means of economic aid takes place in the absence of many of the institutions which assist it in developed countries (e.g. social security and unemployment benefit offices) and in face of many political pressures which obstruct it. Any judgement which is made on the effectiveness of aid as a redistributive tool should reflect awareness of the political constraints to which it is subject.

6.2   IMPACT ON INTER-COUNTRY DISTRIBUTION

We begin by considering the simplest concept of redistribution attempted by aid flows, that which takes place between countries. Table 6.1 relates aid flows to income for all countries for which comparable data exist. These countries are grouped in order of their per capita income in 1981; income rises as we move down the table. The third column of the table, broadly speaking, diminishes as we move from the poorest to the richest income groups: that is, the poorer developing countries receive more aid as a proportion of their GNP than the richer ones. However, there are a number of exceptions to this pattern, which are illustrated by the graph of Figure 6.1. First, the two largest developing countries, China and India, receive far less aid in proportion to their GNP than the norm for countries of their income level. Second, there is a tendency for small countries, particularly but not exclusively in Francophone Africa, to receive more aid than the norm whatever their per capita income. Third, as we saw in Chapter 2, developing countries which are thought to be of particular geopolitical significance to the United States, such as Somalia, Egypt, Syria and most of all Jordan, again get more aid than the norm. So many are the exceptions that the measured statistical relationship between the level of GNP and aid as a percentage of GNP comes out as scarcely significant.[9] Significant it nonetheless is, and we can therefore say that, in the limited sense here considered, the inter-country distribution of aid is progressive. Figure 6.2 formally illustrates this point in the form of a 'Lorenz curve' which is simply a

Table 6.1: *101 developed and less developed countries: classification by income and net aid flows, 1970–80*

(1)	(2)	(3)	(4)		(5)		(6)	(7)
			Share of world GNP, average 1970–80:		Cumulative share of world GNP, average 1970–80:			
Income group (countries in brackets are poorest and richest within each decile)	Average GNP/head, 1981 (US dollars)	Aid flow as a percentage of GNP, average 1970–80 (+ = net inflow) (− = net outflow)	(a) actual	(b) hypothetical, without aid flows	(a) actual	(b) hypothetical, without aid flows	Share of world population, 1981	Cumulative share of population 1981
Poorest 10% (Chad–Uganda)	180	+ 5.6	0.5	0.4	0.5	0.4	6.2	6.2
Second decile (Burundi–Haiti)	273	+ 2.3[b]	5.2	5.1	5.7	5.5	45.2	51.4
Third decile (Sri Lanka–Ghana)	336	+ 4.6	0.6	0.5	6.3	6.0	4.2	55.6
Fourth decile (Kenya–Honduras)	502	+ 3.3	0.7	0.7	7.0	6.7	5.0	60.6

Fifth decile (Zambia–Nigeria)	771	+ 2.5	1.7	1.6	8.7	8.3	6.9	67.5
Sixth decile (Zamabwe–Colombia)	1,137	+ 1.3	0.9	0.8	9.6	9.1	2.4	69.9
Seventh decile (Tunisia–Malaysia)	1,625	+ 1.2	2.6	2.5	12.2	11.6	4.4	74.3
Eighth decile (Panama–Venezuela)	2,835	+ 0.2	5.2	5.2	17.4	16.8	6.9	81.2
Ninth decile (Hong Kong–Finland)	7,595	– 0.2	26.1	26.1	43.5	42.9	7.4	88.6
Richest 10% (Australia–Switzerland)	13,102	– 0.4	56.4	56.6	100	100	11.4	100

Sources and definitions:
GNP and population data for 1981 are from World Bank, *World Development Report 1983*, appendix Table 1. Aid flow is 'net overseas development assistance' as defined by OECD and as reported in their *Geographical Distribution of Financial Flows to Less Developed Countries*, various issues from 1973 to 1983, which is also the source for GNP data for years from 1970 to 1980.

[a]The analysis covers 101 developed and less developed countries for which data are given in successive World Bank *World Development Reports*. Many centrally planned economies, including the Soviet Union, are excluded. A listing of all data is given in Appendix I to this chapter.

[b]This average does not include China, for which aid data are unavailable for most years between 1970 and 1980.

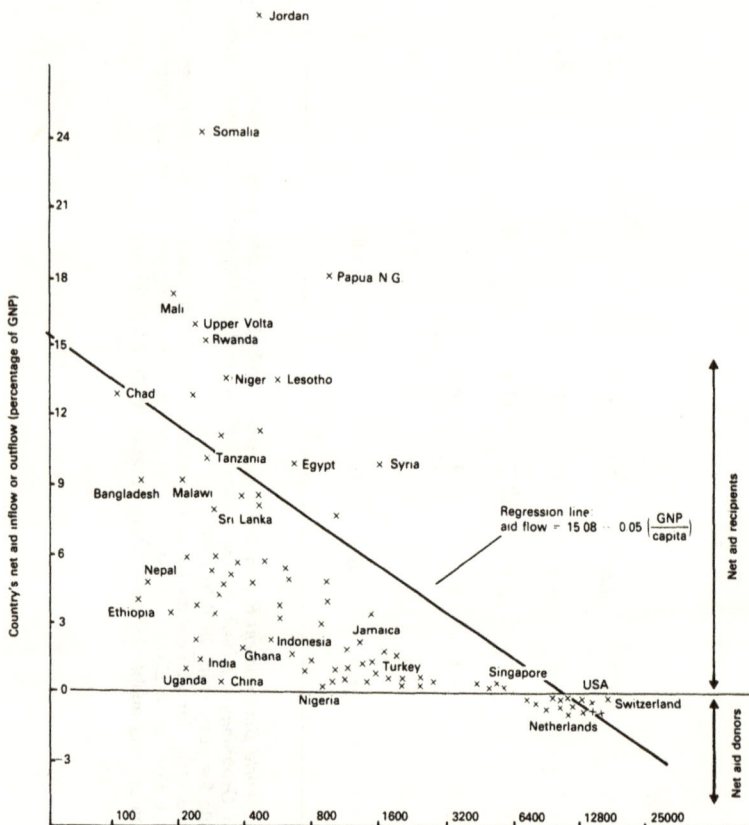

Figure 6.1: 101 developed and less developed countries: net aid inflow or outflow (as percentage of GNP) in relation to per capita GNP, 1970–1980 Source: Appendix I to this chapter.

graph of the cumulative data on population and income for each decile reported in columns 5 and 7 of Table 6.1. The Lorenz curve for the actual inter-country distribution of income lies entirely inside the curve for the distribution which results if each aid recipient's net aid inflow is sub-tracted from, and each aid donor's net aid outflow is added to, its per capita GNP. Thus, if this method of comparing the situation with and without aid flows is accepted, aid does indeed reduce inter-country inequality, perhaps by about one percentage point: the Gini coefficient of inequality, that is, the area between the Lorenz curve and

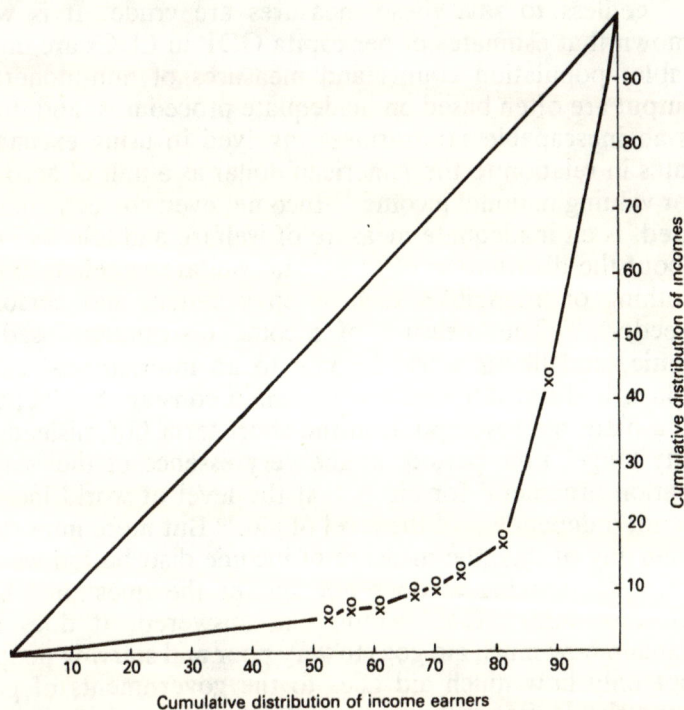

Figure 6.2: 101 developed and less developed countries: inter-country distribution of income with and without aid flows, 1970–80
Source: Table 6.1, columns 5 and 7.
o—o—o Actual distribution of income.
x—x—x Hypothetical distribution of income 'without aid'.

the diagonal as a proportion of the total area under the diagonal, can be calculated from Table 6.1 as 45.3 per cent for the actual situation with aid, and 46.1 per cent for the hypothetical situation without aid flows.[10] By any standards, this represents only mild progressivity; as an illustration, if the current volume of aid were to be concentrated on the poorest countries by removing all aid from countries with a 1981 per capita income in excess of $600—that is to say, countries from the fifth decile upwards—and reallocating it *pro rata* among the forty poorest countries, the Gini coefficient of inequality would fall from 45.3 to 43 per cent.

Needless to say, these measures are crude. It is well known that estimates of per capita GDP in LDCs are unreliable: population counts and measures of non-monetary output are often based on inadequate procedures, and there is an inescapable arbitrariness involved in using exchange rates in relation to the American dollar as a unit of account for valuing national income.[11] Income, even correctly measured, is an inadequate measure of welfare and tells us little about the distribution of assets and welfare benefits, to say nothing of intangibles such as environment and personal freedom.[12] The measure of income distribution used is static, and likens world income to an international cake, which if sliced differently will remain constant in size; this is a plausible assumption in the short term but misleads in any longer time period, as the very essence of the 'stabilisation argument' for aid is that the level of world income is not independent of the level of aid.[13] But more important than any of this, the measure of income distribution we are currently looking at does not answer the question which most students of aid would like answered. It does not explain how much aid goes to very poor and starving people, but only how much aid goes to the governments of poor countries.[14] Bauer has provocatively stated that the distribution of aid between persons: 'is inevitably partly regressive, because many taxpayers in donor countries are poorer than many people in recipient countries ... (and) foreign aid benefits better-off people within the recipient countries'.[15]

The first part of this proposition is dubious, since in every donor country very poor people pay no tax at all, and people who are slightly less poor derive benefits from free health services, housing allowances, education allowances and other welfare benefits which at least counterbalance their tax payments, and hence make no net input to the aid programme. It has been calculated that in the United Kingdom 'no net contribution to the Exchequer and, by implication, to the UK aid programme was made by anyone earning less than 60 per cent of the average national income per capita'.[16] The same assumption probably holds good for other OECD donor countries.[17] Poor people, then, do not finance official aid programmes. But this leaves unanswered the other half of Bauer's claim. Is it the poor who *benefit* from official aid programmes?

6.3 IMPACT ON INTER-PERSONAL DISTRIBUTION: EVIDENCE

We must begin with a warning. The quality of the data available for the analysis of the distributional effects of aid programmes within countries is very poor.[18] The rhetorical arguments presented in support of overseas aid programmes may represent it as a fight against poverty, but out of several thousand aid projects which have been completed since the 1950s there is only a handful on which anyone has even made the attempt to find out whether the poor got any benefit from them, and when the attempt has been made the methods used have often been too weak for the results obtained to be described as a scientific measure of aid effectiveness. The available information on that handful is summarised in Table 6.2, but before we get there it is worth pausing to enquire into the reason for this truly extraordinary gap in our knowledge.

It must first be admitted that poor people in developing countries are not an easy 'target group' about whom to gather information. They live in shanty-towns, or in rural areas well away from the road, so that they are often not even known to government officers, whose job it is to prepare projects for aid finance. If contacted, they often prove to be illiterate, unwell, and suspicious of external agencies, and for this combination of reasons unable to provide reliable information on their material circumstances or 'needs' to such officers.[19] If sympathy and ingenuity do manage to elicit reliable information, then very frequently it will relate—given the usual operating procedures of evaluation agencies[20]—only to one short period, usually at the end of the project, when the evaluation team are present, and hence be unreliable for ascertaining the impact of the project on poverty. There is little doubt that any exercise to find out the effects of an aid project on income distribution does involve much more and much harder work than, for example, finding out *ex post* rates of return, which itself is frequently not attempted.[21]

But the mere difficulty of eliciting information does not explain the decision of aid agencies, except in a very few cases, to capitulate to the problem rather than to try and overcome it. To understand that decision we have to go back to the analysis of the internal politics of aid agencies presented in Chapter 3. We there argued that not one of the major interest groups within a donor agency would have anything to gain from a determined investigation of the poverty impact of aid projects.[22] Administrators wish to move aid money as expeditiously as is consistent with the avoidance of embarrassing technical hitches. Professional advisers (doctors, economists, engineers and so on) wish to help them avoid those technical hitches, but they will work to terms of reference supplied by the administrators, and unless asked to look at a project's effects on target groups they will not think it their job, except in rare cases, to become involved in such investigations on their own initiative. Project staff and aid attachés within developing country embassies, again, will normally work to terms of reference supplied from head office; in the rare cases where such staff exceed themselves and insist on an investigation of poverty focus, they often find themselves asked to stop being a nuisance and if they persist, are shifted elsewhere.[23] This leaves the evaluation department themselves. Formally they work to terms of reference which do instruct them to calculate the income-distribution effects of projects.[24] But they only, in practice, bother to do so in the rare cases (cited in Table 6.2 below) where the evaluator has a strong personal interest in income distribution. In all other cases they are deterred: by the known indifference of other branches of the office, by the technical difficulty of the exercise,[25] or by sheer muddled thinking about the nature of the job involved. The first two of these tendencies have been discussed above; a good example of the third is provided by the World Bank's Report *Focus on Poverty* (World Bank (1982a)) which manages to get through nearly 40 pages without ever saying what effect any of its projects had on any income group. It uses *rate of return on small-farmer projects* and *number of farmers reached by such projects* as indicators of the success of its policy of poverty-focused rural development, indicators which are indeed interesting but which tell us nothing about who got the benefit from those projects.[26] It should be added in conclusion that the governments of developing countries seldom exert any independent pressure for the investigation of income-distribution effects of aid.[27]

Information on who gains from aid, then, is poor and scanty. In our view, this is a disgrace. What we have is summarised in Table 6.2, which lists all the aid-financed projects on which a measurement of poverty impact has been attempted. All of them were explicitly poverty-focused in intention, so the sample is not representative of aid-financed projects as a whole. In addition, the evaluation studies differ in methodology (some comparing the project area 'before and after' and others attempting inferences from a 'snapshot' at a point in time), in their characterisation of income groups (some dividing the population of the project area into income deciles, some into 'rich' and 'poor' and some simply into small farmers and others), and in the precision with which effects on the chosen income groups are measured. Inference is therefore tricky. The pattern which leaps to the surface is that aid projects can help the poor, but not the poorest. Muda irrigation assisted the holders of irrigated rice plots, including small ones, but may have damaged the welfare of migrant casual labourers from Thailand; Nepal Rural Roads increased the income of lorry drivers and commercial farmers but impoverished the hill porters whose services were no longer required; Cajamarca Agricultural Development assisted exclusively dairy farmers, none of whom featured in the bottom two deciles of the income distribution; Noakhali Integrated Rural Development was of assistance to the poorest 40 per cent but not the poorest 10 per cent. And so on, with no exceptions apart from Calcutta Urban Development[28] and Uttar Pradesh Agricultural Credit, where the bottom category of the income distribution is too large for us to know whether the genuinely destitute—say the bottom 10 per cent in the

Table 6.2: Effects of aid-financed projects on poverty

(1) Project	(2) Sponsor	(3) Analyst and bibliographical reference	Method	Categorisation of income groups	Summary of results	Ex post rate of return (%)
Muda, Malaysia	World Bank	Bell et al. (1983)	'Before' and 'after' study with sectoral input-output table	Occupational groups	Benefits to all holders of rice plots; possibly some loss to migrant workers	20
Noakhali Bangladesh	DANIDA	DANIDA Board of Auditors (1982)	'Before' and 'after' study	Deciles	Bottom 40% benefited; bottom 10% did not benefit	N/A
Roads, West Central Nepal	UK/ODA	Blaikie et al. (1977)	'Before' and 'after' study	Occupational groups	Gain to road transporters (mostly rich), loss to foot-porters (mostly poor)	N/A
Lam Pao irrigation	UK/ODA	R. C. Y. Ng and associates (1978)	'Before' and 'after' study	Deciles	Some benefit to all income groups	N/A
Cajamarca agriculture development, Peru	UK/ODA	Mosley and Lawrence-Jones (1984)	Cross-section study	Deciles	Little technical assistance reaching poorest groups	N/A

Project	Source	Study type	Occupational groups	Distribution of benefits	Rate of return
Calcutta urban development, India	World Bank staff (1982c)	Cross-section study	Occupational groups	Some redistribution of urban services to the poor	10[a]
Uttar Pradesh agricultural credit, India	World Bank staff (1980)	'Before' and 'after' study	'Rich', 'medium' and 'poor' farmers	All income groups gained	25–39
Guatemala agricultural development	Juan F. Rada (1979)	Subjective judgement	'Rich' and 'poor' farmers	'Rich' gained, 'poor' lost	N/A
Small farmer development programme, Nepal	Marsh and Dahal (1984)	'Before' and 'after' study	Stratification by landholdings	Little benefit to farmers with below-average landholdings	N/A
Agricultural refinance development corporation I and II, India	World Bank (with ODA, CIDA, EEC)	'Before' and 'after' study	'Large' and 'small' farmers	All income groups gained	23–30

[a] *Ex ante* rate of return, *ex post* re-estimate not made.
Sources: As listed in column 3 (see bibliography for full reference).

project area—actually benefited. It is stressed by more than one aid donor that these achievements in poverty reduction do not have to be traded for reductions in the *ex post* rate of return,[29] but this is really beside the point: official aid seems not to be capable of reaching those at the very bottom of the income scale,[30] except of course with emergency famine relief, which falls outside our direct purview. Why is this and can matters be improved?

Before we proceed let us introduce some new terminology. Let us define the proportion in which the initial aid disbursement is shared out between rich and poor recipients as the *first-round effect*, and the proportion of the first-round effects which accrues to different income groups as the *linkage*. Thus, if we consider an integrated rural development project whose purpose is to increase the incomes of farmers in an underdeveloped region of the Sudan, the first-round effect is the ratio in which the initial aid money divides between rich farmers, poor farmers, government agencies, civil-engineering contractors, and other beneficiaries, whereas the linkage effects measure the extent to which the money thus received by government agencies, rich farmers and so on is spent on purchases from, for example, poor farmers. Money thus transferred between income groups through linkage effects is then spent again on purchases from other income groups, and so on until the entire initial stimulus to the recipient economy administered by aid has been absorbed in leakages such as savings, imports and taxation. What we are considering is a multiplier process analogous to that which is examined in macroeconomics or in input–output analysis.[31] If a donor agency is to help poor people effectively it must understand what keeps them poor, and in particular what determines the shape of the first-round and linkage effects, and whether these effects can be altered by judicious action on the part of aid donors and recipients. These questions are considered in Sections 6.4 and 6.5 respectively.

6.4 DETERMINANTS OF FIRST-ROUND EFFECT AND OF LINKAGE

Conventionally, aid 'aids' by transferring a capital asset, free or at low cost, into the hands of a poor person or group. (It may also transfer consumption goods; this is considered later on.) Whether this can be done successfully depends on at least three considerations. Technology determines whether the capital asset transferred is one which the poor can use; politics determines whether they can retain control over its use; and economic structure, in conjunction with politics, determine the shape of second-round and later linkages. Let us elaborate.

Technology and complementary assets
In most branches of economic activity it is possible to assist the poor directly only if the capital asset transferred to them is of a particular type. Consider energy. This can be generated by various methods: nuclear fission; burning oil, gas or coal in power stations; harnessing hydropower or geothermal energy; utilising crop and animal wastes; and, finally, burning kerosene or wood. Of these methods, only the last two are of any use to a poor household; the others are too big and complex to use within the home or even the village.[32] However, the vast majority of aid-financed energy projects consist of hydroelectric or coal-fired power stations. In Kenya, for example, 73 per cent of final demand for energy (and probably all demand from poor people) takes the form of wood fuel, charcoal and crop wastes, yet only 7 per cent of aid commitments to the energy sector are intended to generate energy by these means.[33] Consider credit. In the shanty-towns of Mathare Valley, Nairobi, 'lack of tools' and 'lack of loans' were cited as two of the three major constraints facing small businessmen by respondents to the one serious empirical survey of the sector that has been done, and the maximum size of loan required was usually (in 1976) 5,000 shillings, or about £300.[34] However, this figure is less than one-third of the minimum loan ever given by any of Kenya's three aid-financed development banks,[35] with the consequence that carpenters and

metalworkers in the shanty-towns effectively have no access to commercial credit, aid-financed or not. In Nepal, an aid-backed group credit scheme explicitly designed to assist poorer farmers has been demonstrated, in the Kosi Hill area, to be making loans to farmers with land-holdings higher than the regional average.[36] Finally, consider housing. The costs of land purchase in almost any urban area in the Third World force any commercial housing company to push rents on even the most modest accommodation up beyond the means of poor families,[37] so that even 'site and service' schemes financed by overseas aid find themselves occupied by people from well outside the bottom decile of the income distribution. A good example is the World Bank's Botswana Second Urban Project where the staff appraisal report is forced to admit that the bottom decile of the population of Gaborone and Francistown had no access even to the cheapest conceivable form of Bank-financed housing.[38] As a consequence they have to continue, as they always have done, in illegal squats.

In short, even if aid helps to remedy a market failure in terms of general lending to the poorest countries, a hole in the market remains at the bottom end. What the poor want to buy is small and simple; what the aid agencies offer them is very often large and complex. The problem has many roots. One is sheer economies of scale: it is much cheaper in terms of administrative cost to supply one loan of $10 million, than ten thousand loans of $1,000, or one giant hydropower station at $20 million rather than twenty micro-hydrogenerators at $1 million, let alone fifty thousand kerosene stoves at $400. Another, of course, is commercial pressure: hydropower stations are much more import intensive than kerosene or wood stoves, and diesel-powered water pumps use more imported spares than shallow wells or protected springs, so that any technical advice which the aid agency takes from sources with an interest in exporting to the Third World will always tend to favour the capital-intensive option. However, the problem is not simply a problem of passive administrators in aid agencies being rolled over by their accountants and by the industry lobby. The accountants have relatively little power in a bilateral agency, as we saw in Chapter 3, since such agencies do not have to worry about profits, nor therefore about cost-effectiveness, which is often not even examined;[39] and the industry lobby is only, even in France and Japan, a lobby, not an arbiter.[40] Moreover, there exist well-documented cases where aid agencies have changed their technology in the course of a project's life so that the poor can benefit from it more, for example a project for rural water supply in Tanzania, which was changed by SIDA from a technology based on diesel pumps and steel pipes to a simpler one based on shallow wells (requiring no pumps) and bamboo pipes when central financial constraints made the former technology inoperative,[41] and a project for rural roads in Kenya, supported by several donors under the leadership of the World Bank, which gradually evolved from a bull-dozer to a crowbar and shovel (labour-intensive) technology between 1975 and 1980.[42] Often the best available technology has been chosen in time where the donors had the percipience to learn on the job;[43] but it was seldom chosen initially. We submit that this is because donor and recipient, having once reached agreement in principle on the desir-ability of a particular project in a particular area, both have a political motive to rush into a quick decision on the technical specification. The donor spends his budget, and the recipient politician (and civil servant) earns the support of his home 'constituency'.[44] In such circumstances the con-tract will go to the first set of consultants who submit a proposal which looks feasible, rather than to those who are best capable of assisting the poor. In the case of multilateral agencies such as the World Bank, things are a little better, in the sense that the contract is put out to competitive tender; but even there the problem remains that projects may be based on imported technology and equipment where a local technology might have done better. Very seldom, in such cases, are poor local people themselves, who often have highly relevant knowledge particularly in relation to agricultural technology, consulted on what they themselves want.[45] I have heard this practice defended by a British aid official on the grounds that 'when you make a decision on how to treat a disease you consult the doctor, not the patient'.

Once aid donors choose the area in which they are going to operate, of course, they often predetermine the choice of technology and scale, and thereby the beneficiary group. We have seen an example of this in the case of energy: once donors have decided that they are going to supply a power station or an aeroplane, they commit themselves to a technical option which is capital-intensive, import-intensive, and cannot help the poor directly; such things simply cannot be engineered any other way.[46] Likewise if an aid donor makes a policy decision to support research on coffee rather than sorghum or on cattle rather than on goats or donkeys, it is clear that the relatively better-off farmers will benefit. The effective choice is made further back, at the sectoral or sub-sectoral rather than the project level: once donors make a decision to specialise in agriculture, in rural roads or in construction more generally they open up the possibility, although only the possibility, of channelling first-round benefits to the poor. The absence of any sectoral strategy is very nearly a guarantee that they will find it difficult to do so.

Local Political and Economic Structure
If donors and recipients between them do manage to design projects that are small, simple, local-cost intensive, and provide what the poor actually want, this is only a necessary, and by no means a sufficient, condition of a positive first-round impact on poverty. There is also the risk, if the input being supplied by aid is wanted by the rich and purchasable by them, that some project benefits will flow to the rich. This description does not apply to 'inferior goods' and services, for example technical help with sorghum, millets, donkeys, brewing local beer. Nor does it apply to services in which property rights cannot be purchased, for example roads, communal forestry development. But it certainly applies to the classical inputs of the process of rural development—land, water, fertiliser, health services, education, transport and most of all credit. In all of these cases the rich will buy what they need on the open market if that is possible, and on the black market if access to the open market is rationed by state action in the interests of the

poor: and if for any reason a black market does not develop, the rich may simply use their control of administrative and legal processes at village level to wreck the entire scheme. Usually it is not necessary. A relevant example is the Small Farmers' Development Programme, instituted to provide credit to groups of farmers in Asian countries who, lacking collateral, would not be eligible for loans from commercial banks. In Nepal finance was provided by the Asian Development Bank, ODA, USAID and UNICEF, and the programme was most conscientiously administered: group organisers, acting on behalf of the Agricultural Development Bank, were required to fill in a questionnaire setting out the income, land holdings, livestock holdings, other capital assets, and non-agricultural income of each inhabitant in every locality where a group stood a chance of being formed. The intention was to exclude from group membership all but poor farmers. But group organisers knew that they would be judged by the speed with which they got groups formed: like their counterparts in overseas aid agencies, they had a budget to spend.[47] Consequently, rather than carry out elaborate field research on village income and expenditure, they made quick rough guesses, and condoned the entry into 'small farmer groups' of a good many rather large farmers. The borrowing groups themselves did the rest spontaneously: frequently they expelled poor or landless farmers from their circles, fearing that people without reserves might be unable to pay their share of the money owed by the group, and thus place a greater financial burden on their own shoulders. The aid donors who financed the Small Farmer Development Programme were powerless to interfere with such processes of self-selection, which themselves were unable to prevent rapidly escalating rates of arrears.[48]

The story just told of the SFDP could be repeated for practically every project which has attempted to make available to the poor means of production which can be freely bought and sold. It illustrates the political balancing act which is required of every agency which tries to implement a poverty-focused development project, namely somehow to make enough concessions to local elites that they are persuaded to abstain from wrecking the project, but not so many concessions that the ultimate objective of assisting poor people is aborted. This is a tightrope which some poverty-focused projects have managed to walk. But many others have fallen off it into the abyss, either destroyed by the opposition of the rich, or less spectacularly diluted into impotence by their too enthusiastic support.[49]

The essence of the argument can be conveyed by Table 6.3. If the population of a rural aid project's target area is arbitrarily divided into the 'village elite' and the 'poor' then the project may have nine possible outcomes, as set out in the Table.

Examples of projects which may lead to each outcome are included in each case. The four in which neither group gains (5, 6, 8 and 9) are, however, of no interest to any party. Cases 4 and 7 are of interest to the village elite but

Table 6.3: Possible distributional outcomes of an aid project

Poor \ Village elite	Gain	Stay in same position	Lose
Gain	1	2 Hospital for untouchables; credit reserved for small farmers	3 Land reform without compensation
Stay in same position	4 Technical assistance with tractor cultivation	5	6
Lose	7 Fencing of communal cattle land	8	9

not, one presumes, to the aid donor. This leaves 1, 2 and 3; but 3 will, one presumes, be blocked by the rural elite: at the village as well as the national level, in all probability, redistribution is only possible from growth if existing power-structures remain in place.[50] Thus project categories 1 and 2 are the only starters; but there is always the risk that the rich will capture the major part of such benefits as are on offer, simply by using their power in the market. There is no way that donors can prevent this except by confining their aid to projects whose output is only produced by the poor (subsistence crops?), or whose services are allocated by a non-market process (roads).

If the local economic and political structure constrains the size and allocation between income groups of the first-round effects of projects, it dominates the linkage effects. The linkages we are interested in are the flows of money and of benefits in kind from the beneficiaries of first-round effects to poor people, particularly poor people within the project area. Each of those flows consists of a quantity multiplied by a price: hence we have two questions to deal with:

(1) What determines the quantity and type of services which beneficiaries of first-round effects will buy from the poor?
(2) What determines the *price* at which they will buy those services?

For one poor Andean village an indication of the answer to the first question is given by Table 6.4, which catalogues the purchases of different income groups by category for the year 1981. Of the village's entire expenditure in that year, only 32 per cent constituted potential linkages, that is, purchases of items which the Poor and Destitute groups were *in principle able* to supply: crops, meat and labour. All the other elements of the village's expenditure demanded, for their production, inputs which the poor and destitute did not possess. Furthermore, only one-tenth of the potential linkages were actually realised, since the actual proportion of total village expenditure which went on pur-

Table 6.4: Catilluc Valley, Peru 1981: pattern of expenditures by income group (in thousands of soles per annum)

Income group Type of expenditure	Rich (most prosperous 10%, average cash income = 4511)	Medium (second to sixth decile, average family cash income = 1523)	Poor (seventh to ninth decile, average family cash income = 419)	Destitute (poorest 10% of sample, average family cash income = 41)
Farm inputs:				
Transport	34.5	22.6	16.9	12.2
Equipment	3.0	0.6	0.8	0.2
Fertilisers	47.7	32.2	17.2	7.6
Labour[a]	241.0	146.5	34.5	—
Livestock	88.5	150.9	42.1	9.5
Consumption goods:				
Food: meat[a] grains and vegetables[a] other	239.9	217.0	170.1	107.3
Drink	165.2	110.9	46.1	24.2
Consumer durables	305.0	206.2	145.2	23.1
Clothing	65.0	49.1	22.0	9.6
Other	140.2	52.0	16.9	0.5

Source: Mosley and Lawrence-Jones (1984), Table IV.13.

[a]Goods and services supplied by the Poor and Destitute income groups.

chases from the Poor and Destitute in 1981 was only 3 per cent. Overwhelmingly these purchases took the form of hiring of unskilled labour.

What will now be obvious is the link between the *form* in which the first-round stimulus is given and the linkage effect to the poor. If that stimulus puts additional means of production in the hands of the poor (land, weaving looms, pumps to lift irrigation water), it will increase the range of goods and services which the poor can produce, and enlarge the potential linkage over the long term. If it leads to large demands for unskilled labour, the thing which the poor can most easily supply (e.g. rural roads, dams, soil conservation works) it will at least enlarge the potential linkage over the short term.[51] If the stimulus consists of consumption goods (e.g. food aid) the effect on linkage will be zero. And if it consists of an investment which reduces the demand for labour (e.g. help with tractor cultivation) then its effect on linkage will be negative.[52]

We now consider the second element of linkages between poor income groups and the immediate beneficiaries of aid, namely the price at which they take place. The essential point here is that most goods and services which the poor supply in the Third World villages, and shanty-towns also, are not traded in a perfect market, but are sold at prices which vary according to the bargaining relationship between buyer and seller.[53] If the buyer has some sort of political hold over the seller, then the price at which the transaction takes place will fall *pro tanto*. One individual amongst the thousand million rural poor will illustrate this. A Peruvian widow aged 26 with three children, she sold the milk produced by her three cows at 35 soles per litre against a village average of over 60 soles, and her labour at 300 soles per day against a village average of 450 soles, in both cases to a neighbouring large farmer, through whose land she had to pass to get to the village. This farmer provided her with Christmas presents, sold her cheap firewood and provided a sort of education for her eldest child.[54] A theoretical economist might well have asked her why she sold her labour and her milk in a market other than the best available, or why she did not seek to enlarge her own income by pooling her milk with other farmers and selling it to the ultimate buyer at a higher price; he would have been told that to do so would certainly have put her concessionary firewood and nursery-school facilities at risk, and might have led to threats against her freedom of movement or even her life. The law, in underdeveloped rural areas, is usually powerless against such threats from powerful people, even if the powerless know how to invoke it.

Hence, as Chambers eloquently argues, the bargaining power of the poor is itself poor.[55] In proportion as this forces them to accept prices below the best available for what little they have to sell, the linkage coefficients between them and other groups will be pushed down. There is nothing external aid agencies can do directly, within the existing framework of law and society in developing countries, to subvert such quasi-feudal social relationships.

But awareness of those relationships should encourage them to do what they can to place productive assets in the hands of the poor at the first-round, and not to delude themselves that the poor will eventually benefit through mechanisms of 'linkage' or 'trickle-down'. Those mechanisms can readily be seen, except perhaps in the fast-growing and labour-intensive economies of the Far East, to be virtually inoperative. And those are not the countries which are currently in need of aid.

Possibilities for Fiscal Redistribution

Awareness of the difficulties of achieving a first-round redistribution to the poor, or of augmenting linkage, through projects has caused some commentators to despair of this avenue of approach to the problem. Hayter and Watson, for example, argue as follows:

The 1974–9 Labour Government in Britain had a policy of 'aid to the poorest people in the poorest countries'. The philosophy was not much different from that expounded by McNamara when he was President of the World Bank ... (but) in practice it nearly always ends up in the pockets of the elites or the relatively well-off, when they control the state ... The policy is unworkable.[56]

In the light of the discussion so far, that view, which is

backed up by no empirical evidence of its own, is over-pessimistic. But it is important to consider the alternative avenue of approach to redistribution through aid, which is to confine it to those governments which redistribute income through public expenditure and taxation. Such governments, as Jolly argues, do not need to be subjected to the discipline of project tying:

Much greater priority (in aid policy) should be provided to countries whose development policies showed an open and effective commitment to poverty-focussed strategies ... If a country's policies are clearly set in this direction and it has the capacity to implement them, then effective, genuine, untied programme aid support is the most effective assistance that can be given.[57]

And so say all of us; but where are those governments? Again, we are handicapped by bad data—on income distribution in LDCs as such and *a fortiori* on the ability of their governments to influence such distribution.[58] But the following consensus is discernible.

Tax policy in most countries redistributes only between the rich and the urban (formal-sector) working class; it is often regressive in relation to the rural areas, reinforcing 'urban bias'.[59] Public expenditure policy may reach further down the income scale, providing selectively with one hand what the systems of taxation and crop pricing take away less visibly with the other, but most of its benefits probably go to the urban middle classes, as in developed countries[60] all but the poorest of all, lying largely outside the cash economy, are neither taxed nor the recipients of a social wage and hence affected neither one way nor the other. Papanek's conclusion is that: 'apparently ... Sri Lanka represents the only case among less developed countries where income distribution became significantly more equal as a result of deliberate government policies, short of a revolutionary change'.[61] This is probably harsh on Jamaica, Malaysia[62] and Tanzania in the 1970s. But any attempt to expand the list to a size where it will account for even a large part of an existing aid programme quickly runs into embarrassment. The only donor to have explicitly announced an intention to concentrate aid on countries

whose governments were redistributive is Holland under
the inspiration of Jan Pronk betwen 1973 and 1977. But the
need to spend the aid budget somehow forced the Dutch
government into announcing a list of 'concentration countries',[63] some of which, such as Kenya, Indonesia and Bangladesh, could scarcely be described as having redistributive
governments by the most generous possible standard. The
task of donors is even harder now. All three of the countries
identified above as most progressive—Sri Lanka, Tanzania
and Jamaica—have been forced to cut back severely on
their welfare payments and food subsidies since 1978 in
stabilisation programmes whose detail was actually drafted
and imposed on them by the aid donors themselves.[64] As
members of the Executive Board of the World Bank and
IMF, who provided the spearhead of the pressures towards
a reduction of government welfare spending in each of those
countries, those donors bear responsibility for erasing at the
macro-level much of the good they have attempted to do
by concentrating their aid on the most fiscally progressive
of Third World governments.

All is not lost. Not all aid passes through central governments, and in many cases it has proved possible to increase
the redistributive effect of aid by channelling it through the
government of a state, city council or development authority
which has a better reputation for concern with the poor
than the central government: for example, the state governments of Maharashtra, Kerala and West Bengal in India.[65]
More than this, the donor can actually make such authorities
more progressive by imposing on them policies that will
assist the poor, for example by requiring a water authority
to supply free water to the poorer villages, as SIDA
attempted to do in Kenya. For such conditionality to stick
the donor needs to be in a strong bargaining position in
relation to the recipient, and not to be in competition with
other donors offering conflicting advice. But such situations
exist. If aid donors were to use conditionality less to impose
'outward-looking' policies on the recipient and more as an
instrument to persuade them to do more for their own
disadvantaged groups then, in the present author's view,
that might help the device to retrieve something of its

currently tarnished reputation. This theme is further developed in Chapter 8.

6.5 CONCLUSION: WHAT CAN BE DONE?

Desire to help the very poor in the Third World is—still—at the centre of every aid agency's rhetoric. But that desire does not penetrate very far into administrative procedures, so that such help as the poor and destitute get from aid is largely adventitious rather than the consequence of rational action to that end by the donors. In our view it is none the worse for that. Perhaps, in these spheres, the right thing always has to be done for the wrong reasons.

Perhaps, however, it can be better done. Our statistical work suggests that *between countries* aid does manage to shift resources in favour of the poor, although, to put matters in perspective, even an annual flow of resources in excess of $40 billion reduces inter-country inequality, as conventionally measured, by less than 1 per cent. More could be achieved at this level by cutting the middle-income countries out from aid altogether; but apart from the opposition this would encounter from the defence and commercial lobbies, it may even be regressive as between persons. Brazil is a middle-income country, but it still contains in the north-east of the country a large number of people who are close to starvation.

A more meaningful measure of aid's redistributive ability, then, is its impact on the welfare of very poor people. The very inadequate evidence which we have suggests that that minority of projects which are aimed at them, help the poor but not the poorest. We identified three likely explanations for this: inappropriate technology, born of simple lack of awareness but aided and abetted by commercial pressure and local cost constraints within donor agencies; opposition to poverty-focused projects from local elites; and a tendency for districts in which poverty-focused projects take place to be 'very open economies', with the consequence that local linkage effects are very small. These difficulties have appeared to some observers so deep rooted as to make them despair of aid projects as a vehicle for assisting the poor. Such observers, asked to suggest an alternative, usually recommend programme aid for governments which can be trusted to act in support of the poor; but of these, as we saw, there are very few. Another alternative frequently suggested is that official agencies should disburse more of their budget through non-governmental organisations such as OXFAM, Save the Children Fund and World Vision, which are widely believed to be 'good at reaching the poor'.[66] They may be, although we do not know this, since voluntary organisations have so far done very little to evaluate their own operations.[67] But even if the proposition is accepted, they account for only some 2 to 5 per cent of all resource flows to LDCs,[68] and hence there is no possibility that a large proportion of present aid flows (see Table 6.5, Appendix I) could be redirected to the poor by switching them to private voluntary agencies. A small proportion certainly could, and the recent success of the 'Live Aid' concerts in raising £70 million from the public for famine relief in 1985 (or more than the sum raised by all voluntary agencies in Britain during the year) may be taken as an indicator of the public's anxiety to redirect aid money towards the direct relief of poverty.

It is far from clear, in any case, that the 'project approach' to poverty alleviation has been pushed to its politically feasible limit. Of the constraints to the effectiveness of poverty-focused aid mentioned earlier, three at least seem to derive more from lack of thought than from the existence of any interest group opposed to the removal of the constraint. Local cost quotas for aid projects no longer have any validity in an environment where the balance of payments is no longer a policy target in developed countries, and are essentially an institutional hangover from the era of fixed exchange rates. The spending of aid money on technology biased against the poor, and on research into products which the poor neither produce nor consume, often reflects mere failure to consider alternative blueprints to the first one submitted, rather than a conspiracy to defraud the poor of the Third World. And finally, the fact that the benefits of many projects intended for the poor have been hijacked by the rich reflects, more often than not, failure to think about and anticipate that threat by working out compensatory measures that would deprive the rich of a motive for wrecking tactics. As Chambers has observed, amidst all their sophisticated appraisals of technical and economic feasibility, aid agencies very seldom ask their projects to pass a political feasibility test.[69] It is the more important to stress that such faults of procedure are remediable, because one response to the various initiatives in favour of poverty-focused aid announced in the last dozen years has been to suggest that they have failed, and that therefore we should return to trickle-down.[70] In our view, that inference is mistaken, because the effect of those initiatives has never been properly tested. Agencies have not yet had the opportunity to incorporate the lessons of experience, including those mentioned above, into the new generation of poverty-focused projects. Until they have, any judgement on what aid can do as a redistributive tool would appear to be premature. We are still, for better or worse, in the experimental stage.

APPENDIX I

Table 6.5: Statistics on aid flows and a note on the data

		Average GDP per head 1981 (US dollars)	Population (millions) 1981	Aid flows as a percentage of GNP (average for period stated; – : net outflow) 1970–80
1	Chad	110	4	13.3
2	Bangladesh	140	91	9.0
3	Ethiopia	140	32	3.9
4	Nepal	150	15	4.7
5	Burma	190	34	3.6
6	Afghanistan	250	16	3.8
7	Mali	190	7	17.2
8	Malawi	200	6	9.0
9	Zaire	210	30	5.9
10	Uganda	220	13	0.8
Group average		180		5.6

Table 6.5 (continued)

		Average GDP per head 1981 (US dollars)	Population (millions) 1981	Aid flows as a percentage of GNP (average for period stated; – : net outflow) 1970–80
11	Burundi	230	4	13.2
12	Upper Volta	240	6	15.8
13	Rwanda	250	5	15.2
14	India	260	690	1.4
15	Somalia	280	4	24.3
16	Tanzania	280	19	9.9
17	Vietnam	no data	55	6.1
18	China	300	991	no data
19	Guinea	300	6	3.3
20	Haiti	300	5	5.9
	Group average	273		2.3*
21	Sri Lanka	300	15	7.8
22	Central African Rep.	320	2	11.2
23	Sierra Leone	320	4	4.4
24	Madagascar	330	9	4.6
25	Niger	330	6	3.5
26	Pakistan	350	85	4.7
27	Mozambique	350	12	2.1
28	Sudan	380	19	5.6
29	Togo	380	3	8.6
30	Ghana	400	12	1.7
	Group average	336		4.6

Table 6.5 (continued)

		Average GDP per head 1981 (US dollars)	Population (millions) 1981	Aid flows as a percentage of GNP (average for period stated; – : net outflow) 1970–80
31	Kenya	420	17	4.8
32	Senegal	430	6	8.1
33	Mauritania	460	2	29.2
34	Yemen AR	460	7	8.5
35	Yemen PDR	460	2	11.6
36	Liberia	520	2	5.4
37	Indonesia	530	150	2.1
38	Lesotho	540	1	13.6
39	Bolivia	600	6	3.3
40	Honduras	600	4	3.9
	Group average	502		3.3
41	Zambia	640	6	4.5
42	Egypt	650	43	10.3
43	El Salvador	650	5	1.9
44	Thailand	770	48	1.0
45	Philippines	790	50	1.0
46	Angola	no data	8	1.1
47	Papua NG	840	3	18.1
48	Morocco	860	21	3.0
49	Nicaragua	860	3	4.0
50	Nigeria	870	88	0.2
	Group average	771		2.5
51	Zimbabwe	870	7	0.6
52	Cameroon	880	9	5.1
53	Congo-Brazzaville	1,110	2	7.8
54	Guatemala	1,140	8	1.1
55	Peru	1,170	17	0.9
56	Ecuador	1,180	9	1.0
57	Jamaica	1,180	2	2.0
58	Ivory Coast	1,200	9	2.2
59	Dominican Rep.	1,260	6	1.3
60	Colombia	1,380	26	0.6
	Group average	1,137		1.3

Table 6.5 (continued)

		Average GDP per head 1981 (US dollars)	Population (millions) 1981	Aid flows as a percentage of GNP (average for period stated; – : net outflow) 1970–80
61	Tunisia	1,420	7	4.2
62	Costa Rica	1,436	2	1.3
63	Turkey	1,540	46	0.7
64	Syria	1,570	9	10.4
65	Jordan	1,620	3	27.8
66	Paraguay	1,620	3	1.8
67	South Korea	1,700	39	0.9
68	Iran	no data	40	0.04
69	Iraq	no data	13	0.15
70	Malaysia	1,840	14	0.70
	Group average	1,625		1.2
71	Panama	1,910	2	1.6
72	Lebanon	no data	3	2.9
73	Algeria	2,140	20	0.8
74	Brazil	2,220	121	0.1
75	Mexico	2,250	71	0.1
76	Chile	2,560	11	0.3
77	Argentina	2,560	28	0.1
78	Uruguay	2,820	3	0.3
79	Trinidad	3,670	1	0.02
80	Venezuela	4,220	15	0.4
	Group average	2,835		0.2
81	Hong Kong	5,100	5	0.04
82	Singapore	5,240	2	0.3
83	Ireland (Rep.)	5,230	3	negl.
84	Spain	5,640	38	negl.
85	Italy	6,960	56	−0.13
86	New Zealand	7,700	3	−0.36
87	United Kingdom	9,110	56	−0.43
88	Japan	10,080	118	−0.25
89	Austria	10,210	7	−0.20
90	Finland	10,680	5	−0.17
	Group average	7,595		−0.20

Table 6.5 (continued)

		Average GDP per head 1981 (US dollars)	Population (millions) 1981	Aid flows as a percentage of GNP (average for period stated; – : net outflow) 1970–80
91	Australia	11,08	15	−0.54
92	Canada	11,400	24	−0.48
93	Netherlands	11,790	14	−0.85
94	Belgium	11,920	10	−0.52
95	France	12,190	54	−0.61
96	United States	12,820	230	−0.26
97	Denmark	13,120	5	−0.64
98	Germany, Fed. Rep.	13,450	62	−0.39
99	Norway	14,060	4	−0.75
100	Sweden	14,870	8	−0.81
101	Switzerland	17,430	6	−0.20
Group average		13,102		

Sources: Average GNP per head and population from World Bank, *World Development Report 1983* (Washington 1983). Aid flows as percentage of GNP from OECD, *Geographical Distribution of Financial Flows to Less Developed Countries*, successive issues from 1971 to 1983. Definition of aid used is grant element of net ODA.
*Excludes China.

APPENDIX II   AN ANALYTICAL MODEL OF DISTRIBUTION EFFECTS AND ITS APPLICATION TO ONE RURAL DEVELOPMENT PROJECT IN PERU

We wish to measure the effects of an external injection of money and technical assistance on different income groups within a defined geographical area, in this case the Catilluc valley in the Peruvian Andes, 500 miles north-north-east of Lima. A necessary first step, therefore, is to identify the income groups in which we are interested and the nature of the resource flows between them. Income groups can be defined in relation to some arbitrary classification such as deciles of the income distribution, or in relation to functional categories such as 'the landless', 'tractor owners' and so on. In what follows we shall use the categories 'rich', 'medium', 'poor' and 'destitute' to denote those in the top 10 per cent, the next 50 per cent, the next 30 per cent and the poorest 10 per cent of the income distribution respectively. It happens that in the Andean valley which forms the subject-matter of our empirical case study these divisions mark the major discontinuities in the income distribution, and also correspond to functional divisions: the 'rich' are ex-hacienda owners and farm managers, the 'medium' farmers occupy a privileged position in the marketing structure in the sense of being able to sell their own produce direct to the ultimate buyer, the 'poor' lack this privileged position but own sufficient land and livestock for self-sufficiency, and the 'destitute', all of whom are below the absolute poverty line, have insufficient assets for self-sufficiency and must scrape a living together from casual labour, liquor brewing, sales of handicrafts and so on. The subdivisions in the distribution of income and wealth which are appropriate for an analysis of this sort will, of course, vary from place to place according to the prevailing system of production and exchange.

For the moment, let us consider the pattern of income flows between the four income groups mentioned above. Table 6.6 presents these flows within an input–output framework: A_{ij} stands for a flow of income, in cash or in kind, from one income group to another, the subscripts 1, 2, 3, 4 stand for the rich, medium,

Table 6.6: Income flows between income strata: schematic representation

Purchases from other income groups:	Sales to other income groups:				Sales to outside world
	To rich	To medium	To poor	To destitute	
From rich	A_{11}	A_{12}	A_{13}	A_{14}	Y_1
From medium	A_{21}	A_{22}	A_{23}	A_{24}	Y_2
From poor	A_{31}	A_{32}	A_{33}	A_{34}	Y_3
From destitute	A_{41}	A_{42}	A_{43}	A_{44}	Y_4
Purchases from outside world (plus saving)	P_1	P_2	P_3	P_4	

poor and destitute respectively, and the ordering of the subscripts reflects the direction of a flow. Thus A_1 is an income flow from the rich to the destitute and A_{23} is an income flow from the poor to the middle-income farmers. P_1, P_2, P_3 and P_4 are the purchases of the different income groups from the outside world and Y_1, Y_2, Y_3 and $\bar{Y}_4$ are 'final demands' made by the outside world on the different income groups, that is, the value of the output sold by those income groups to the rest of the world outside the project area. The income of any group is, by definition, the sum of the incomes which it derives from different sources: any income which is derived by the destitute in an Andean valley must come either from the different group within that valley or from the outside world. Thus, letting X_1 stand for the total output of an income group (and disregarding for the moment purchases from the outside world) we may write:

income of the rich: $$X_1 = A_{11} + A_{12} + A_{13} + A_{14} + Y_1$$

income of the medium
farmers: $$X_2 = A_{21} + A_{22} + A_{23} + A_{24} + Y_2$$

income of the poor
farmers: $$X_3 = A_{31} + A_{32} + A_{33} + A_{34} + Y_3$$

income of the destitute
farmers: $$X_4 = A_{41} + A_{42} + A_{43} + A_{44} + Y_4.$$

If we now express each of the flows between income groups as proportions of total output for that income group, and denote these proportions by means of lower-case letters, for example $a_{12} = A_{12}/X_1$ and so on, we have:

income of
the rich $$X_1 = a_{11}X_1 + a_{12}X_2 + a_{13}X_3 + a_{14}X_4 + Y_1$$

income of
the medium $$X_2 = a_{21}X_1 + a_{22}X_2 + a_{23}X_3 + a_{24}X_4 + Y_2$$
farmers:

income of
the poor $$X_3 = a_{31}X_1 + a_{32}X + a_{33}X_3 + a_{34}X_4 + Y_3$$
farmers:

income of
the destitute $$X_4 = a_{41}X_1 + a_{42}X_2 + a_{43}X_3 + a_{44}X_4 + Y_4$$
farmers:

(6.1)

which simplifies to:

$$(1 - a_{11})X_1 \qquad - a_{12}X_2 \qquad - a_{13}X_3 \qquad - a_{14}X_4 = Y_1$$

$$-a_{21}X_1 + (1 - a_{22})X_2 \qquad - a_{23}X_3 \qquad - a_{24}X_4 = Y_2$$

$$-a_{31}X_1 \qquad - a_{32}X_2 + (1 - a_{33})X_3 \qquad - a_{34}X_4 = Y_3$$

$$- a_{41}X_1 \qquad - a_{42}X_2 \qquad - a_{43}X_3 + (1 - a_{44})X_4 = Y_4$$

or in matrix notation:

$$(I - A)x = y \qquad (6.2)$$

where:

$$I = \begin{bmatrix} 1 & 0 & 0 & 0 \\ 0 & 1 & 0 & 0 \\ 0 & 0 & 1 & 0 \\ 0 & 0 & 0 & 1 \end{bmatrix} \qquad A = \begin{bmatrix} a_{11} & a_{12} & a_{13} & a_{14} \\ a_{11} & a_{22} & a_{23} & a_{24} \\ a_{31} & a_{32} & a_{33} & a_{34} \\ a_{41} & a_{42} & a_{43} & a_{44} \end{bmatrix}$$

$$x = \begin{bmatrix} x_1 \\ x_2 \\ x_3 \\ x_4 \end{bmatrix} \qquad y = \begin{bmatrix} y_1 \\ y_2 \\ y_3 \\ y_4 \end{bmatrix}$$

From (6.1) it is possible to solve for the levels of each output x_t given the level of final demands y_i:

$$x = (I - A)^{-1}y \qquad (6.3)$$

or, writing (6.3) in first differences,

$$\Delta x = (I - A)^{-1} \Delta y$$

which may alternatively be written:

$$\Delta x = (I - A + A^2 + A^3 + \ldots A^n)\Delta y. \qquad (6.4)$$

This is the first result which we shall wish to explore; it is nothing more, of course, than the simplest possible input–output model re-interpreted in such a way that the coefficients a_{ij} represent flows between deciles of the income distribution rather than between productive sectors. It enables us to forecast, subject to the usual restrictions of input–output models such as fixed coefficients, what the consequences for given income groups will be if the demand for the output of those income groups is raised, for example by an overseas aid project, by an amount Δy. The elements of the vector Δy represent the amounts by which the incomes of different income groups are *directly* increased by the aid project; in our simple four-sector model Δy_1, Δy_2, Δy_3 and Δy_4 represent the amount by which the incomes of the rich, the medium, the poor and the destitute are increased by the project. We shall refer to these henceforward as the *first-round effects* of the project, and to its other effects, that is $(A + A^2 + \ldots + A^n)$ Δy, as the *linkage or 'trickle-down' effects*. 'The theory of trickle-down', as it has been described, has never been given any kind of precise formulation—it is more of a suggestive metaphor than a theory—but it can be sharpened into a theory by stipulating that the linkage effects for certain lower income groups must exceed some specified magnitude, for example:

effect on poor: $\Delta x_3 - \Delta y_3$ = third element of
$(A + A^2 + \ldots + A^n)\Delta y \geqslant Z_1$

$$(6.4')$$

effect on destitute: $\Delta x_4 - \Delta y_4$ = fourth element of
$(A + A_2 + \ldots + A^n)\Delta y \geqslant Z_2$

where Z_1, Z_2 are arbitrary fixed numbers.

Expanding (6.4^1), the linkage effects of a boost to demand Δy on the poor may be expressed as:

$$\Delta x_3 - \Delta y_3 = (a_{31}\Delta y_1 + a_{32}\Delta y_2 + a_{33}\Delta y_3 + a_{34}\Delta y_4) + (a_{31}a_{11} + a_{32}a_{21} + a_{33}a_{31} + a_{34}a_{41})\Delta y_1 + \ldots$$
$$+ \text{ higher-order terms}$$

and the indirect effects of a boost to demand Δy on the destitute may be expressed as:

$$\Delta x_4 - \Delta y_4 = (a_{41}\Delta y_1 + a_{42}\Delta y_2 + a_{43}\Delta y_3 + a_{44}\Delta y_4) + (a_{41}a_{11} + a_{42}a_{21} + a_{43}a_{31} + a_{44}a_{41})\Delta y_1 + \ldots$$
$$+ \text{ higher-order terms}$$

In other words, if one is interested in the trickle-down effects of a project on the poor it is the linkage coefficients a_{31}, $a_{32} \ldots$ representing the purchases of other income groups from the poor which are critical, and if one is interested in the trickle-down effects on the destitute it is the coefficients a_{41}, a_{42} . . . representing the purchases of other income groups from the destitute which are critical. In the next section we proceed to an empirical measurement, and to a discussion of the factors determining the size, of these linkage coefficients.

The Size of Linkage Coefficients

During the 12 calendar months of 1981 the author was a member of a team which conducted an income and expenditure survey in the Catilluc valley. This valley, an area of some 300 square kilometres, had for some 2 years been the scene of an agricultural development project financed by the United Kingdom ODA. This project, the Agricultural Development Project of Cajamarca, provided technical assistance, plus very limited capital aid in the form of bridge improvements and water supplies, to a rural community whose principal cash activities are dairy farming and, to a much lesser extent, potato production. A sample of approximately 25 per cent of the farmers in the valley was selected for analysis; within this sample, the flow of funds between the income strata identified earlier (Table 6.4) is estimated to have been as set out in Table 6.7.[71]

Table 6.7 demonstrates the Catilluc valley to be a very open economy, with a very high propensity to 'export' to, and 'import' from, the outside world. The export and import propensities increase as income rises. Such openness, carrying the implication of low linkage coefficients within the national input–output production matrix, has often been noted as a characteristic of LDC *national* economies, for example, by Peacock and Dosser (1957). Within the present theoretical context the high degree of openness and small degree of inter-sectoral linkage imply that 'trickle-down effects' are likely to be low. If we express such income group's sales to other income groups, as set out in Table 6.7, as a proportion of total output for that income group, we derive the **A**-matrix, in the notation of equations (6.1) to (6.4) above. This is:

	Rich	Medium	Poor	Destitute
Rich	0.047	0.044	0.079	0.265
A = Medium	0.156	0.141	0.251	0.585
Poor	0.025	0.023	0.071	0.445
Destitute	0.001	0.001	0.005	0.117

Table 8.7: Canillac Valley, Peru 1981: estimate of cash flows between income groups (thousands of Peruvian soles)[a]

Purchases from other income groups	Sales to other income groups:				Sales to outside world (exclusive of purchases of farm inputs)	Total income (value added)
	Rich	Medium	Poor	Destitute		
Rich	1,492	2,045	502	59	27,069	31,167
Medium	4,859	6,496	1,587	130	32,902	45,974
Poor	787	1,089	452	99	3,882	6,309
Destitute	42	49	30	26	75	222
Purchases from outside world (exclusive of farm inputs)	14,553	24,432	2,961	148		
Net savings 1981	9,434	11,863	777	−240		

'Income' in column 6 is an estimate of total value added on-farm; it consists of gross farm revenue *net* of cash purchases of the following inputs: animal medicines; insecticides and fungicides; fertilisers; tools and agricultural equipment.

'Rich' = most prosperous 10 per cent of sample, average 1981 cash income =4511 thousand soles

'medium' = deciles 2 to 6 of sample, average 1981 family cash income 1523 thousand soles
'Poor' = deciles 7 to 9 of sample, average 1981 family cash income = 419 thousand soles
'Destitute' = poorest 10 per cent of sample, average 1981 family cash income = 41 thousand soles
[a]In 1981 on average, 800 soles = £1 = $1.85.
Cash income in 1981 consisted 54 per cent of milk sales, 34 per cent of livestock sales, 7 per cent of potato sales, and 5 per cent of sales of labour for cash (Mosley and Lawrence-Jones, 1984, Table IV.1).
Source: Mosley and Lawrence-Jones (1984), Tables IV.7 and IV.3.

It so happens that on this particular project the direct, or 'first-round' benefits, as we have called them, accrue almost entirely to the 'rich' and 'medium' income groups. The principal benefits offered by the project consisted of technical help with matters such as animal health, planted pastures and milk quality, benefits which were of no value to that substantial proportion of the poorest farmers who kept no dairy cattle, and which were in any case taken up more confidently and with less suspicion by farmers whose previous personal contact with external markets and external agencies was substantial. In particular, we estimate that for 1981 the 'first-round' benefits received from the project were distributed as follows between the four income groups:

$$\Delta y = \begin{Bmatrix} 400 \\ 650 \\ 200 \\ 0 \end{Bmatrix} \text{ thousand soles per annum to } \begin{Bmatrix} \text{rich} \\ \text{medium} \\ \text{poor} \\ \text{destitute} \end{Bmatrix} \text{ farmers respectively.}$$

Using equation (6.4) above and the data contained in Table 6.7, we estimate that if those sample data are a true reflection of the inter-group flows in the population at large, then the 'linkage' or 'trickle-down' effects are:

$$= \Delta x - \Delta y = (A + A^2 \ldots + A^n)\Delta y \qquad (6.4'')$$

$$= \begin{Bmatrix} 68 \\ 242 \\ 35 \\ 4 \end{Bmatrix} \text{ thousand soles per annum for } \begin{Bmatrix} \text{rich} \\ \text{medium} \\ \text{poor} \\ \text{destitute} \end{Bmatrix} \text{ farmers respectively.}$$

These are small trickle-down effects indeed, implying a multiplier of only just over one for the valley as a whole, but what needs to be stressed is not this special case, but the general point, which is that a structure of linkages such as that set out in Table 6.7 cannot but produce small trickle-down effects. An exactly even share-out of benefits, in which the first-round benefits of 1,250 thousand soles were shared out at the rate of 9,200 soles per farmer per annum, or:

$$\begin{Bmatrix} 125 \\ 625 \\ 375 \\ 125 \end{Bmatrix}$$ between the different income groups, rather than the actual figures set out on p. 194, would, using equation (6.4) once again, have produced 'indirect' changes in income of only:

$$\begin{Bmatrix} 103 \\ 350 \\ 106 \\ 19 \end{Bmatrix} \begin{matrix} \text{thousand soles} \\ \text{per annum for} \end{matrix} \begin{Bmatrix} \text{rich} \\ \text{medium} \\ \text{poor} \\ \text{destitute} \end{Bmatrix} \begin{matrix} \text{farmers} \\ \text{respectively.} \end{matrix}$$

This is more indirect benefit for each group, and in particular for the poor and destitute groups, than in the real-life case where the first-round benefits are unequally distributed, because the redistribution shifts income to those whose propensity to buy from others within the valley is relatively high. However, the trickle-down effect remains small in absolute terms, at less than half the total first-round effect. If we stipulate, indeed, that the indirect benefits for the poor and destitute groups from the project must in each case be not less than 20 per cent of the total first-round benefits of 1,250 thousand soles (i.e. $Z=250$ in the notation of equation (6.4'), then it can quickly be demonstrated that there is no possible allocation of first-round benefits which will allow this requirement to be satisfied. All tests of the trickle-down hypothesis are arbitrary, since the hypothesis has never been formulated in any strict way, but this model and this community comfortably fail all such tests which require more than one-third of first-round benefits to 'trickle-down' in 1 year to the lowest 40 per cent of the income distribution.

Extensions of the Model: 'Downstream Effects'
The foregoing analysis has worked with the simplest possible static input–output model: it has attempted to measure the 'multiplier' effects of an aid-financed income inflow on different income groups, that is, those effects which result from the diffusion of that income flow through the local community. It has made no attempt to consider the impact on different income groups of forces operating through time such as:

(1) the extent to which the initial income flow stimulates local investment, in imitative or complementary efforts;
(2) the extent to which the lowest income groups respond to their inadequate income by migrating out of the district;
(3) the alleged vicious circle of impoverishment and environmental depletion in poor rural areas;
(4) remittances from outside and voluntary transfers between income groups.

In what follows we attempt to extend the analysis by designing and estimating a simulation model which includes these relationships. Limitations on the available data mean that in many cases the formulation we have adopted must be regarded as provisional and unsatisfactory. But, as Bell and Hazell (1980) have noted in the case of Muda irrigation project in Malaysia,[72] the 'downstream' effects of a project on the income distribution may cause those effects as measured well after a project's completion to differ significantly from those observable at the conclusion of disbursements; hence some measurement of these effects is necessary for any assessment of the trickle-down hypothesis.

We begin from our original input–output model, now with time subscripts:

Income of
the rich:
$$X_1(t) = a_{11}X_1 + a_{12}X_2 + a_{13}X_3 + a_{14}X_4 + Y_1(t)$$

Income of
medium farmers:
$$X_2(t) = a_{21}X_1 + a_{22}X_2 + a_{23}X_3 + a_{24}X_4 + Y_2(t)$$

Income of
poor farmers:
$$X_3(t) = a_{31}X_1 + a_{32}X_2 + a_{33}X_3 + a_{34}X_4 + Y_3(t)$$

Income of
destitute farmers:
$$X_4(t) = a_{41}X_1 + a_{42}X_2 + a_{43}X_3 + a_{44}X_4 + Y_4(t)$$

$$(6.1)$$

where $X_i(t)$ = income; $Y_i(t)$ = final demand; a_{ij} = transfers between income groups.

The link between time periods is provided by productive investment out of the 'surplus' which is left over after inter-sectoral purchases and essential purchases of food, fuel, etc. from the external economy have been made. Formally:

$$\left.\begin{array}{ll}
\text{Investment of the rich:} & I_1(t) = B_1\left(X_1(t) - \sum_{i=1}^{4} a_{i1} X_1(t) - \gamma_1 X_1(t)\right) \\[2em]
\text{Investment of medium farmers:} & I_2(t) = B_2\left(X_2(t) - \sum_{i=1}^{4} a_{i2} X_2(t) - \gamma_2 X_2(t)\right) \\[2em]
\text{Investment of poor farmers:} & I_3(t) = B_3\left(X_3(t) - \sum_{i=1}^{4} a_{i3} X_3(t) - \gamma_3 X_3(t)\right) \\[2em]
\text{Investment of destitute farmers:} & I_4(t) = B_4\left(X_4(t) - \sum_{i=1}^{4} a_{i4} X_4(t) - \gamma_4 X_4(t)\right)
\end{array}\right\} \quad (6.5)$$

where I = investment; B_i = 'propensities to reinvest';
γ_i = each income group's propensity to buy consumer goods from outside the local community.

In Catilluc $B_1 > B_2 > B_3 > B_4$, and we imagine that this will be the case in most places; but the absolute size of the B-coefficients will vary between communities, reflecting in particular, in places where external development assistance has recently been provided to a community, the extent to which it stimulates and supports, or alternatively supplants, local investment efforts.[73] In many communities—certainly in Catilluc—the 'investible surplus' left behind after essential consumption expenditures, and hence investment also, will be zero or negative;[74] 'disinvestment', in such cases, will characteristically take the form of sales of livestock.

For each farm family, the next period's income depends on the last period's investment, plus remittances from outside. The size of the coefficient which turns investment into income for each income group will, in any given year, depend on extraneous forces such as weather, the level of output prices, and the productivity of the soil. Several writers (for example, Blaikie *et al.*, 1977) have suggested that the last of these three variables will exhibit a different pattern through time for different income groups, and specifically that the poorest groups are likely to be subjected to a 'reproduction squeeze', in which they are forced to move on to progressively steeper and less fertile land simply in order to maintain a subsistence, so that productivity per acre diminishes over time.

Thus we write:

$$
\left.
\begin{aligned}
Y_1(t+1) &= \text{constant}^{75} + \delta_1(I_1(t)) + R_1 \\
Y_2(t+1) &= \text{constant} + \delta_2(I_2(t)) + R_2 \\
Y_3(t+1) &= \text{constant} + \delta_3(I_3(t)) + R_3 + \text{time trend} \\
Y_4(t+1) &= \text{constant} + \delta_4(I_4(t)) + R_4 + \text{time trend}
\end{aligned}
\right\} \quad (6.6)
$$

where the δ_i are 'incremental output–capital ratios', the R_i represent transfers of surplus out of the community through the export of capital and in by means of remittances,[76] and the time trend reflects the deterioration of land yields for the lower income classes. Empirically, the rate of decline in crop yields in Cajamarca seems to be very close to that noted by Blaikie *et al.* (1977) for West-Central Nepal, namely 0.65 per cent per annum.[77]

There is one difficulty with which we have not yet reckoned, namely that we have treated the four income classes as water-tight compartments and made no allowance for movement between them, or indeed for movement in and out of the project area by means of birth, death or migration. The empirical data for Cajamarca district suggest that it will be appropriate if we work with the simplest imaginable population-growth function:

$$
N_i(t) = N_i(0)e^{rt} + \sum_{4=0}^{t} M_i(t) \qquad (6.7)
$$

where N_i = population within an income class ($N_i(0)$ = population in year 0), r = rate of natural increase for all classes, $M_i(t)$ = net gain or loss ($-$) to that income class through migration in each time period, as, within the rural community with which we are here concerned, population growth rates and family sizes do not seem to vary with income level.[78]

There is migration out of the valley from an income class if and only if the total income of that income class declines:

$$
M_i(t) = m_i[X(t) - X(0)] \quad \text{if} \quad X(0) < X(t), i = 1, \ldots 4. \,(6.8)
$$

We work with the figures for m_i which represent the highest and lowest levels recorded in the valley over the last 5 years. If migration takes place in a given year, the income of all migrants is lost to that income group for that year.

Table 6.8: *Measurement of 'Downstream Effects' of initial values and coefficients of the model*

| Income group | Estimated income at end of first year of project | | | Purchases from outside district γ_i | Investment coefficients B_i | Constant in earnings function Y_i | 'Rate of return' on investment δ_i | | | Balance of Remittances R_i | Time trend of crop productivity | | Initial Population $N_i(o)$ | Rate of population growth per annum r | Migration coefficient: m_i | |
	Without project	With project (1)	With project (2)				Good weather + crop prices	Moderate weather + crop prices	Bad weather + crop prices		Optimistic assumptions	Pessimistic assumptions			Assumption (1)	Assumption (2)
Rich	30,698	31,167	30,926	0.47	0.71	22,300	1.65	1.33	0.95	−200	—	—	1,300	2.9%	−3.1	−1.5
Medium	45,082	45,974	46,057	0.53	0.62	34,400	1.65	1.33	0.95	+50	—	—	6,600	2.9%	−5.6	−2.8
Poor	6,074	6,309	6,555	0.47	0.57	5,850	1.65	1.33	0.95	+200	—	−0.65%	3,980	2.9%	−7.3	−3.6
Destitute	147	222	291	0.66	0.44	145	1.65	1.33	0.95	+150	—	−0.65%	1,450	2.9%	−5.5	−2.0

Sources: Initial income $Y(o)$: 'with Project (1)' are the actual values given in Table 6.7. 'Without project' subtracts the 'first-round' and 'trickle down' effects of the project reported on p. 194; 'with project (2)' adds to this the 'first-round' and 'trickle down' effects of a hypothetical project, with equal distribution of direct benefits, reported on p. 195.
Purchases from outside world γ_i: from Table 6.7.
Investment coefficient B_i: from Mosley and Lawrence-Jones (1984), Table IV.6.

Table 6.9: '*Downstream effects' after 5 years on different income groups of an initial stimulus of 1,250 thousand soles (=$2,000). Simulation results based on 1981 data. 'Downstream effects' are difference between total income after 5 years and income after 1 year as measured in Table 6.8.*

(a) Worst case: bad weather, low milk price, declining soil quality, no out-migration.

| Income group | Downstream effects (thousand soles) | |
	Project (1)	Project (2)
Rich	−624	64
Medium	−728	300
Poor	540	−392
Destitute	−120	−640

(b) Intermediate case: moderate weather, moderate milk price, no change in soil quality, out-migration at present level.

| Income group | Downstream effects (thousand soles) | |
	Project (1)	Project (2)
Rich	13,636	14,212
Medium	17,736	18,992
Poor	1,328	440
Destitute	140	−376

(c) Best case: good weather, high milk price, slight improvement in soil quality, increased level of out-migration.

| Income group | Downstream effects (thousand soles) | |
	Project (1)	Project (2)
Rich	25,644	26,128
Medium	33,096	34,532
Poor	1,900	1,032
Destitute	244	172

For definition of 'Project (1)' and 'Project (2)' see Table 6.8.

There are, of course, remittances in Table 6.8, but we do not postulate any link between migration m_i and remittances R_i in any time period, as so large a proportion of remittances comes from migrants already settled outside the project area at the start of the time period under examination.

We now proceed to run the model consisting of equation systems numbers (6.1), (6.5), (6.6), (6.7) and (6.8), with coefficients set out in Table 6.8. These parameters are in nearly all cases derived either from actual measurement of data from the Catilluc project area, or from our previous analysis; the exceptions are the 'rate of return on investment' coefficients δ_i, where we have set out a variety of alternative values dependent on different states of nature.

By running the model we can forecast the downstream effects of different 'projects', that is, alternative sets of income stimuli to different economic groups. In Table 6.9 we measure the effect after 5 years of the two different 'projects' already considered in this paper: one, corresponding to the actual Cajamarca project, in which the direct effects of the project are concentrated largely on the rich and medium income groups, and a second hypothetical project in which the same initial stimulus of 1.25 million Peruvian soles is evenly spread between all members of the population as described on p. 195. The table suggests that the downstream effects of a project are no more likely to trickle-down to the poorest groups of society than the indirect effects examined in Section 6.3, *whether or not* the project is explicitly targeted on those groups. This is the consequence of the extremely low propensity to save and reinvest of the poor and destitute groups, as manifested in Table 6.8, and of an assumption, in equation (6.5) that those propensities can be taken as fixed parameters. If aid projects could be designed which could raise the savings and reinvestment propensities of the poorest groups, this result would no longer hold; but there is no evidence of such a change in savings propensities over the period in which we have been carrying out surveys in Cajamarca.

NOTES

1. 2.7 per cent in 'low-income economies' against 2.5 per cent in 'industrial market economies': World Bank, *World Development Report 1985*, Appendix Table 1.
2. This seems to be true within individual countries, as well as in the world as a whole; Lipton reports that 'the proportion of Indians in poverty, and the average severity of that poverty, have not changed much since independence': Lipton and Toye (1984), paragraph 2.7.

3. Bowles (1978), p. 55. The same report shows (at p. 70) that out of the minority who were *unfavourably* disposed towards British aid to developing countries, 86 per cent gave as a reason 'the help we give to the poorest countries of the world often fails to reach the people who really need it.'

4. This was the group stressed by Robert McNamara while he was President of the World Bank. *See* his Addresses to the World Bank Board of Governors, at Washington in 1971, pp. 6–19, and 1972, pp. 8–15; and at Nairobi in 1973, pp. 10–14, 19.

5. For a discussion of different measures of inequality, and of how they may be in mutual conflict, *see* the essay by Sen (1974).

6. For description of these and other kinds of projects which 'may assist the poor at the expense of the poorest' *see* Devitt (1978).

7. Chenery *et al.* (1974), p. 53.

8. *See* Chambers (1983), Chapter 1.

9. For the 101 countries on which data is given in summary form in Table 6.1, the measured relationship between income level and aid flows as a proportion of GNP is:

$$\begin{array}{c}\text{aid flow} \\ \text{(as percentage of GNP)}\end{array} = 15.08 - \underset{(3.17)}{0.005^{**}} \left(\frac{\text{GNP}}{\text{capita}}\right); \quad r^2 = 0.14$$

Ordinary least-squares estimation; t-statistic in brackets beneath coefficient; 101 observations, as listed in Appendix I to this chapter which presents full data arrays.

10. The Gini coefficient of inequality is measured as $G = \Sigma_{i=1}^{n}(X_i - Y_i)$ $(X_{i-1} - X_{i+1})$ where X_i are cumulative income shares, Y_i are cumulative population shares, and there are n (in this case ten) class intervals.

11. For a discussion of these arbitrarinesses *see* Usher (1968).

12. Chenery *et al.* (1974), p. 44.

13. *See* Chapter 1, pp. 10–11.

14. The UK Overseas Development Administration, aware of the importance which the public attach to aid reaching the poorest, use the phrase 'aid to the world's poorest countries' in their publicity material. But their posters no longer make any claims that British aid is reaching poor *people*.

15. Bauer (1972), p. 115.

16. Healey and Clift (1980), p. 10. This would mean, in 1981 to which the figures of Table 6.1 relate, a personal income of $5500.

17. *See* O'Higgins and Ruggles (1981).

18. *See also* Lipton and Toye (1984) paragraphs 5.10 and 5.121 ff.

19. These arguments are elaborated in Mosley (1981a) and, more eloquently, by Chambers (1983), in particular Chapters 1 and 5.

20. These procedures vary, but much the most common practice is for

evaluation reports to be compiled by a team from the donor agency who fly out at the end of the project period, stay in the host country for a hectic 3 or 4 weeks, and then fly back again, producing their report within a month or two of their return. A few aid-financed projects do contain a provision for 'built-in monitoring and evaluation', including a baseline study at the beginning of the project; and a few, nearly all financed by the World Bank, are subjected to so-called 'impact evaluation' several years after the termination of external finance on the project. But one-shot evaluation studies at the project's end are still the norm. For more detail on evaluation procedures *see* Mosley (1983).

21. *See* Chapter 3, pp. 60–66, and Mosley (1983), Table 1 and pp. 594–6.
22. *See* p. 64 above, also note 42, p. 83.
23. Such cases occurred in the British Overseas Development Administration even during the period of formal 'poverty focus' from 1975 to 1979. One project which ODA approved for aid financing during that period was the Mbeya regional hospital in Tanzania. The UK's First Secretary (Aid) in Dar es Salaam argued that such a hospital was likely to be of benefit only to citizens of Mbeya and the immediately surrounding district and hence could not be of much help to the rural poor. He was told that some poor rural patients would be referred to the Mbeya hospital from outlying clinics (in fact, very few have been), warned that his muck raking, as it was described, was causing embarrassment both to ODA and to the Tanzania Government, and finally, when he persisted with 'embarrassing' minutes about the Mbeya Hospital, transferred to a safe berth within the United Nations Department of the ODA.
24. The ODA's *Guidelines for the Preparation of Evaluation Studies* (London, 1981, revised edn.), p. 5, asks that evaluation studies should 'compare the intended and achieved:

    — rate of return (economic and financial)
    — total cost
    — output levels
    — completion dates
    — effect on target groups'.

25. Particularly on agricultural projects, where income and welfare may change for reasons unconnected with the project, a baseline study must be done at the start and a control group selected to net out 'non-project-related' changes in income. But the control group, which by definition does not share in the benefits of the project, may for that reason refuse to answer questions about its income and welfare.
26. World Bank (1982a), pp. 35–7.
27. Mosley (1981), p. 217.
28. For a discussion of Calcutta First Urban Development, *see* Lipton and Toye (1984), paragraphs 5.62 to 5.65.

29. Average *ex post* rates of return are reported to be as follows:

ODA–financed projects	Poverty-focused projects	Non-poverty-focused projects
1974–9	13.5 (*n* = 31)	18.3 (*n* = 24)
World Bank–financed projects	(agriculture only)	
1961–81	17.4 (*n* = 71)	16.5 (*n* = 150)

Source: for ODA data, Mosley (1981a): for World Bank data, World Bank (1982a).

30. This judgement is corroborated by the official commentators; Morris and Gwyer (1983, p. 158) assert that 'experience suggests that official aid can rarely reach the poorest of the poor' and the World Bank (1982c) p. 34 claim that 'it has proved extremely difficult to benefit the very poorest groups who lack productive assets'.

31. For a formal analytical model of the distributional effects of one rural development project based on the idea of an input–output analysis between income groups, *see* Appendix II to this chapter.

32. In principle, energy generated by the other means may be of indirect benefit to the rural or urban poor by lowering the price of electricity to them (*see* Porter in evidence to United Kingdom 1979a, evidence of 13 December 1978, p. 42). But this argument is abstract and impractical: most poor people in rural villages or shanty-towns are nowhere near an electrical connection.

33. Duncan and Mosley (1984), p. 117.

34. William J. House, 'Nairobi's informal sector: a reservoir of dynamic entrepreneurs or a residual pool of surplus labour?' University of Nairobi: Institute for Development Studies, working paper 347, p. 25. The third major constraint was 'establishing a market'.

35. Kenya Industrial Estates, Industrial and Commercial Development Corporation, and the Industrial Development Bank. ICDC imposes a floor on its loans of 2,000 shillings, and IDB a floor of 40,000 shillings.

36. Mosley and Dahal (1985).

37. *See* the essay by D. C. Rao in Chenery *et al.* (1974), pp. 152–3.

38. 'Household budget data supplied by the Government indicate that households with incomes below P60 (about £40) per month are willing to pay 15 per cent of their income for shelter and services and those with incomes above P60 per month 20 per cent. Based on this information, which is considered reasonable, the minimum charges for upgraded (squatter) and settlement plots are affordable by (only) 90 per cent of the residents of Gaborone and Francistown.' World Bank, *Botswana: Second Urban Project Staff Appraisal Report* (1975a -BT), p.41. Compare the statement by Rao that 'experience with public housing projects has shown that they rarely reach even the poorest 40 per cent (and very rarely the poorest 20 per cent) of the population' (Chenery *et al.*, 1974, p. 152).

39. *See* Chapter 3, pp. 56–57, also Tendler (1975), pp. 87–94.
40. However, donor country administrators are subject to constraints on the proportion of the aid budget for a particular country which can be spent within the recipient country, which may force technology in a capital-intensive direction. The severity of local cost ceilings varies from donor to donor; they are relatively generous in Scandinavia, Germany and Holland, and relatively tight in the US and Japan. In Britain, local cost ceilings vary from recipient to recipient: they are 100 per cent for most countries in sub-Saharan Africa, but 60–80 per cent for much of Asia and far less in the Caribbean and Latin America. It is possible to cite a number of cases—Guyanan sea defences/irrigation, SCARP V in Pakistan, Brazilian rural electrification, and finally all aid to India until the introduction of Retrospective Terms Adjustment on outstanding debt—which caused potentially poverty-focused projects, particularly in the better-off developing countries, to be delayed, truncated or else simply passed over in favour of other projects with a lower local-cost content. For more detail of the Indian case *see* United Kingdom (1979a) pp. XXIV and 110 ff.
41. *See* Independent Group on British Aid (1982), p. 39.
42. *See* Duncan and Mosley (1984), p. 115.
43. Recall Rondinelli's observation that 'most projects scoring high on success experienced at least one major revision after the project managers decided the original plan was not working' (1983), p. 5.
44. For more detail of this argument, *see* Chapter 4, pp. 93–97.
45. An eloquent plea for the use of more indigenous knowledge in the design of poverty-focused rural development projects is made by Chambers (1983), Chapter 4.
46. For a most valuable analysis of the causes of, and a sectoral comparison of 'technical rigidity' *see* the paper by Forsyth (1977).
47. *See* Chapter 3, p. 52.
48. For a full account of the SFDP *see* Mosley and Dahal (1985).
49. Of India—a more hopeful country than most for initiatives in poverty reduction, given the support that exists at state level—Michael Lipton has written:

   The 'dilemma of politics', that has defeated poverty-reducing efforts by many honest and immensely capable Indians since Pandit Nehru, is this. Enlist the power groups that gain from privilege in State policy against poverty, and they subvert that policy—by emasculation (e.g. by writing loopholes into most land reform legislation) or by capturing its benefits (e.g. credit allegedly subsidised 'to help the poor'). Exclude them from such policy and they prevent its implementation—e.g. by using the courts against genuine land reform; or by insisting on central action to impede radical reforms by State governments. (in Lipton and Toye, 1984, paragraph 2.20).

50. Chenery *et al.* (1974), as one might expect, endorse this view: 'the chances of a specific intervention coming off successfully depend significantly on whether or not the situation affected is perceived as an essentially zero-sum game, with one party losing what the other wins' (p. 58).

51. This is the logic of the case for investment in rural public works made by Lewis (1977).
52. Lipton and Toye (1984), paragraph 2.37. There is a radical–pessimist argument which seeks to extend this argument to *any* asset which the rich acquire through aid, on the grounds that this will increase their purchasing power and thereby enable them to buy up the poor's land until they lose it all (*see* for example, Hayter and Watson (1985), *passim*; United Kingdom (1979a), evidence of 13 December 1978, pp. 6–13. This may indeed happen to farmers who experience sudden distress; but not to all, and to those to whom it does happen it does at least provide an escape route to survival. The argument scarcely justifies the cessation of rural capital investment by aid agencies, although it certainly warns them to keep an eye on the distribution of benefits inasmuch as that lies within their control.
53. Within a single village of Uttar Pradesh, India in 1975–7, Bliss and Stern recorded interest rates varying from 11 to 50 per cent, wage rates for unskilled agricultural labour from 3 to 5½ rupees per day and rentals for water pumps from 8 to 12 rupees per acre (1982), pp. 96, 108 and 112.
54. For more detail of this case study *see* Mosley (1982b), p. 288.
55. Chambers (1983), pp. 128 and 135.
56. Hayter and Watson (1985), p. 252.
57. Jolly, in Chenery *et al.* (1974), p. 177. A variant on this argument is provided by Papanek, in Parkinson (1982), p. 181, who argues in favour of programme aid, not for countries whose governments are redistributive, but rather for countries whose private sectors follow a labour-intensive production function.
58. For a general survey of such data *see* Chenery *et al.* (1974), Chapter 1.
59. *See* Lipton (1977), Chapters 12 and 13.
60. The same principle (that public expenditures are paid for by all income groups, but benefit largely the middle classes) also applies in developed countries, where it is known as 'Director's Law'. *See* Heald (1982), p. 146.
61. Papanek, in Parkinson (1982), p. 181.
62. On Malaysia *see* Meerman (1979). Meerman concluded that Malaysia had been very successful in directing its social welfare programmes towards the poor; much of this success could be ascribed to the fact that the politically dominant Malays were typically rural and poor whereas the politically subordinate Chinese were urbanised and better off.
63. Kenya, Colombia, Bangladesh, India, Pakistan, Indonesia, Tanzania, Sri Lanka, Sudan, Upper Volta, Cuba, Egypt, Jamaica and Zambia.
64. The detail is different in each case. Sri Lanka was forced into austerity measures earliest, in an economic crisis in 1978/9; the detail was worked out as part of the conditionality on an IMF stand-by agreement. For more detail *see* Nelson (1984). Jamaica has had three IMF stand-bys and three World Bank Structural Adjustment Loans

since its change of government in 1980, each of which has demanded a reduction of government expenditure; for more detail *see* the case study in Killick (1984), Vol. II.

65. Lipton and Toye (1984), paragraphs 2.2 and 2.83.
66. For one of many instances of this claim, *see* Gorman (1983), p. 56.
67. Gorman (1983), pp. 42 and 144. Certainly non-governmental organisations are free from local-cost constraints and high-technology bias. But they face the problem of potential opposition from local elites, and of low linkage, in just the same way as official agencies do; *see ibid.* Chapter 6.
68. Gorman (1983), p. 54.
69. Chambers (1983), p. 163.
70. *See* the reference to 'the failure of the integrated rural development approach' in Cox (1984), p. 159 and the claim that 'experience shows that it is seldom possible for official aid to reach the poorest of the poor' in Morris and Gwyer (1983), p. 158. The authors of these two statements are, respectively, employees of the World Bank and of the United Kingdom Overseas Development Administration.
71. The working out of these flows between income classes presented some novel problems of data collection as the data relate only to a 25 per cent sample of the population. Essentially all questions about income and expenditure were accompanied by questions concerning the origin of purchases and destination of sales. If origin or destination were either within the sample or in the outside world there were no problems of attribution. If on the other hand origin or destination were a household *within* the valley but *outside* the sample then the household in question had to be labelled as 'rich', 'medium', 'poor' or 'destitute' not according to measured income but rather according to number of cattle, which is known for all households in the valley from Ministry of Agriculture data and correlates closely with income (Mosley and Lawrence-Jones (1984), Table IV.6).
72. Bell and Hazell (1980), p. 86.
73. The latter tendency was observable, in 1980–1, on the Cajamarca project discussed in this appendix. Part of the project area was cut off from the other part, and from the market, by an unfordable river, for 4 months of the rainy season. Members of the local community accordingly began, in the late 1970s, to build a bridge across the river, but work was suspended when word got round that the resources for the bridge might be supplied from overseas aid funds. After 2 years of complicated negotiation, in the autumn of 1981, the bridge was built with British overseas aid money.
74. In Table 6.7 p. 193, net savings of the destitute income group for 1981 are estimated at *minus* 240,000 soles.
75. The constant reflects existing asset stocks, which make it possible for a household, in the short term, to reproduce itself without any expenditure on capital investment.
76. By the standards of the Peruvian Sierra, which is notorious for capital transfers to the coastal region and even out of the country, Catilluc

has relatively low capital 'exports'; but coefficient R_1 seems empirically to be negative, and R_2 close to zero. *See* data in Table 6.8.
77. Blaikie *et al*. (1977), p. 25.
78. Ahluwalia and Chenery, in Chenery *et al*. (1974), pp. 216–223, assume that population growth rates will vary according to income, but their model is of the entire national economy. Within a small rural community it is more probable that population growth rates will be similar as between classes; certainly in Catilluc the annual rate of population growth for all classes seems to be of the order of 3 per cent.

7 Aid as Export Subsidy

7.1 INTRODUCTION

Since its inception the practice of aid giving has been underpinned by the argument that it is not only beneficial to the recipient but also serves the donor's commercial and political self-interest. We have examined the extent of benefit to the recipient in the two preceding chapters, and of political benefit to the donor in Chapter 2. It remains to consider, in this chapter, the available evidence on the degree to which aid is responsible for increasing exports and employment in the donor country. As we argued earlier[1] those export orders which aid is able to win will usually be 'trade diverting', that is at the expense of exporters in other countries, rather than 'trade creating', and hence the commercial benefits which aid is able to generate must be seen as particular to the donor, and not as universal. However, it has been argued that the existence of a commercial interest in aid giving, and of specific institutional arrangements to put leverage behind that interest, cause the aid budget to be expanded to a larger size than it would otherwise have, and hence to convey spin-off benefits to development; by the same token, these arrangements may also impose costs on development through the distortions which they inflict on incentives in the recipient country. We shall therefore examine the positive and negative spillovers from using aid as an export subsidy, inasmuch as the data will allow.

Outline History

The classical instrument which donors have used to extract trade gains from their aid programmes is *source-tying*, that is, the requirement that the import content of an aid project or programme be procured in the donor country. As Table 7.1 demonstrates, about a third of OECD members' bilateral aid has been source-tied ever since its inception, but around this average there is considerable inter-donor variation, with some donors, notably Britain, France and Canada, disbursing a large part of their aid budget as a tied bilateral transaction, and others, such as West Germany and the Scandinavian countries, disbursing their aid either through multilateral agencies, who put nearly all procurement contracts up for free international bidding, or in untied bilateral form.

We have already noted[2] that in times of international recession governments come under protectionist pressure from the industrial and commercial lobby. But protectionism, in an international trading environment still nomin-

Table 7.1: OECD countries: tying status of overseas development assistance, 1972 and 1982–3

	Percentages of gross ODA disbursements					
	1972			1982–3		
	Bilateral:			Bilateral:		
	Tied	Untied	Multi-lateral	Tied	Untied	Multi-lateral
Canada	36.0	41.1	22.9	51.7	10.6	37.7
France	18.0	72.9	9.1	53.8	31.1	15.0
West Germany	19.8	67.1	13.1	21.1	50.1	28.8
Japan	55.0	29.3	15.7	32.8	40.6	26.6
Netherlands	17.3	57.3	25.4	30.1	40.1	29.7
Sweden	3.2	64.1	32.7	11.9	51.3	36.8
United Kingdom	18.0	67.7	14.3	41.9	13.0	44.9
United States	46.8	39.4	13.8	41.0	23.9	35.0
Total DAC countries	29.0	54.6	16.4	37.2	31.5	31.2

Source: OECD, Development Assistance Committee, *Development Assistance*, 1974 and 1985 issues.

ally governed by the free-trade understandings of the Bretton Woods Agreements, cannot be implemented without subterfuge. Any selective import tariff or export subsidy runs counter to the provisions of the General Agreement on Tariffs and Trade and, more to the point, invites retaliation. The secret of successful protectionist action, therefore, is to implement it under the cloak of an internationally accepted practice,[3] such as national quality control legislation or tax policy, a common market agreement, or overseas aid. This last appears particularly important to chambers of commerce and of industry as the means of unlocking new markets in the Third World. As Table 7.2 demonstrates, the share of Third World countries in the total market for OECD exports is scarcely growing; but for individual Western exporters the market of Third World countries, being less well known, will appear to offer more potential for purposive action by Western governments than the established markets in the West. Many of those governments, in the most recent recession of 1980–3, have considered that mere tying of their aid is insufficient, and have turned to the practice known as mixed credit.

Mixed credit is the practice of combining commercial credit and aid money in the financing of export sales. The practice appears to have been initiated by the governments

Table 7.2: OECD countries: share of exports taken by less developed countries 1967–79

Country	Year			
	1967	1972	1979	1983
United States	30.1	28.1	34.6	34.7
Canada	7.1	8.4	8.6	9.1
Japan	43.7	38.2	45.1	42.3
United Kingdom	22.6	20.5	21.2	20.6
Netherlands	10.6	9.2	10.2	10.4
France	22.7	17.6	22.5	25.5
West Germany	13.7	11.4	14.3	16.1
OECD	20.9	18.5	23.6	23.8

Source: United Nations. *Yearbook of International Trade Statistics*, 1970, 1976, 1979, 1983.

of France and Japan during the recession of 1974–5 in order to capture for domestic suppliers export contracts in Third World countries which might otherwise have gone elsewhere.

As an export subsidy, mixed credit, like any other measure of protection, is contrary to the spirit of the General Agreement on Tariffs and Trade, but since this particular subsidy is debited to the aid budget and can be justified as developmental, it does not contravene the letter of the agreement. However, its success as an instrument of commercial policy depends on other donor countries not retaliating, and retaliate they have, especially during the still graver recession of 1980–3, which saw a large increase in the volume of mixed credit[4] and the initiation of new lines of mixed credit by the aid agencies of West Germany, Canada, Britain,[5] Australia, Holland and even Sweden. Some donors, however, as Table 7.3 demonstrates, still make no use of the practice. The OECD has done what it can to regulate the mixed credit race by setting up 'Guiding Principles' in 1976 under which the members of its Development Assistance Committee:

undertook to confine associated financing to priority projects and programmes which are carefully appraised against the developmental standards and criteria applicable to official development assistance programmes. They also undertook not to extend associated financing transactions with a grant element of less than 20 per cent.[6]

'Mixed credit' is analytically distinct from ordinary tied aid, formally speaking, inasmuch as:

(1) aid finances less than 100 per cent of the export deal, the balance being made up by credit on commercial terms;
(2) the aid is given in response to the prospect of an export order, instead of the export orders being given as a voluntary, or contractual,[7] response to the award of aid.

In practice the distinction has become blurred. Some awards of aid from donor agencies' lines of 'mixed credit' have not been mixed at all, as aid has paid for 100 per cent

Table 7.3: OECD countries: disbursements of 'associated financing' (mixed credit) 1983–4

Country	'Associated financing' disbursements 1984 ($m)	Share of bilateral aid budget (%)
United States	0	0
Canada	157	10
Japan	44	1
United Kingdom	137	14
Netherlands	54	6
France	484	11
West Germany	28	1
Sweden	17	3
OECD total	1054	4

Source: OECD, *Twenty-five years of Development Co-operation*, Paris, 1985, Table X-2, p. 246.

of the export deal,[8] and a good quantity of aid inspired by the prospect of winning export orders has been awarded out of the bilateral aid budget, not the mixed credit budget.[9] The importance of this dilution is that not only mixed credit, but *all* aid packages mounted in response to an export opportunity have to be assembled very quickly, so that there is no time to assemble the information required for a proper appraisal of the project's development prospects. A 'snap judgement', as a senior British administrator has described it,[10] is all that can be made. In such increasingly common circumstances any developmental benefit which does materialise will be a lucky by-product, and by no means a planned outcome, of the decision to give aid.

7.2 TRADE AND EMPLOYMENT BENEFITS

From the point of view of the individual donor country, aid can be described as 'commercially beneficial' if it generates, over time, *additional* commercial exports whose value, discounted to the present, exceeds the value of the initial capital investment, just as it can be described as 'developmentally beneficial' if it yields net developmental benefits with a positive present value.

But how should those 'commercial benefits' be measured? Are we speaking of gains to domestic *income and employment*, of gains to *exports*, or of gains to the *balance of payments*, in which case the import content of aid-financed exports must be considered? In what follows we shall neglect balance-of-payments effects, which arguably are of small importance in a world of floating exchange rates, and concentrate on the effects on exports and income. To measure the effect of aid on exports we must measure:

(1) exports directly financed by the aid transaction, *plus*
(2) follow-up orders from the same source, *plus*
(3) 'reflection effects', or exports generated by the gain in income which the aid makes possible, *plus* (arguably)
(4) exports generated by the untied portion of other donors' aid.

The last three of these are scattered over a long period of time and hence difficult to measure. Furthermore, to go from gross exports generated to *net* (i.e. *additional*) exports generated we need to subtract:

(5) the exports which would have materialised with or without the aid, and also,
(6) the exports to Third World markets which are lost as a consequence of fuelling aid-financed orders.[11]

Both of these magnitudes are hypothetical, and for that reason measurements of them are necessarily arbitrary. In particular, any assessment of the incremental exports won by an offer of mixed credit depends crucially on the nature of the offers which competing tenderers and aid donors are making at the same time, and these, in the nature of the case, are usually shrouded in mystery.[12]

If instead of *exports* we are looking at the effects of aid on income and employment we encounter the same difficulties but we need to measure some additional magnitudes. We must begin by measuring (1) exports generated by aid, plus (2) follow-up orders, plus (3) reflection effects *net* of (5 + 6) exports which would have occurred anyhow, or are lost because of aid business. But in addition to these 'direct' effects on income we are also interested in the 'indirect effects' of aid-induced business on the donor's industry: for example, an aid-financed order given to the shipbuilding industry will cause the shipbuilding industry to buy more steel, and generate more jobs in steel-making. So the increment to final demand measured by (1 + 3 + 4 − 5 − 6) needs to be fed through an input–output table to find out what indirect effects it will generate. In practice, as we shall see, most studies simply calculate the indirect effects which are due to effect (1) and do not worry about the other elements in the study.

Anyone who sets out to look at the effects of aid on exports (to say nothing of the developmental spin-offs, which are considered in the next section) therefore needs in principle to add up six numbers, of which two are hypothetical. Of the few studies which exist, none gets this far, perhaps because the uncertainties are so daunting. However, a good deal of information can be gleaned from the five studies, three for Britain and two for West Germany, of which details are reproduced in Table 7.4. In the four studies of complete capital aid programmes, between a half and two-thirds of the initial disbursement comes back to the donor economy in the form of exports; in the study of mixed credit two-and-a-quarter times the initial investment comes back as the result of the contractual linkage between aid and commercial credit. One of the British and the two German studies calculate, by means of an input–output table, the 'indirect changes in domestic output' stimulated by these export orders; they are in all cases smaller than the value of the export orders themselves, but if added on to those initial orders they can be used to justify the claim that an increase in capital aid of £x leads to an increase in domestic *output* of more than £x.[13]

Some of the studies are more concerned with the effect of aid on exports or the balance of payments than with its effect on domestic output. Of these, only the study by

Hopkin *et al.* (1970) attempts to measure reflection effects, which it finds, in the late 1960s, small but positive; however, the evidence presented in Chapter 5 suggests that the net effect of aid on growth in most recipient countries is broadly neutral,[14] in which case the net reflection effect, now, will be zero. There have also been three attempts to check on follow-up orders; their results are disappointing. May and Dobson asked suppliers to the UK aid programme:

whether there had been any follow-up orders not financed out of the aid budget. Seventy-five per cent of companies reported no such orders. Many companies said they hoped for further (spare part) orders, but very few seem(ed) to expect anything more ... In any case it is difficult to ascribe subsequent orders directly to the influence of earlier aid-financed business.[15]

In similar vein a study of six projects financed in 1977–8 under the British line of mixed credit, the Aid/Trade Programme, found that by 1985 only one of these projects had generated follow-up orders.[16] Finally, an earlier study by the British Office of Population Census and Surveys (United Kingdom, 1972) reported that:

out of sixteen cases in which aid was essential or helpful in securing the original contract, new commercial business has been secured in three cases and is expected in another four. The study was thus generally inconclusive in demonstrating the extent of any causal relationship between the provision of aid and the award of subsequent commercial business.[17]

Discouraging though these results are for exporters, they are scarcely surprising.

The mere existence of aid tying—rather pervasive, as we saw, in the case of the UK aid programme—makes follow-up orders rather unlikely, since if tying is necessary it logically follows that supplies from the tying country must be uncompetitive, and incapable of winning orders in an environment where the donor is no longer injecting official aid into the competition for orders. The advent of mixed credit, under which technical assistance is seldom supplied with the capital goods, makes it still more probable that after-sales service from the donor will be found wanting, and prejudice the supplier's chance of winning follow-up orders.[18] We conclude that the balance of evidence is against the proposition that aid can enable exporters to win *and retain* a foothold in a market previously closed to them. Hence the effect of aid on exports must be inferred from its direct effects, without any large allowance being made for putative 'follow-up order' or 'reflection' effects. These direct effects alone, as Table 7.4 demonstrates, do not compensate for the outflow of aid.

What is more serious, all the studies we have considered proceed, explicitly or implicitly, on the assumption that exports which in Table 7.4 are ascribed to aid business are *generated* by that business in the sense that they would not have occurred in any case, and also that they are not pushing out any exports which would otherwise have gone to other markets. Nobody, perhaps wisely, has attempted to quantify the extent to which aid orders were a necessary condition for the award of export business. But May and Dobson, on the basis of their 1979 study, do stress

the fact that 90% of firms said that the market to which the aid order was supplied was an already established one, often with a long history of goods supplied under usual commercial arrangements to that particular country, and that they could not explain why it was that one of this long series of orders should suddenly be financed in this way (i.e. by aid). They were usually certain that they would have received the order in any case eventually, and that aid finance had not won them any extra business.[19]

If May and Dobson's sample is at all representative, the estimates of export business cited in Table 7.4 must be regarded as large overestimates of the amount of export business which aid actually makes possible.

We may conclude by taking a look at the effects of aid on domestic employment summarised in the bottom row of Table 7.4. These suggest that it costs between £7,500 (in the case of mixed credit) and £25,000 to create a man-year of employment in the aiding country. So far, in Britain at any rate, the jobs thus created seem to have been no more concentrated in declining industries with excess capacity, or in development areas receiving regional support from cen-

Table 7.4: Effect of aid on donor's exports: Method I

Study	Hopkin et al., 1970	May and Dobson, 1982a	ODA Evaluation Unit, 1985	Ashoff et al., 1979	Schumacher, 1981
Donor country	United Kingdom	United Kingdom	United Kingdom	West Germany	West Germany
Portion of aid programme evaluated	Entire aid programme	Entire aid programme	Sample of mixed credit projects only	Capital aid only	Capital aid only
A. Effects on exports: (per £1,000 of aid disbursed)					
1. Exports directly financed by the aid transaction *plus*	725	605	2270[a]	457[b]	690
2. (a) Follow-up orders from same manufacturer *plus*		Yes in about 25% of cases	Yes in one case out of six		
(b) Indirect effects, *i.e.* orders elsewhere in the economy induced by aid[c] *plus*	38	(414)[b]		(395)[b]	(540)[b]
3. Exports attributable to untied portion of other donors' aid	Not measured	513	N/A	Not measured	Not measured

plus 4. 'Reflection effects' = exports generated by aid-induced increase in income	49	Not measured	Not measured	Not measured	Not measured
less 5. Exports within which would have occurred in any case[c]	⎱ 236	Not measured	Not measured	Not measured	Not measured
less 6. Exports to third markets sacrificed by acceptance of aid orders	⎰	Not measured	Not measured	Not measured	Not measured
B. *Effects on employment:* (man years per £1,000 of aid disbursed)	Not measured	0.086[e]	0.13	0.041[d]	0.06[d]

[a]In most cases of mixed credit, including five of the six covered by this sample, aid finances only a fraction of the total transaction, so that it 'automatically' generated a greater volume of exports.

[b]'Indirect effects' consist of orders placed in the donor country by exporters, and of subsequent rounds of the multiplier; hence they do not represent a net gain to the balance of payments.

[c]In an earlier paper (1979, p. 9) May and Dobson indicate that "90% of firms were certain . . . that they would have received the order anyway, and that aid finance had not won them any extra business."

[d]These estimates use the exchange rate DM4 = £1.

Sources: As indicated in top line of table.

[e]From May and Dobson (1979) p. 19.

tral government, than the national average.[20] Moreover, it seems to be more expensive, if creating jobs is the objective, to do so by increasing overseas aid rather than by reflating domestic demand or by special domestic employment measures. One of the German studies, by Schumacher, puts the number of jobs created by an expansion of DM100m in the aid budget as 1,200, by comparison with 1,800, 1,600 and 2,300 which would be created by an expansion of DM100m in private investment, private consumption and public consumption respectively.[21] And a study by Byatt of the cost of export subsidies gives the cost per job-year created by mixed credit as £33,000, by contrast with £3,000 for the Youth Employment Programme, £5,000 for the Community Enterprise Programme and £7,000 for the Young Workers Scheme.[22] It should come as no surprise that the export of capital goods such as aircraft, power stations and steelworks to developing countries is not exactly labour-intensive. But it should discourage governments from using job creation as an argument for trade-related aid, even if they insist, contrary to the evidence, that every job derived from an aid order in fact owes its existence to that order.

An Alternative Approach

Enough has already been demonstrated to justify scepticism about the efficiency of aid as an instrument of commercial policy. However, there are sufficient gaps in the methodology of the studies so far considered[23] to warrant an alternative approach to the measurement of its effects; we shall therefore take four of the main aid donors and see whether there is any relationship between the amount of aid they give and the degree to which they are able to penetrate the market for capital goods of the Third World countries to which they give that aid. Clearly this approach also cannot yield conclusive results, as many factors are at work to determine market share and the lag in effect of aid is uncertain, but it will be useful to see whether it gives results consistent with those so far attained.

It does. On Figure 7.1 are set out data on aid flows from West Germany, Japan, France and the United States to two each of their main aid recipients, in relation to data on the donor's penetration of the recipient's total market for imports.[24]

We find that the *German* trade share in Turkey increased from 18 to 21 per cent between 1971 and 1976 despite a falling aid programme; subsequently, between 1977 and 1981, an enormous boost in aid to both that country and Brazil was accompanied by a fall in market share. *Japan*, between 1977 and 1979, trebled the real value of its aid to Thailand but its share of the market fell throughout those years and did not thereafter rise until 1983. The boost in *French* aid to the Ivory Coast between 1978 and 1980 was equally ineffective in promoting her share of that country's market. In Chile in 1974 and in Brazil in 1973, a peak in *American* aid followed and did not precede an improvement in the donor's market penetration.

Examples could be multiplied simply from the scanty information in Figure 7.1. These data cannot of course yield hard and fast conclusions on their own. None the less they suggest very strongly that aid has no appreciable effect on trade share. In several cases a rising trade share is associated with a falling or constant aid programme. Major boosts in aid are not associated with positive changes in trade share, with or without a lag. The tendency for peaks in aid to *follow* increases in trade share may testify to effective lobbying by exporters, but not to a causal relationship from aid to the unlocking of markets. Whereas once trade followed the flag, in these days of lost empire it seems to be commoner for the flag—in the shape of pressure on the aid programme from commercial attachés in embassies overseas—to follow trade opportunities.

7.3 TRADE-RELATED AID: DEVELOPMENTAL AND OTHER SPIN-OFF EFFECTS

Effects on the Recipient Country

It is a major theme of this book that effects, whether of aid or of anything else, cannot be inferred from motives. A mere decision 'to give greater weight in the allocation of our aid to political, industrial and commercial considerations

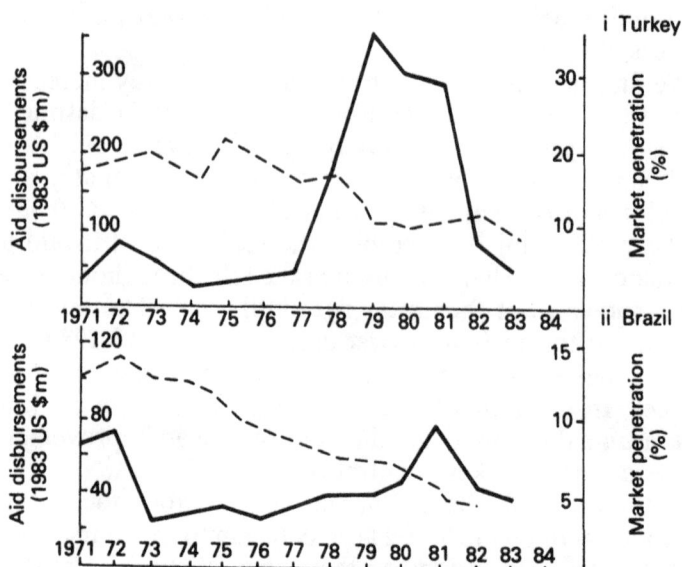

Figure 7.1(a): West Germany: aid flows (left scale, solid line) and market penetration (right scale, broken line), 1971–84

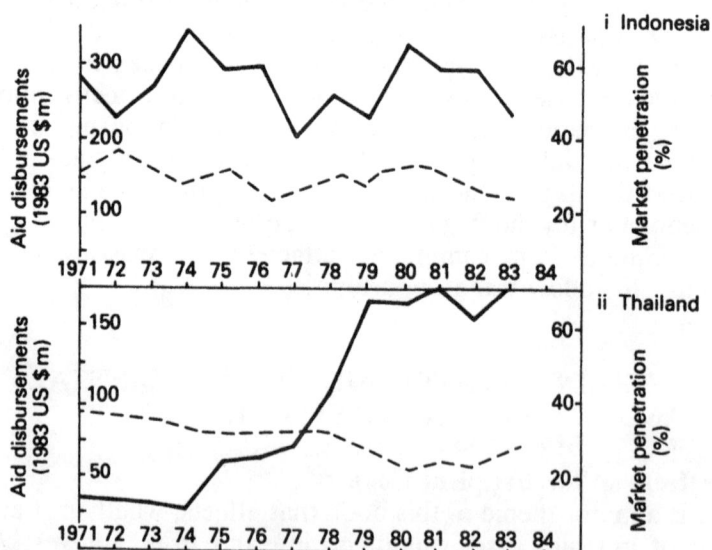

Figure 7.1(b): Japan: aid flows (left scale, solid line) and market penetration (right scale, broken line), 1971–84

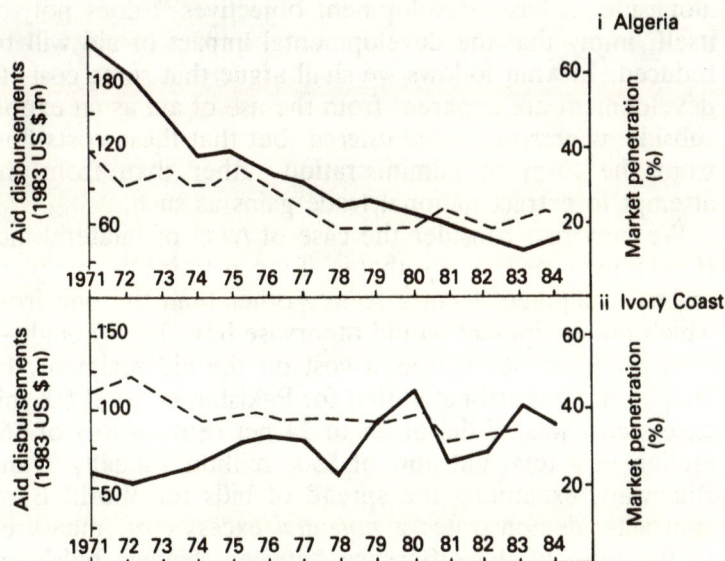

Figure 7.1(c): France: aid flows (left scale, solid line) and market penetration (right scale, broken line), 1971–84

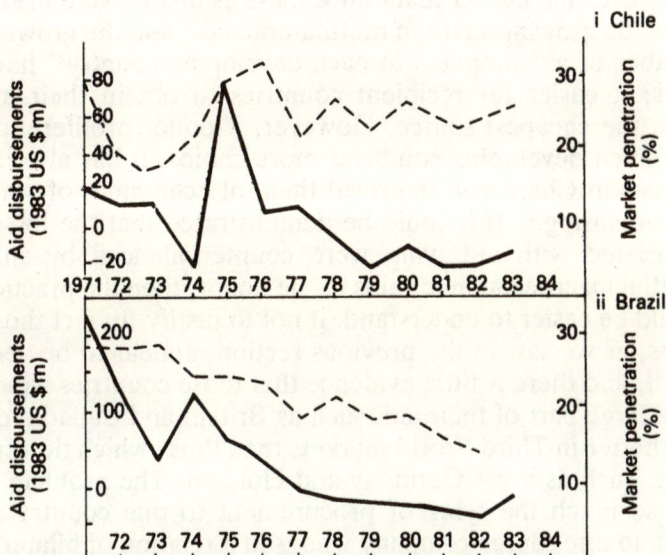

Figure 7.1(d): United States: aid flows (left scale, solid line) and market penetration (right scale, broken line), 1971–84

alongside ... basic development objectives'[26] does not, of itself, imply that the developmental impact of aid will be reduced. In what follows we shall argue that some costs to development are apparent from the use of aid as an export subsidy *as presently administered*, but that these costs flow from the form of administration rather than from the attempt to extract national trade gains as such.

We may first consider the case of *tying* of bilateral aid. If aid tying is necessary—that is, if it constrains the recipient to buy equipment from a source other than the one from which the equipment would otherwise have been bought—then *pro tanto* it imposes a cost on the aid recipient. Ul Haq (1965) has estimated that for Pakistan in the 1960s this excess cost was of the order of 14 per cent, 'a loss of $60 million in a total aid flow of $500 million annually'[25] and Bhagwati, examining the spread of bids for World Bank contracts, demonstrates a *potential* excess cost, measured as the ratio of the difference between 'highest bids' and 'successful bids', of 49 per cent.[26] It is possible that the actual cost of tying to recipient countries may have diminished over the last 15 years since these estimates were made, since the growing share of multilateral aid[27] and the growing number of aid suppliers to each developing country[28] have made it easier for recipient countries to obtain their aid from the cheapest source. However, if donor proliferation has given developing countries more choice, it has also, as we saw in Chapter 4, deprived them of economies of scale in purchasing.[29] If it could be demonstrated that the losses associated with aid tying were counterbalanced by substantial macroeconomic gains to the donor, then the practice would be easier to understand, if not to justify. In fact those gains, as we saw in the previous section, appear to be very small, and there is little evidence that those countries which tie a large part of their aid, such as Britain and Canada, do any better in Third World markets than those which tie very little, such as West Germany and Holland. The problem is not so much the tying of procurement to one country as tying to one source company who is in a relation of bilateral monopoly *vis-à-vis* the aid agency and can name its own price. If it were the normal practice of aid administrations to put supply contracts out to competitive tender within their own country, rather than simply to nominate a supplier who may easily not be the most efficient, many of the costs associated with tying could be reduced.

The developmental costs inherent in aid tying are very often augmented in the special case of tying known as mixed credit. Since mixed credits usually consist simply of a lump of capital equipment (often a lump which the donor country cannot otherwise sell) without any associated training and maintenance component, they have the effect of aggravating the bias towards capital intensity in Third World production which is inherent, we have argued, in most aid.[30] (Where the equipment supplied consists, for example, of a ship or an aeroplane, this absence of a training and maintenance component may have consequences which are tragic as well as wasteful of scarce resources.) Since goods supplied under mixed credit are explicitly offered in competition with other donors, they offer little opportunity for policy dialogue, since if a donor attempts to attach side-conditions to his offer of mixed credit in order to make the aid work better developmentally, the recipient can gain room for manoeuvre by switching to another donor who is not trying to impose side-conditions. Since mixed credit packages are rapidly assembled to fit in with a deadline imposed by the purchasing authority in the recipient country, and since in the nature of the case only the haziest information is usually available about competitors' bids, it is not possible for aid ministries to carry out a proper appraisal of whether aid is helpful to the country's development, or even necessary to win the contract.[31] What is certain is that donors, when vetting mixed credit projects, lower their standards of appraisal. A number of cases can be cited of projects which, having been explicitly rejected by aid ministries as ordinary bilateral aid projects, were later accepted when proposed for mixed credit transactions.[32]

In all three of the respects we have mentioned—reduced maintenance input, reduced scope for policy dialogue and reduced rigour of economic and technical appraisal—mixed credit transactions go in precisely the opposite direction to the recommendations for improving the quality of aid propounded by the World Bank in their recommendations, in particular, for sub-Saharan Africa.[33]

If mixed credit scarcely conduces to development by improving the allocation of resources, neither does it do so through an improvement in the distribution of income. Because a majority of lucrative orders for capital goods are in the better-off developing countries, and because these countries find it easier to pay market rates of interest on their overseas debt, these are countries which are the main beneficiaries of mixed credit deals. Of twenty-nine mixed credit arrangements concluded under the United Kingdom's Aid and Trade Provision (ATP) between 1981 and 1984, 8 per cent, representing 41 per cent of the total value, were given to countries with a 1983 per capita income of over $1,000, that is, countries for which there is very little redistributive case for aid.[34] They included countries such as Malaysia, Thailand, Jordan, Colombia, Brazil, Mexico and Paraguay, which have long been excluded from the British bilateral aid programme because they are simply too rich. It scarcely needs to be added that very few mixed credit projects, in any country, have anything to offer to poor people, either as producers or as consumers. They meet, not 'basic needs', but needs created in the minds of profligate Third World public authorities by equipment salesmen who cannot meet the test of the market unassisted.

One of the greatest ironies of mixed credit, indeed, is that over the medium term it risks having effects quite opposite to those intended even among the rich-country exporters who are meant to be the primary beneficiaries. Although created by governments who claim to value business efficiency and the free market above all things, the practice actually offers a reward to inefficiency by encouraging exporters to look to government patronage rather than to the reduction of their own costs as a means of competing in Third World markets. Firms whose product is unsaleable in Western markets because of poor design or low productivity now find themselves offered an incentive to lobby their ministry of trade and industry to try and sell it for them in the Third World rather than to improve the design, the technology or the price tag. And like any other form of protection, mixed credit funds become contagious as retaliation develops: each successive provision which has been brought in by OECD donors has been justified by 'the aggressive use of aid funds by other donors'[35] even though, once introduced, it can be used to initiate a bid rather than to match the offers of other donors.[36] Meanwhile recipient governments can become so hooked on mixed credit that they ask firms tendering for contracts, as a matter of routine, to indicate the proportion of aid funds in the proposed financial package.[37] And as we have seen, the principle of allowing commercial interest to dictate the design of aid projects has spread from mixed credit funds so defined to the rest of the bilateral aid programme. By a variant of Gresham's Law, bad aid runs the risk of driving out good.

7.4 CONCLUSIONS

We have persistently stressed that the mere existence of a commercial advantage for the donor in an aid transaction does not imply a loss for the recipient. What we have argued, rather, is that the concept of commercial advantage has been imprecisely specified by donors, and that of late it has been pursued without the proper tests of developmental soundness which are necessary to avoid such losses. The classical case for all protection has been based on the idea of a *temporary* shelter from market forces, which can enable producers to descend their cost curve by taking advantage of economies of scale or of learning by doing effects. But the standard methods of subsidising exports by way of the aid budget do not offer this kind of shelter. Rather, they offer *permanent* protection to those firms who are lucky enough to get aid orders, with the consequence that a firm which needs tied aid as a means of gaining a foothold within an export market has no incentive to cut its costs to the point where it can gain follow-up orders without such assistance. It is perhaps not surprising, therefore, that there is so little evidence of such follow-up orders, nor that sharp increases in aid by bilateral donors are so seldom followed by an increase in those donors' penetration of Third World markets for capital equipment. The OECD's general judgement is that 'considering the orders of magnitude involved, it is improbable that aid tying provides significant macro-economic benefits to any donor's domestic or balance of payments aggregates'.[38] Perhaps so, but tying could be made a less blunt instrument if:

    first, it were confined, if practised at all, to procurement in specific regions and/or industries of the donor country, rather than to the entire donor country. Thus, British tied aid in the heavy-industry sector could be restricted to procurement in Wales, Scotland or Northern England;

    second, it were practised on a temporary basis, with donors announcing an intention gradually to untie all their aid over a period of years, starting with aid to the least developed countries. This would deprive suppliers of the comfort of a permanent export subsidy, and restore to tying its basic rationale, which is to secure for exporters an initial footing in a new market;

    third, orders for goods to be supplied under tied aid were put out to competitive tender in the donor country.

The most important requirement of all is that any commercial advantage secured through aid should be secured without prejudice to development in the recipient country. Of late, some aid agencies have made it more difficult for themselves to satisfy this condition by allowing commercial pressures to dictate the design and management of aid projects rather than simply tying, as of old, to extract whatever commercial advantage was possible from projects already certified as developmentally sound in concept. This not only lets bad projects through the net but does so in such transparent manner as to damage the credibility of the policy advice which bilateral donors, with increasing frequency, offer to recipients in order to try and increase the effectiveness of their aid. In other words, the cutting edge of an entire aid programme may be damaged by the patent inadequacy of a small part of it. In such cases, perhaps the best one can recommend is an acceleration of the existing trend towards aid disbursement through multilateral agencies.

NOTES

1. *See* Chapter 1, p. 12.
2. Chapter 3, p. 57.
3. For a discussion of the many legal ways (including tied aid and mixed credit) in which the principle of free trade is breached by the countries which profess it, without the appearance of discrimination, *see* the book by Shutt (1985).
4. The volume of mixed credit or 'associated financing', as it is known to the OECD, has grown as follows:

	Commitments in $ billion	Percentage of bilateral ODA
1981	3.5	4.0
1982	4.6	6.0
1983	1.9	3.0
1984	2.7	4.0

Source: OECD, *Development Co-operation* 1984, p. 10; OECD (1985), p. 243.
5. The British line of mixed credit to developing countries—the Aid–Trade Contingency Programme or ATCP—was set up in 1977.
6. OECD (1985), p. 243. The OECD claim (*ibid.*) that 'the provisions of the Guiding Principles have by now been largely absorbed into members' policies and practices', but scrutiny of some of those policies suggests otherwise (p. 225 above).
7. In the case of tied aid.
8. For example the sale of fifty buses to the Zambian government under UK aid; *see* United Kingdom (1982), p. 100.
9. For early cases *see* Independent Group on British Aid (1982), p. 14.
10. R. M. Ainscow to the Overseas Development Sub-Committee of the House of Commons Foreign Affairs Committee: United Kingdom (1982), p. 36, paragraph 71.
11. For example, if a British company producing diesel engines suddenly receives, and fulfils, a large aid financed order from Indonesia this may prevent it from accepting an order from the United States which arrives the following week.
12. For an account, by mixed-credit negotiators, of the environment surrounding such negotiations, *see* the inquiry by the House of Commons (United Kingdom, 1982) especially questions 31 and 93 to 99.
13. Except in the case of the study by Ashoff and Weiss (1979) which suggests a sum of direct and indirect effects which is about 95 per cent of the initial aid outflow. However, if 'income multiplier effects' from these stimuli to domestic income are added in, the total impact of aid on domestic income comfortably exceeds the value of the aid itself.

14. *See* Table 7.5.
15. May and Dobson (1979), p. 19.
16. The study was financed by the Evaluation Department of ODA but its results have not been made available to the public.
17. United Kingdom (1972), p. 5.
18. Mixed credit also (*see* p. 225) frequently supplies capital goods which remain under-utilised for long periods of time. In this event the supplier, even if competitive on price, quality and after-sales service, will necessarily have to wait a long time for any follow-up order.
19. May and Dobson (1979), p. 9.
20. The percentage increase in the index of production for aid-financed goods, in the period 1966–76, was more or less the same, at 14.9 per cent, as the index of production for manufactured goods as a whole (May and Dobson, 1979, p. 13); and 'most (companies gaining aid orders) are located in the non-development areas of England and Wales, mainly in fact in the South-East region' (*ibid*. p. 11).
21. Schumacher (1981), p. 125 and Note 8.
22. Byatt (1983), p. 175. Note that the figure of £33,000 here quoted is much greater than the figure of £7,500 given for the ATP in Table 7.4; this is because Byatt's figures (a) consider the whole expenditure on ATP, not just a sample of projects and (b) consider the expense of export subsidy to sustain a person's job over the entire period (assumed to be 10 years) before s/he finds re-employment through the normal operation of market forces. Different assumptions about re-employment periods are considered by Byatt, but all lead to the conclusion 'that export-credit subsidies are an extremely expensive way of reducing unemployment' (*ibid*. p. 175).
23. For example, all of the effects 'not measured' in Table 7.4.
24. The phrase is that of the British Minister for Overseas Development, Neil Marten, speaking in the House of Commons on 20 February 1980; but a similar switch in aid policy has taken place in a number of countries since the onset of the 1980–3 recession.
25. Bhagwati (1970), p. 268.
26. Bhagwati (1970), p. 267.
27. *See* Table 1.1.
28. *See* Chapter 5, Note 22.
29. *See* pp. 100–103.
30. *See* Chapter 4, Table 4.2. A particularly important case of this problem is where mixed credit enables a recipient to implement stop-gap measures which rescue him, at high cost, from the need to confront more fundamental development problems. For example, the Egyptian government has obtained under mixed credit gas turbines for base-load electricity generation. These turbines deflect the Egyptian government from the correct policy, which is to generate base-load power at lower cost, for example by hydroelectric schemes. But they cannot get an aid donor to finance schemes of this sort, and they cannot finance them from internal resources because they set the price of electricity, for political reasons, too low. Mixed credit

has released them from the need to consider these basic roots of the problem.

31. The OECD's Guiding Principles require 'members to confine associated financing to ... programmes which are carefully appraised against the developmental standards and criteria applicable to official development assistance programmes' (1985, p. 243). Some members manifestly do not comply with this recommendation. The UK's Overseas Development Administration, for example, applies to its mixed credit projects a 'minimum test of developmental soundness' which, in practice, frequently consists not of a test of any sort, but of a bland assertion that services of the type it is hoped to supply are a good thing.

32. Within the portfolio of the UK Overseas Development Administration one could cite the Majes irrigation project in Peru (*see* Moran (1979)) and the supply of gas turbines to the Egyptian power sector (see United Kingdom (1982), appendix).

33. *See* for example World Bank (1981), Chapter 9; (1984), Chapter 5).

34. Data for 1982–4 from United Kingdom, Overseas Development Administration, *British Overseas Aid* 1982, 1983 and 1984. Tables 6.1, 8.1 and the unnumbered table on p. 39 respectively.

35. The phrase used by the UK Overseas Development Administration in evidence to the Foreign Affairs Committee: United Kingdom (1982), p. 9.

36. In 1983, 40% of ATP allocations took the form of direct initiatives, and as of 1 October 1984, 45% of ATP funds were available for offers by UK firms at the initial stage of tendering (Toye and Clark, 1986, forthcoming).

37. United Kingdom (1982), question 43, p. 28.

38. OECD (1985), p. 241.

8 The Case for the Defence

Foreign aid is perhaps the least questioned form of state spending in the West. It is never questioned in principle. The mainstream advocacy of aid rarely addresses itself to its actual operation and notably not to its efficiency in terms of its proclaimed objectives. The advocates do not examine whether aid actually promotes development or improves the lot of the poor. Nor do they examine its adverse repercussions.

P.T. Bauer, *Equality, the Third World and Economic Delusion* (p. 89)

8.1 SUMMARY OF FINDINGS

This book has been an attempt to respond to Bauer's challenge. It starts from the moral premiss that anything which can be done to improve the living conditions of very poor people, and to narrow the gap between the living standards of the average person in the West and the average person in Ethiopia or Bangladesh, is in principle worth doing. It has examined the contribution which official overseas aid has made towards these and other more narrowly nationalistic objectives. It has also, in some detail, examined its adverse repercussions.

Its findings have been as follows:

As an instrument of *political leverage*, as we saw in Chapter 2, economic aid has been conspicuously unsuccessful. When used by the superpowers on a large scale (e.g. by the US in Vietnam and by Russia in Somalia) it has failed to prevent the defection of allies, and when withdrawn from client states (e.g. by the US in Brazil) it has seldom been followed by any erosion of political support in the United Nations. It may be natural to seek political support by buying it, but on the available evidence that is not an easy thing to do.

As an instrument of *export promotion*, the record of aid is no better. Aid seldom seems to induce follow-up orders or a lasting increase in market share: the benefits it confers on the companies which it subsidises are transient and hence do not justify government intervention. Employment in the donor country can more efficiently be increased by almost any other form of policy tool than aid. Finally, trade-related aid can have serious negative spin-off effects both on the efficiency of supplier firms in the donor country and on the quality of development in the recipient, which have been documented in Chapter 7.

The empirical picture becomes a little brighter when we move from selfish to altruistic objectives of aid. In Chapter 6 we found that it did achieve a modest but palpable redistribution of income between countries. Between persons the picture is less clear, since the data are so bad, but the evidence we have is sufficient to acquit aid of the charge of redistributing money from the poor in the West to the rich in the Third World. It appears to redistribute from the reasonably well-off in the West to most income groups in the Third World *except* the very poorest, and it supports a number of governments, such as Tanzania, Sri Lanka and Zimbabwe, whose tax and expenditure policies are genuinely redistributive. Bauer's statement that 'official aid does not go to poor people'[1] is therefore, at the level of generalisation he has chosen, simply wrong.

Finally, in Chapter 5 we considered the efficiency of aid in *promoting growth* in the recipient country. At the world level, this appears to be neutral: neither significantly and automatically positive, as many defenders of aid assume, nor negative, as argued both by Bauer and by many writers on the extreme left. We found reasons for this, including the possibility of leakages of aid into unproductive public expenditure and of negative effects on the private sector through the price mechanism. But these effects are by no means universal, as Bauer assumes.[2] The statistical analysis of Chapter 5, for example, supports the widespread folk-wisdom of the development community that over the last fifteen years aid has had a significant effect on development in Asia and very little in Africa. But within Asia itself there are countries where aid appears to have replaced domestic development effort, such as Nepal, Cambodia and arguably the Philippines; by the same token there are a number of African countries where it has manifestly supplemented those efforts, such as Kenya, Malawi and Botswana. Public-sector behaviour in developing countries is not, we submit, subject to general laws of behaviour which predetermine the effectiveness of aid; rather, it varies from country to country and from period to period. Because it varies, blanket statements to the effect that aid 'does good' or 'does harm' to growth ought to be avoided. In different places and at different times it has clearly done both, sometimes with a very long lag which has made snap judgements subsequently look very silly. In the early 1950s one country in receipt of a large quantity of American aid money was castigated as a 'bottomless pit' into which that money was being uselessly poured, and in which a 'mendicant mentality' was being created.[3] The country was South Korea, now acknowledged as one of the great success stories of aid in particular and of Third World development efforts in general.

Stripped to its bare essentials, then, the case for development aid is that it increases growth rates in some developing countries, improves the living standards of some poor people, and offers the prospect of doing better in future on both counts. That is all. It is beyond doubt that some advocates of aid, with their hearts very much in the right place, have claimed more for aid than it was actually delivering.[4] But the case against aid has been just as much overstated, either by the use of purely anecdotal evidence to support claims of worldwide failure or by outright a priori theorising.[5] It has been a major purpose of this book to purge the case for aid of these excesses of claim and counter-claim, and to rebuild it on more secure, if more modest, foundations.

8.2 DIAGNOSIS

It will be clear from all of the preceding chapters that aid, even if on balance a good thing, has consistently fallen far short of the expectations of its supporters. Before making any recommendations about what should be done to make things better we may reasonably ask what has gone wrong.

One constraint on effectiveness must be faced at the start. Aid is given to sovereign governments, who have the power to do what they wish with the instruments of government policy; hence the power of a donor is limited. He can tie aid to specific projects, but he cannot stop the recipient reshuffling the rest of his spending pattern in response to a donation: aid is fungible. He can ask the recipient to comply with specific policy conditions, but monitoring of compliance takes so long and is so tricky that by artful juggling the recipient can often confine his policy changes to the ones he would have undertaken anyway: conditions too are fungible.[6] All that he can do is to support with aid the governments he trusts to use aid money well and to switch the aid budget from the countries and sectors which use it badly to the countries and sectors which use it well.

Our first hypothesis concerning the disappointing performance of aid is that donors, as a broad generalisation, do not do this. As we saw in Chapter 5, aid is far more effective in Asia than in Africa, both in macro and in rate-of-return terms; but donors are switching their aid budgets from Asia to Africa to deal with the 'crisis of sub-Saharan Africa'. Within Africa, the outstanding successes of aid are Malawi and Botswana, but these countries have in recent years experienced a decline in real aid flows, whereas problem countries such as Mozambique and the Sudan have had large increases.[7] This is not necessarily bad: it suggests that the allocation of aid is motivated more by awareness of difficulties, and hopes of doing something about them, than by a desire to back tested solutions to those difficulties. But it does reduce the effectiveness of aid as an instrument of growth generation.

If donors are slow to switch aid resources from unsuc-

cessful to successful fields, this is partly because the information available to them is so poor. Of all development
agencies, the World Bank is the only one which subjects all
its projects to *ex post* evaluation, and worldwide probably
only a quarter of all aid-financed projects have publicly
available evaluation reports written on them. Many of these
reports, in turn, as we saw in Chapter 3, simply do not
ask the questions which have to be answered if a rational
reallocation of aid resources is to be achieved: for example,
many do not attempt to estimate an *ex post* rate of return
on projects, and only a very tiny minority try to find out
the impact of projects on the poorest groups. In the absence
of proper information, many allocative decisions have to be
based on hunch rather than on accurate information, and
this has led to a number of blunders in aid policy, such as
the premature withdrawal from the concept of integrated
rural development.[8]

A further problem, however, lies not in the measurement
of results but in the specification of objectives. Not only
aid programmes in the aggregate, as we have seen, but also
individual projects are expected at the same time to advance
the donor's political and commercial interests, assist the
recipient's economic growth, and reallocate resources to
poor people. These separate objectives are loaded on to
individual projects like baubles on to a Christmas tree,
without any concern for the conflicts which may exist
between individual objectives. Indeed, the overload is
increasing, as donor agencies become increasingly orien-
tated towards the pursuit of national self-interest without
admitting to the costs involved. When the British Minister
for Overseas Development in 1980 expressed an intention to
'give greater weight to political, commercial and industrial
objectives *alongside* our basic developmental objectives'[9]
he nicely demonstrated the ability of sloppy language to
conceal a conflict of interests. It is a cardinal principle of
the theory of economic policy that the number of instruments must be equal to the number of policy targets;[10] and
yet one policy instrument, the entire aid budget, is routinely
expected to chase at least *four* targets of policy simultaneously. It is no wonder that some of them, some of

the time, are not achieved. A full listing of the biases to which this can lead is given in Table 4.2 on page 110. The logical solution to the problem is either to drop some of the objectives, or else to partition the aid budget into separate funds, each of which is aimed solely at one particular policy target. This proposal will be further developed later in the chapter.

If it is difficult to achieve a focus on a particular policy target within the aid programme of a particular donor, it is ten times more difficult to achieve such a focus within the 'aid programme' of the OECD aid donors as a whole. The inverted commas need emphasis, since that programme, so far from being a co-ordinated effort, is a collection of isolated endeavours within the Third World which at best bear little relation to one another and at worst, as in the case of mixed credit, are actually dedicated to the cause of driving other aid donors out of a particular market sector. In such an environment, the effectiveness of aid is damaged not only by the contradictory instructions and incompatible technologies of different aid donors, but also by the loss in credibility which attaches to their advice when it is seen to be commercially partisan. This problem alone constitutes a strong argument in favour of multilateral aid.

8.3 PRESCRIPTION

If an institution is not performing as well as it should there are, as Hirschman has reminded us, three possible responses. *Exit*—the termination of all concessional aid transfers, as recommended by Bauer—we oppose, partly because in a limited degree aid does achieve its developmental and redistributive objectives, and partly because its ultimate aim of reducing poverty is so important. If a problem is serious enough, and current remedies against it are not working too well, you do not give up the fight: you try harder, and bring new ingenuity to bear on the problem. Nobody suggests abandoning the fight against cancer because the existing treatments do not always achieve a cure, and by the same token, it is no argument against international aid that some projects which it finances have failed. However, the results of aid so far as portrayed in this book scarcely justify blind *loyalty* to the existing institutions of aid transfer, or to increases in aid volumes without reference to the mechanisms of aid distribution. This leaves *voice*, or efforts towards reform. But in what direction should the efforts be made? Our prescriptions follow on directly from the diagnoses of the last section.

First, aid donors need better information. If they do not know what their aid is achieving, they have no basis on which to spend their money better in future. They must budget enough for *ex post* evaluation of projects to be able to know how well each of the activities which they finance has achieved its stated objective.

Second, the stated objectives must themselves be reduced in number. Export subsidy through the aid budget, as we saw in Chapter 7, is an inefficient means of export or employment creation, reduces the developmental impact of aid, and cannot be justified even in terms of its stated objectives. Ideally, it should be abolished altogether; failing this it should at least be moved out of the aid budget where it makes a pretence of satisfying developmental objectives which it cannot, in the nature of the case, hope to meet. Once relieved of an obligation to promote exports, bilateral aid programmes should then be formally partitioned between a budget whose major objective is the encouragement of growth and the plugging of gaps in the recipient's capital market, and a budget whose major objective is the direct relief of poverty. Aid donors who try to satisfy the second objective purely from 'trickle-down', as is currently fashionable, are abdicating their responsibility towards the poor and the starving by invoking a mechanism which, in most Third World rural environments, varies between the feeble and the non-existent.[11]

Third, the current shift from bilateral towards multilateral aid must be encouraged and accelerated. If this could be done without a reduction in aid volumes, it would reduce both the harmful side-effects on the recipient country of aid given for geopolitical or commercial motives, and also the waste caused by a proliferation of incompatible technologies and policy recommendations from different bilateral donor countries. It is customary at this point in the argument to call also for 'better co-ordination' between aid donors, but since such co-ordination is in general desired neither by bilateral donors (whose commercial interests are opposed) nor by recipients (who resent the thought of being dictated to by a donors' cartel) we see little merit in such recommendations.

Fourth and last, donors must show willingness to move aid money from those countries where their money is doing no good to the countries where it is. The obstacles to this are: (1) lack of information about where it *is* doing good (as discussed earlier), (2) diplomatic staff who can be relied on to kick and scream against any proposed cuts in the aid budget for 'their' country, and (3) sheer unquenchable optimism that countries where aid is achieving little can, if the support is sustained for long enough, 'turn the corner' and show a return on that support. The first of these obstacles can be removed, and the second overridden, but the third demands to be taken more seriously since the willingness of members of the aid community to take a long view, and not give up hope in face of reverses, is in fact one of the most attractive aspects of the entire development assistance operation. However, there is no doubt that those in charge of concessional aid money frequently stay with lost causes longer than they should, partly of course because they have no material incentive to do otherwise. A businessman who invests money unwisely loses that money; a civil servant who recommends the adoption of a Groundnut Scheme loses only professional status, and sometimes not even that because data are missing or decision processes collective.

The dilemmas associated with making aid a more efficient instrument of development are well illustrated by the case of sub-Saharan Africa, the poorest, most heavily aided and least successful region of the Third World.[12] A literal application of the principle of 'aid for those who use it best' would dictate a redirection of aid flows away from the region towards Asia, just when its need appears greatest. We do not recommend that, but we would support a redirection of aid from countries which are poor and have incompetent and corrupt administrations (such as Zaire) towards countries which are poor but have competent administrations (such as Malawi). An alternative approach to the dilemma, a half-way house much stressed by the World Bank,[13] is conditionality: the tying of aid flows to specific policy reforms by the recipient, which are expected to improve his development performance. In principle, this is a valuable and powerful instrument for increasing the effectiveness of aid. In practice, its success in changing policy in sub-Saharan Africa has so far been limited. The reasons for this include the difficulty of monitoring compliance with conditions and disagreements between donor and recipient concerning appropriate economic policy. If the policy change being requested is 'raise the price of sugar, and the rate of return on sugar projects will rise' compliance can be easily monitored and all involved can see the connection between the conditionality proposed and its desired objective. But if it is 'rationalise the structure of protection' or 'privatise the marketing of specific crops' the connection between target and instrument is less obvious and the administrative implications highly complex, so that it is relatively easy for a recipient to conceal a determination to do nothing in particular behind an appearance of collaboration with the donor.[14]

We do not believe, therefore, that too much should be expected of our recommendation to switch aid from 'failures' to 'successes' or to put pressure on the 'failures'. For many 'failures' of development derive not from obvious and quickly remediable incompetence in government but rather from sheer bad luck (e.g. with weather or commodity prices) or alternatively from the presence of political vested interests and economic structures too deeply ingrained to be susceptible to quick action by an aid donor. The catastrophic famines in Ethiopia and the Sudan in 1984/5 are a case in point. Countries in such a position, if abandoned or threatened too hard by aid donors, will almost certainly revert to the vicious circle of poverty and dependence in which they have long been trapped; if supported on a long-term basis, they may escape. While that support continues the 'return' on aid will be low and possibly negative, but it may in the long term bring about a transformation in the ability of the country to support itself, as occurred in India in the 1970s. The long-term and risky nature of such processes constitutes both a justification for aid flows and a warning to donors not to expect quick or certain results from them.

NOTES

1. Bauer (1981), p. 111.
2. Here is a characteristic statement of Bauer's position:

   Foreign aid ... cannot appreciably promote the growth of the national income. It promotes the disastrous politicisation of life in the Third World. People divert their resources and attention (sc. because of aid) from productive economic activities into other areas, such as trying to forecast political developments, placating or bribing politicans and civil servants, and operating or evading controls. (Bauer (1981), pp. 100 and 103)

3. By Hahm Pyong-Choon in 1954; *see* Steinberg (1984), p. 31.
4. These include Hollis Chenery: 'One of the principal means for poor countries to accelerate their development is by using external resources to supply additional exports and to finance a higher level of investment' (Chenery and MacEwan 'Optimal patterns of growth and aid: the case of Pakistan'; *Pakistan Development Review*, Summer 1966, p. 209) and Jack Parkinson: 'It is almost impossible to think that the principle of providing for the poor could or should be refuted': in Parkinson (1982), p. 1.
5. The style of discourse of (Lord) Peter Bauer, the major exponent of this position, is particularly strange: he denounces the reluctance of defenders of aid to give empirical support to their position (witness the quotation at the beginning of this chapter) but offers none for his own position. Indeed, at one point he doubles back on his challenge to defenders to provide more evidence and argues that there is no point in ever doing so:

   It is often thought that the effects of aid could be established from statistical evidence with the help of statistical analysis. This is not so ... Even if it were established (which is in practice impossible) that aid funds over a period proved highly productive in their overall effects, the maximum contribution of aid would still be restricted to the avoided cost of borrowing as the funds could have been obtained commercially from abroad. Thus the statistical exercises at times undertaken to establish the contribution of aid to development are beside the point. (Bauer (1981), pp. 102–3)

   This passage, of course, begs a number of questions, such as whether countries such as Upper Volta and Nepal can borrow commercially from abroad and whether the contribution of, for example, aid to starving children is simply 'the avoided cost of borrowing'. But most strangely of all, it appears to deny that any scientific method whatever can be used to find out whether aid is effective. If this contention is taken seriously, it invalidates his attacks on aid as much as the defences of others, since none of them, *ex hypothesi*, can be given any empirical support, and all debate about aid becomes otiose. In fact, aid and the targets it is meant to influence can be measured, and hypotheses concerning their mutual relationship can be tested: hence Bauer's contention of the impossibility of applying scientific method is absurd.

6. For a discussion of conditionality which lays particular emphasis on this point, *see* Mosley (1985c).
7. Between 1981 and 1984 Malawi's total receipts of net ODA from OAC countries have declined from $82m to $51m and Botswana's from $76m to $65m, whereas in the Sudan they have increased from $64m to $121m and in Mozambique from $6m to $16m: OECD, *Geographical Distribution of Financial Flows to Less Developed Countries 1981 to 1984*, individual country tables.
8. *See* Chapter 3, p. 64 and Chapter 6, p. 204.
9. Neil Marten: *House of Commons Debates*, 20 February 1980.
10. *See* Tinbergen (1952, 1955).
11. *See* Chapter 6, especially p. 178.
12. *See* World Bank (1981, 1984).
13. *See* World Bank (1981), Chapter 9 and (1984), Chapter 5.
14. For development of this argument, *see* Mosley (1985c).

Bibliography

Abbott, George C.
  1970 'Economic aid as a unilateral transfer of resources', *Journal of Political Economy*, vol. 78, pp. 1213–27.
  1971 'A re-examination of the 1929 Colonial Development Act', *Economic History Review*, vol. 24, pp. 68–81.
Akerlof, George
  1970 'The market for "lemons": quality uncertainty and the market mechanism', *Quarterly Journal of Economics*, vol. 84, pp. 488–500.
Anderson, Dennis and Khambata, Farida
  1985 'Financing small-scale agriculture in developing countries: the merits and limitations of "commercial" policies', *Economic Development and Cultural Change*, vol. 33 (January), pp. 349–72.
Arrow, Kenneth
  1962 'The economic implications of learning by doing', *Review of Economic Studies*, vol. 29, pp. 155–73.
Ashoff, Guido and Weiss, D.
  1979 'Effects of German development aid on the internal economy', *Intereconomics*, vol. 14, pp. 215–20.
Bates, Robert A.
  1981 *Markets and States in Tropical Africa*, Berkeley: University of California Press.
  1983 *Essays on the Political Economy of Rural Africa*, Cambridge: Cambridge University Press.
Bauer, P. T.
  1954 *West African Trade*, Cambridge: Cambridge University Press.
  1965 (with Barbara Ward) *Two Views on Aid to Developing Countries*, London: Institute of Economic Affairs.

1972 *Dissent on Development*, London: Weidenfeld and Nicolson.

1981 *Equality, the Third World and Economic Delusion*, London: Methuen.

Baum, Warren C. and Stokes, M. Tolbert

1985 *Investing in Development: Lessons from the World Bank's Experience*, Oxford: Oxford University Press.

Beenstock, Michael

1980 'Political econometry of official development assistance', *World Development*, vol. 8, pp. 137–44.

Bell, C. L. G. and Hazell, P. B. R.

1980 'Measuring the indirect effects of an agricultural development project on its surrounding region', *American Journal of Agricultural Economics*, vol. 62, pp. 75–86.

Bell, C. L. G., Hazell, P. B. R. and Slade, R.

1983 *The Evaluation of Projects in Regional Perspective*, Baltimore: Johns Hopkins University Press.

Bhagwati, Jagdish

1970 'The tying of aid' in Bhagwati, J. and Eckaus, R. S. (eds.) *Foreign Aid*, Penguin Modern Economics Readings, Harmondsworth: Penguin.

Bird, Richard and Hirschman, Albert

1968 *Foreign Aid: a Critique and a Proposal*, Princeton Studies in International Finance, Princeton, NJ: Princeton University Press.

Blaikie, Piers, Cameron, J. and Seddon, J. D.

1977 'The effects of roads in West-Central Nepal: a summary', unpublished report, Overseas Development Group, Norwich.

Bliss, Christopher and Stern, Nicholas H.

1982 *Palanpur: the Economy of an Indian Village*, Oxford: Oxford University Press.

Bornschier, V., Chase-Dunn, C. and Rubinson, R.

1976 'International evidence of the effects of foreign investment and aid on economic growth and inequality: a survey of findings and a reanalysis', *American Journal of Sociology*, vol. 84, pp. 651–83.

Bowles, T. S.

1978 *Survey of Attitudes Ttowards Overseas Development*, London: Her Majesty's Stationery Office.

Brandt Commission

1980 *North–South: a Programme for Survival*, London: Pan Books.

1983 *Common Crisis*, London: Pan Books.

Braybrooke, D. and Lindblom, C. E.
1963 *A Strategy of Decision: Policy Evaluation as a Social Process*, London: Collier-Macmillan.

Breton, Albert
1974 *The Economic Theory of Representative Government*, London: Macmillan.

Bridger, G. A. and Winpenny, J. T.
1983 *Planning Development Projects*, London: Her Majesty's Stationery Office.

Brown, C. V. and Jackson, Peter M.
1982 *Public Sector Economics*, second edition, Oxford: Martin Robertson.

Byatt, I. C. R.
1983 'Byatt report on subsidies to British export credits', *World Economy*, vol. 7, pp. 163–78.

Cable, Vincent and Weale, Martin
1982 'Trade and aid policy analysis: use of the Cambridge Growth Project model', *ODI Review*, vol. 1 (May), pp. 50–70.

Caiden, Naomi and Wildavsky, Aaron
1974 *Planning and Budgeting in Poor Countries*, Englewood Cliffs, NJ: Prentice-Hall.

Carruthers, Ian (ed.)
1983 *Aid to Irrigation*, Paris: OECD.

Cassen, Robert *et al.*
1982 *Rich Country Interests and Third World Development*, London: Croom Helm.
1986 *Does Aid Work? Report of the Independent Consultants' Study of Aid-Effectiveness*. Oxford: Oxford University Press.

Chambers, Robert
1983 *Rural Development: Putting the Last First*. London: Longman.

Chenery, Hollis and Strout, A. M.
1966 'Foreign assistance and economic development', *American Economic Review*, vol. 56, pp. 679–733.

Chenery, Hollis, Bell, C., Duloy, J. H. and Jolly, Richard
1974 *Redistribution with Growth*, Oxford: Oxford University Press for World Bank and Institute of Development Studies.

Cox, Pamela
1984 'Implementing agricultural development policy in Kenya', *Food Research Institute Studies*, vol. 19, pp. 153–76.

Dacy, D. C.
1975 'Foreign aid, government consumption, savings and

growth in less developed countries', *Economic Journal*, vol. 85, pp. 548–61.

DANIDA
1982 *Noakhali Integrated Rural Development Project: Evaluation Report*, Copenhagen: DANIDA Board of Auditors.

Devitt, Paul
1978 *The Role of Sociological Factors in Four ODM Projects: an Evaluation*, London: Overseas Development Administration Evaluation Unit (document EV 101).

Dudley, Leonard and Montmarquette, C.
1976 'A model of the supply of bilateral foreign aid', *American Economic Review*, vol. 66, pp. 132–42.

Duesenberry, James S.
1949 *Income, Saving and the Theory of Consumer Behaviour*, Cambridge, Mass.: Harvard University Press.

Duncan, Alex and Mosley, Paul
1984 'Aid effectiveness: Kenya case study'. Unpublished report, Queen Elizabeth House, Oxford and University of Bath.

Ehrhardt, R.
1983 *Canadian Development Assistance to Bangladesh*, Ottawa: Canadian International Development Agency.

Faaland, Just
1981 *Aid and Influence: the Case of Bangladesh*, London: Macmillan.
1984 'Norwegian aid and reaching the poor', *Development Policy Review*, vol. 2 (May), pp. 1–12.

Fishlow, Albert
1972 'Brazilian size distribution of income', *Papers and Proceedings of the American Economic Association*, vol. 62, pp. 391–402.

Forsyth, David
1977 'Appropriate technology in sugar manufacturing', *World Development*, vol. 5, pp. 189–202.

Frey, Bruno S.
1984 *International Political Economics*, Oxford: Basil Blackwell.

Galbraith, John Kenneth
1968 *The New Industrial State*, Harmondsworth: Penguin Books.

Gasper, Des
1985 'Bargaining in project appraisal and evaluation'. Unpublished paper presented to Development Studies Association annual conference, Bath, September.

Gorman, Robert F.
1983 *Private Voluntary Organisations as Agents of Development*,

Boulder, CO.: Westview Press.

Griffin, Keith
1970 'Foreign capital, domestic savings and economic development', *Bulletin of the Oxford University Institute of Economics and Statistics*, vol. 32, pp. 99–112.

Griffin, Keith and Enos, J. L.
1970 'Foreign assistance: objectives and consequences', *Economic Development and Cultural Change*, vol. 18, pp. 313–27.

Harlow, V. and Chilver, E. M. (eds.)
1965 *History of East Africa*, vol. II, Oxford: Oxford University Press.

Hayter, Teresa
1971 *Aid as Imperialism*, Harmondsworth: Penguin Books.

Hayter, Teresa and Watson, Catharine
1985 *Aid: Rhetoric and Reality*, London: Pluto Press.

Heald, David
1982 *Public Expenditure: its Defence and Reform*, Oxford: Martin Robertson.

Healey, John M.
1971 *The Economics of Aid*, London: Routledge.

Healey, J. M. and Clift, Charles
1980 'The development rationale for aid re-examined', *ODI Review*, no. 2, pp. 14–34.

Heclo, Hugh and Wildavsky, Aaron
1979 *The Private Government of Public Money*, second edition, London: Macmillan.

Heller, Peter S.
1975 'A model of public fiscal behavior in developing countries: aid, investment and taxation', *American Economic Review*, vol. 65, pp. 429–45.

Heller, Peter S. and Aghevli, Joan M.
1985 'The recurrent cost problem: an international overview', Chapter 1 in Howell (1985).

Hewitt, Adrian and Kydd, Jonathan
1984 'A study of the effectiveness of aid to Malawi', unpublished study, Overseas Development Institute, London and Wye College, London.

Hirschman, Albert O.
1964 'The stability of neutralism: a geometrical note', *American Economic Review*, vol. 54, pp. 94–100.

Hodd, Michael
1976 'Income distribution in Kenya', *Journal of Development Studies*, vol. 12, pp. 221–8.

Holtham, Gerald and Hazlewood, Arthur
1976 *Aid and Inequality in Kenya*, London: Croom Helm.

Hopkin, Bryan and associates
   1970 'Aid and the balance of payments', *Economic Journal*,
   vol. 80, pp. 1–23.
Howell, John (ed.)
   1985 *Recurrent Costs and Agricultural Development*, London:
   Overseas Development Institute.
Independent Group on British Aid
   1982 *Real Aid: a Strategy for Britain*, London: Independent
   Group on British Aid.
   1984 *Aid is Not Enough*, London: Independent Group on Brit-
   ish Aid.
   1986 *Missed opportunities: Britain and the Third World 1984–86*,
   London: Independent Group on British Aid.
Jackson, Peter M.
   1982 *The Political Economy of Bureaucracy*, Deddington: Philip
   Allan.
Jennings, Anthony
   1984 'Measuring the success or failure of aid: an experiment in
   the scoring method for aid evaluation', unpublished paper,
   University of Leicester.
Jones, David
   1977 *Aid and Development in Southern Africa*, London: Croom
   Helm.
Kay, John and King, Mervyn
   1982 *The British Tax System*, third edition, Oxford: Oxford
   University Press.
Killick, Tony and associates
   1984 *The Quest for Economic Stabilisation: the IMF and the
   Third World*. 2 vols. London: Heinemann Educational Books.
Kitching, Gavin
   1982 *Development and Underdevelopment in Historical Per-
   spective*, London: Methuen.
Kleemeier, L.
   1984 'Domestic policies versus poverty-oriented foreign assist-
   ance in Tanzania', *Journal of Development Studies*, vol. 20
   (January), pp. 179–201.
Lappe, Frances Moore
   1980 *Aid as Obstacle: Twenty Questions about our Foreign
   Aid and the Hungry*, San Francisco: Institute for Food and
   Development Policy.
Lele, Uma
   1983 'Growth and development of foreign assistance and the
   effect on African agricultural and food production strategies',

paper presented to conference on Accelerating Agricultural Growth in sub-Saharan Africa, Victoria Falls, Zimbabwe, 29 Aug.–1 Sept.

Leonard, David, Cohen, J. and Pinckney, T.
1983 'Budgeting and financial management in Kenya's agricultural ministries', *Agricultural Administration*, vol. 14, pp. 105–20.

Lewis, J. P.
1977 'Designing the public works mode of anti-poverty policy', in Frank, C. R. and Webb, R. C. (eds.) *Income Distribution and Growth in Less Developed Countries*, Brookings Institution, Washington DC.

Linear, Marcus
1985 *Zapping the Third World: the Disaster of Development Aid*, London: Pluto Press.

Lipton, Michael
1973 'Aid allocation when aid is inadequate: problems of the non-implementation of the Pearson Report', in Byres, T. (ed.), *Foreign Resources and Economic Development*, London: Frank Cass.
1977 *Why Poor People Stay Poor: Urban Bias in World Development*, London: Maurice Temple Smith.
1986 'Introduction: aid-effectiveness, prisoners' dilemmas, and country allocation', *IDS Bulletin*, vol. 17 (April), pp. 1–6.

Lipton, Michael and Toye, John
1984 'Aid-effectiveness: India'. Unpublished report, Institute of Development Studies, Sussex and Centre for Development Studies, Swansea.

McKinley, R. D. and Little, R.
1978a 'The German aid relationship: a test of the recipient need and the donor interest models of the distribution of German bilateral aid 1961–1970', *European Journal of Political Research*, vol. 6, pp. 235–57.
1978b 'A foreign policy model of the distribution of UK bilateral aid 1960–1970', *British Journal of Political Science*, vol. 8, pp. 313–32.
1979 'The US aid relationship: a test of the recipient need and donor interest models', *Political Studies*, vol. 27, pp. 236–50.

McKinnon, Ronald I.
1964 'Foreign exchange constraints in economic development and efficient aid allocation', *Economic Journal*, vol. 74, pp. 388–409.

Marsh, D. K. V. and Dahal, R. P.
1984 *Evaluation of the Small Farmer Development Programme in the KHARDEP Area*, unpublished report, Kathmandu: Agricultural Development Bank of Nepal.

Mason, Edward S. and Asher Robert E.
1973 *The World Bank since Bretton Woods*, Washington, DC: Brookings Institution.

May, R. S. and Dobson, N. C.
1979 'The impact of the United Kingdom's bilateral aid programme on British industry', *ODI Review* no. 2 (October), pp. 1–22.
1982a 'The UK development aid programme and the British domestic economy', *Intereconomics*, vol. 17, pp. 20–5.
1982b 'Some trade aspects of aid: the British experience' *National Westminster Quarterly Review*, February 1982, pp. 46–58.

Meerman, Jacob
1979 *Public Expenditure in Malaysia: Who Benefits and Why*, Oxford: Oxford University Press for World Bank.

Mende, Tibor
1973 *From Aid to Recolonisation: Lessons of a Failure*, London: Harrap.

Mikesell, R. F.
1983 *The Economics of Foreign Aid and Self-sustaining Development*, Boulder, CO.: Westview Press.

Moran, James
1979 *Majes Irrigation Project, Peru: A Desk Study*. London: ODA Evaluation Unit, document EV 115.

Morgan, D. J.
1980 *The Official History of Colonial Development*, 5 vols., London: Macmillan.

Morgenthau, H. J.
1962 'A political theory of foreign aid', *American Political Science Review*, vol. 56, pp. 301–25.

Morris, John and Gwyer, George
1983 'UK experience with identifying and implementing poverty-related aid projects', *Development Policy Review*, vol. 1 (November) pp. 147–62.

Morss, Elliott
1984 'Institutional destruction resulting from donor and project proliferation in Sub-Saharan Africa', *World Development*, vol. 12, pp. 465–70.

Morss, Elliott R. and Victoria, A.
1983 *US Foreign Aid: an Assessment of New and Traditional*

Development Strategies, Boulder, CO.: Westview Press.

Morton, Kathryn A.
1975 *Aid and Dependence: British Aid to Malawi*, London: Croom Helm.

Mosley, Paul
1974 'The economics of colonialism, 1870–1939', *Journal of Economic Studies*, n.s. vol. 1 (1974), pp. 150–61.
1980 'Aid, savings and growth revisited', *Oxford Bulletin of Economics and Statistics*, vol. 42, pp. 79–97.
1981a 'Aid for the poorest: early lessons of UK experience', *Journal of Development Studies*, vol. 17, pp. 214–25.
1981b 'Models of the aid allocation process', *Political Studies*, vol. 29, pp. 245–53.
1982a 'The quality of overseas aid', *ODI Review*, no. 2, pp. 46–55.
1982b 'Marketing systems and income distribution: the case of milk producers in highland Peru', *Food Research Institute Studies*, vol. 18, pp. 275–92.
1983 'The politics of evaluation: a comparative study of World Bank and UKODA evaluation procedures', *Development and Change*, vol. 14, pp. 593–608.
1985a 'The political economy of foreign aid: a model of the market for a public good', *Economic Development and Cultural Change*, vol. 33, pp. 373–94.
1985b 'Towards a predictive model of overseas aid expenditures', *Scottish Journal of Political Economy*, vol. 32, pp. 1–19.
1985c 'On persuading a leopard to change his spots: optimal strategies for donors and recipients of conditional development aid', *Bath University Papers in Political Economy* 35.
1986 'The politics of liberalisation: the World Bank and USAID in Kenya 1980–84', *African Affairs*, vol. 85, pp. 107–19.

Mosley, Paul and Dahal, R. P.
1985 'Lending to the poorest: early lessons from the Small Farmers' Development Programme, Nepal', *Development Policy Review*, vol. 3 (November), pp. 193–207.

Mosley, Paul and Hudson, John
1984 'Aid, the public sector and the market in developing countries', *Bath University Papers in Political Economy* 23.

Mosley, Paul and Lawrence-Jones, W.
1984 *Cajamarca Agricultural Development Project, Peru: Baseline Survey Report*, Overseas Development Administration, London, Evaluation Unit: document EV 242A.

Mosley, Paul, Hudson, John and Horrell, Sara
1986 'Aid, the public sector and the market in less developed countries', forthcoming *Economic Journal*, vol. 96.
Myrdal, Gunnar
1957 *Economic Theory and Underdeveloped Regions*, London: Methuen.
Nelson, Joan M.
1984 'The political economy of stabilisation: commitment, capacity and public response', *World Development*, vol. 12, pp. 983–1006.
Ng, R. C. Y. and associates
1978 *The Impact of Irrigation in the Lam Pao Project Area: Evaluation Report*. Overseas Development Administration, London, Evaluation Unit: document EV 134.
Niskanen, William
1971 *Bureaucracy and Representative Government*, Chicago: Aldine Press.
OECD
1984 *Development Assistance Committee: report of the expert group on aid evaluation on lessons of experience emerging from aid evaluation—note by the Secretariat*. Document DAC (84) 11, 17 July.
1985 *Twenty-five Years of Development Co-operation*, Paris: OECD.
O'Higgins, M. and Ruggles, P.
1981 'The distribution of public expenditure and taxes among households in the United Kingdom', *Review of Income and Wealth*, series 27 (September).
Over, A. M.
1975 'An example of the simultaneous-equations problem: a note on "Foreign assistance: consequences and objectives"', *Economic Development and Cultural Change*, vol. 24 (July), pp. 751–6.
Pack, Howard
1976 'The substitution of labour for capital in Kenyan manufacturing', *Economic Journal*, vol. 86 (March), pp. 45–58.
Papanek, Gustav
1972 'The effect of aid and other resource transfers on savings and growth in less developed countries', *Economic Journal*, vol. 82, pp. 863–74.
1973 'Aid, private foreign investment, savings, and growth in less developed countries', *Journal of Political Economy*, vol. 81, pp. 120–31.
1982 'Aid, growth and equity in Southern Asia'. In Parkinson (1982).

Parkinson, Jack (ed.)
1982 *Poverty and Aid: Essays in Honour of Just Faaland*, Oxford: Basil Blackwell.
Rada, Juan F.
1979 'San Martin Jilotepeque agricultural project: evaluation report'. Unpublished report, OXFAM.
Rondinelli, Dennis
1983 *Development Projects as Policy Experiments*, London: Methuen.
Rosenstein-Rodan, P.
1961 'International aid for underdeveloped countries', *Review of Economics and Statistics*, vol. 43, pp. 107–38.
Sandilands, Roger J. and Dudley, Leonard
1975 'The side effects of foreign aid: the case of PL480 assistance to Colombia', *Economic Development and Cultural Change*, vol. 23, pp. 325–36.
Schumacher, D.
1981 'Development aid and employment in the Federal Republic of Germany', *Intereconomics*, vol. 3 (May–June), pp. 122–5.
Sen, A. K.
1974 *On Economic Inequality*, The Radcliffe Lectures, Oxford: Basil Blackwell.
Shutt, Harry
1985 *The Myth of Free Trade*, Oxford: Basil Blackwell.
Steinberg, David
1984 *On foreign aid and the development of the Republic of Korea: the effectiveness of concessional assistance*. Unpublished report, Washington: USAID.
Stern, Ernest
1983 'World Bank financing of structural adjustment', Chapter 5 in J. Williamson (ed.) *IMF Conditionality*, Washington DC: Institute for International Economics.
Stewart, Michael
1983 *Controlling the Economic Future: Policy Dilemmas in a Shrinking World*, Brighton: Wheatsheaf Books.
Stokke, Olaf
1984 *European Development Assistance*, vol. I: Policies and performance, vol. II. Third world perspectives, Oslo: Norwegian Institute of International Affairs.
Sugden, Robert
1982 'Hard luck stories: the problem of the uninsured in a laissez-faire society', *Journal of Social Policy*, vol. 11, pp. 201–16.
Sumner, D. and Erickson, E. W.
1984 *The Theory and Practice of Development Aid*. North Caro-

lina State University: Department of Economics and Business, Faculty Working Paper 60.

Tait, Alan, Gratz, Werner and Eichengreen, Barry
1979 'International comparisons of taxation for selected developing countries 1972–76', *IMF Staff Papers*, vol. 26, pp. 123–56.

Tendler, Judith
1975 *Inside Foreign Aid*, Baltimore: Johns Hopkins University Press.
1982 *Rural Projects Through Urban Eyes: an Interpretation of the World Bank's New-style Rural Development Projects*, Washington DC: World Bank Staff Working Paper 532.

Thorp, Rosemary and Bertram, Geoffrey
1977 *Peru: Economic Development and Structural Change 1890–1965*, Oxford: Oxford University Press.

Tinbergen, Jan
1952 *On the Theory of Economic Policy*, Amsterdam: North-Holland.
1955 *Economic Policy: Principles and Design*, Amsterdam: North-Holland.

Toye, John and Clark, Graham
1986 'The Aid and Trade Provision: origins, dimensions and possible reforms', *Development Policy Review* 4 (September).

Ul Haq, M.
1967 'Tied credits: a quantitative analysis', in Adler, J. and Kuznets, S. (eds.) *Capital Movements in Economic Development*, London: Macmillan.

United Kingdom (*n.b. ODA evaluation unit reports are listed under author's name*)
1955 *Report of the East Africa Royal Commission*, London: HMSO (Cmnd. 9475).
1960 HM Treasury. *Assistance from the United Kingdom for Overseas Development*, London: HMSO (Cmnd. 974).
1964 Central Office of Information. *Financial and Technical Aid from Britain*, London: HMSO.
1972 *Programme Analysis and Review: Trade and Aid*. London: HMSO.
1975 Overseas Development. *The Changing Emphasis in British Aid Policies: More Help for the Poorest*. London: HMSO (Cmnd. 6270).
1979a House of Commons. *First Report from the Select Committee on Overseas Development: the Pattern of UK Aid to India*. London: HMSO (H.C. 338).

1979b Overseas Development Administration. 'Aid and Trade'. Unpublished paper.

1981 House of Commons. *Third Report from the Foreign Affairs Committee, Session 1980–81: Turks and Caicos Islands: Hotel Development*, London: HMSO (H.C. 26, 2 vols.).

1982 House of Commons. *Second Report from the Foreign Affairs Committee, Session* 1981–82: *Supply estimates 1982–83* (class II, votes 10 and 11), London: HMSO (H.C. 330).

1983 House of Commons. *Fourth Report from the Treasury and Civil Service Committee, Session 1982–83: International Monetary Arrangements.* 3 vols. London: HMSO (H.C. 21).

1984a Foreign and Commonwealth Office. *Soviet, East European and Western Development Aid 1976–83*. Foreign Policy Document no. 108. London: FCO.

1984b Overseas Development Administration. *The Evaluation of Aid Projects and Programmes*. London: HMSO.

1985 House of Commons, All-Party Parliamentary Group on Overseas Development, *UK Aid to African Agriculture*, London: Overseas Development Institute for the All-Party Group.

United Nations
1951 *Measures for the Economic Development of Under-developed Countries*; report by a group of experts appointed by the Secretary-General (document ST/ECA/10). New York: United Nations.

Usher, Dan
1968 *The Price Mechanism and the Meaning of National Income Statistics*, Oxford: Oxford University Press.

van Arkadie, Brian and de Wilde, K.
1984 'Aid effectiveness in Bangladesh'. Unpublished report, Institute of Social Studies, The Hague.

van der Laar, Aart
1980 *The World Bank and the Poor*, The Hague: Martinus Nijhoff Publishers.

van Wijnbergen, Sweder
1985 *Macroeconomic Aspects of the Effectiveness of Foreign Aid: on the Two-gap Model, Home Goods Disequilibrium and Real Exchange-rate Misalignment*. Centre for Economic Policy Research, London: discussion paper 45.

Veitch, Michael
1985 'The budgetary process of resource allocation among competing projects: the case of Sri Lanka'. Unpublished paper presented to Development Studies Association Conference, Bath, September 1985.

Wall, David
1973 *The Charity of Nations: the Political Economy of Foreign Aid*, London: Macmillan.
Walters, Robert S.
1970 *American and Soviet aid: a Comparative Analysis*, Pittsburgh: University of Pittsburgh Press.
Weisskopf, Thomas
1970 'Income distribution and economic growth in Puerto Rico, Argentina and Mexico', *Review of Income and Wealth*, vol. 16, pp. 303–32.
Wheeler, D.
1984 'Sources of stagnation in sub-Saharan Africa', *World Development*, vol. 12, pp. 1–24.
White, John 1974
The Politics of Foreign Aid. London: Bodley Head.
Wiggins, Steven
1985 'Integrated rural development revisited: early lessons from Kenya's Arid and Semi-Arid Lands Programme', *Public Administration and Development*, vol. 5, pp. 91–108.
Wildavsky, Aaron
1964 *The Politics of the Budgetary Process*, Boston: Little, Brown.
Wolff, Richard D.
1974 *The Economics of Colonialism. Britain and Kenya 1870–1930*, New Haven: Yale University Press.
World Bank
1979 *India: Agricultural Refinance and Development Corporation: First Credit Project, Project Performance Audit Report*, Operations Evaluation Department, Report no. 2702, October.
1980 *India: Uttar Pradesh Agricultural Credit Project. Project Performance Audit Report*, Operations Evaluation Department, Report no. 3081, August.
1981 *Accelerated Development in Sub-Saharan Africa*, Washington DC: World Bank.
1982a *Focus on Poverty*, Washington DC: World Bank.
1982b *IDA in Retrospect: the First Two Decades of the International Development Association*, Oxford: Oxford University Press.
1982c *India: First Calcutta Urban Development Project: Project Performance Audit Report*, Operations Evaluation Department, Report no. 4023.
1983a *World Development Report 1983*, Washington DC: World Bank.

Index

References to material in the notes at the end of each chapter are *italicised*, thus: *17*

1983b *Ninth Annual Review of Project Performance Audit Results*, Operations Evaluation Department, Report no. 4720, September.

1984 *Towards Sustained Development in Sub-Saharan Africa: a Joint Program of Action*, Washington DC: World Bank.

1985 *Sustainability of Projects: First Review of Experience*, Operations Evaluation Department, Report no. 5718, June.

www.ingramcontent.com/pod-product-compliance
Lightning Source LLC
Chambersburg PA
CBHW021535260326
41914CB00001B/24

* 9 7 8 0 8 1 3 1 1 6 0 8 2 *